OPUS DEI

A HISTORY (1928–2016)

From the Foundation to the Second Vatican Council

VOLUME ONE

OPUS DEI

A HISTORY (1928–2016)

VOLUME ONE

From the Foundation to the Second Vatican Council

José Luis González Gullón
and John F. Coverdale

Scepter

Opus Dei: A History (1928–2016) Volume One © 2022 José Luis González Gullón and John F. Coverdale

The total or partial reproduction of this book is not permitted, nor its informatic treatment, or the transmission of any form or by any means, either electronic, mechanic, photocopy, or other methods without the prior written permission of the owners of the copyright.

Unless otherwise noted, Scripture texts from the New and Old Testaments are taken from The Holy Bible Revised Standard Version Catholic Edition © 1965 and 1966 by the Division of Christian Education of the National Council of the Churches of Christ in the United States. All rights reserved. All copy-righted material is used by permission of the copyright owner. No part of it may be reproduced without permission in writing from the copyright owner.

Published by Scepter Publishers, Inc.
info@scepterpublishers.org
www.scepterpublishers.org
800-322-8773
New York

All rights reserved.

Text and cover design by Rose Design

Library of Congress Control Number: 2021947549

ISBN: (pbk.) 9781594174360
ISBN: (eBook) 9781594174377

Printed in the United States of America

CONTENTS

Introduction ix
Background xix

    Section 1. Discovering his Calling / xx
    Section 2. Priest and Jurist / xxv

PART I
Foundation and Early Years (1928–1939) / 1

Chapter 1. The Foundation of the Work 5

    Section 1. The Original Foundational Event / 5
    Section 2. Initial Development / 7
    Section 3. New Lights and First Followers / 13

Chapter 2. The DYA Academy-Residence 24

    Section 1. The Beginning of the St. Raphael Work / 26
    Section 2. The DYA Residence / 32

Chapter 3. The Spanish Civil War 41

    Section 1. Republican Spain / 41
    Section 2. In the Rebel Zone / 46

PART II
Approvals and Initial Expansion (1939–1950) / 53

Chapter 4. Growth of the Men's Branch 59

    Section 1. From Madrid to the Provinces / 60
    Section 2. Opus Dei Becomes a Pious Union / 65

Section 3. In the University World / 70
Section 4. Opposition within the Church / 74

Chapter 5. **Development of the Women's Branch** 82

Section 1. At the "Third Attempt" / 82
Section 2. The Administration / 87

Chapter 6. **Priests of Opus Dei and Growth in Europe** 93

Section 1. Priests of Opus Dei / 93
Section 2. Consolidation in Spain / 99
Section 3. The Founder Moves to Rome / 108
Section 4. Expansion in Western Europe / 112

Chapter 7. **Pontifical Approvals** 120

Section 1. An "Entirely" Secular Institute / 121
Section 2. Government and Organization / 124
Section 3. Variety of Members / 129
Section 4. Developments and Difficulties / 133

PART III

Spreading throughout the World (1950–1962) / 143

Chapter 8. **Organization of Opus Dei** 145

Section 1. The Work as a Family / 145
Section 2. The Administration of the Centers / 150
Section 3. The "Battle of Formation" / 153
Section 4. Moving the Central Government of Opus Dei
    to Rome / 159

Chapter 9. **Worldwide Expansion** 172

Section 1. Common Patterns / 172
Section 2. Western Europe / 179
Section 3. Latin America / 183
Section 4. The United States / 185
Section 5. Kenya, Japan, and Australia / 187

Chapter 10. Individual Action in Society 194

Section 1. Apostolate of "Friendship and Confidence" / 197
Section 2. Freedom and Responsibility in Public Life / 199

Chapter 11. Institutional Apostolic Activities 209

Section 1. Corporate Works / 212
Section 2. Common Apostolic Works / 219
Section 3. Auxiliary Companies / 225
Section 4. Office of the Apostolate of Public Opinion / 228

Epilogue 233
Index 235

INTRODUCTION

Opus Dei is a way of incarnating and radiating the gospel.* It reminds people of all conditions, creeds, and cultures that God calls them to be his children, to be saints and apostles, in the midst of the world, in the framework of work, family, and daily life. This mission has a charismatic component at its origin. Its founder, Josemaría Escrivá, felt called by God to transmit a spiritual and universal message linked to the first Christians—one that expressed the vitality of the Church.†

Our book narrates the birth and initial development of Opus Dei under the guidance of the Founder and his first two successors, Álvaro del Portillo and Javier Echevarría. During that period, which

---

* Escrivá used the expression "Opus Dei" beginning in the 1940s, when he had to translate the first statutes into Latin. Until then, he had used the Spanish phrases *"la Obra de Dios"* ["the Work of God"] or, simply, *"la Obra* ["the Work"]. We use *Opus Dei, the Work of God*, and *the Work* interchangeably.

† The Founder of Opus Dei was baptized with four first names as José, María, Julián, and Mariano. In his manuscripts, as early as the 1930s, and on his letterhead from December 1963, he united his first two names into one, "Josemaría," out of devotion to the Holy Family. Since he joined them together at a very early date, we will use "Josemaría" throughout our book.

On formal occasions and in legal documents, Spaniards use their father's last name followed by their mother's. Following this convention, as a youth the future Founder of Opus Dei was known as Escrivá Albas. With respect to the first surname, in October 1940 the family changed *Escrivá* in the civil registry to *Escrivá de Balaguer* to distinguish themselves from other family branches. (Balaguer is the region of Lérida from which the Escrivá lineage originated). To avoid confusing English-speaking readers, the English version of this book generally uses simply *Escrivá*. The Founder's first successor, Álvaro Portillo y Diez de Sollano added "del" to his first last name after 1939. See Nota general (General Note) 104/63, AGP E.1.3, 243–3; José Luis González Gullón, *DYA: La Academia y Residencia en la historia del Opus Dei (1933–1939)*, 4th ed. (Madrid: Rialp, 2016), p. 11. We will refer to him throughout this book as Del Portillo.

runs from 1928 to 2016, the Work spread to countries on five continents with members from diverse cultural, social, and political environments. It established its juridical position in the Church as a personal prelature. It celebrated the canonization of Josemaría Escrivá and the beatifications of Álvaro del Portillo, his successor, and of a lay member, Guadalupe Ortiz de Landázuri. And it promoted corporate activities in the areas of education, health, and social service. The goal of this historical monograph is to analyze how the message of Opus Dei spread in the Church and in society through the institution and its members, as well as those who participate in its apostolates.

Writing a history of Opus Dei is a complex task for many reasons. What was born in Spain in the 1920s with a handful of members has become a worldwide phenomenon with 93,000 members and 175,000 cooperators. Its charismatic origin makes it necessary to distinguish essential elements that comprise its message or spirituality from other elements that are transitory or of minor importance. We will need to give theological and legal explanations, and explore the continuities and discontinuities of its spirit and practice with traditional and modern forms of spirituality. Distinctions will need to be drawn between the characteristics of the foundational stage and later developments. We will have to address controversies in the media and in the popular imagination about Opus Dei and its founder. Finally, the fact that the authors belong to Opus Dei means that our study also is in some ways an expression of the self-understanding of the people of the Work. More specifically, it reflects our conviction that the charismatic origin of Opus Dei manifests the presence of the divine in our lives, although this goes beyond the limits of strictly historical method.

Research on Opus Dei requires a precise methodology typical of religious history, because it contains intangible aspects related to the mystery of the Church. Its message refers to God and to our relationship with him. It views the world as a sphere of contact between the temporal and the sacred. And those who share the teachings of the Work are men and women who base their thinking, their forms of prayer, and their relationship with others on a message that unites the human and the religious.

Certain topics will reappear throughout the book: the fact that the faithful of the Work are normal Christians, not members of a religious order; the relationship between personal and corporate activity; and the unity and variety of its membership, made up of priests and laity, men and women.

When a person is baptized, he or she is incorporated into the Church and becomes a participant in its mission, called to follow Jesus Christ in order to spread the kingdom of God. The mere fact of being baptized gives a person a position in the Church, as a member of the faithful or, colloquially, as an *ordinary Christian*. Among these Christians are the people of Opus Dei, who try to take seriously their call to holiness and apostolic service. They try to imitate the virtues of Jesus, attend Mass daily, devote time to prayer, and speak of God's goodness, beauty, and love to their relatives, friends, and colleagues. Their way of living is one particular concrete response, among others, to Jesus' invitation to follow him.

In the law of the Church, some men and women take a public position by professing the evangelical counsels of poverty, chastity, and obedience and give a public witness of prayer and apostolate. These are called *consecrated persons*.* The vast majority of the faithful are called to seek holiness and to spread the kingdom of God in

---

* In this monograph, we will often distinguish between consecrated persons and secular Christians. Before 1983 consecrated persons were often called "religious." We will frequently use the word religious in this special sense rather than in its generic meaning of taking God and the things of God seriously. When Opus Dei was founded, the term *religious* meant a person who belonged to a religious order or congregation. In the terminology of the Code of Canon Law in force at the time, "The religious state or stable form of common life" was proper to those who, "in addition to the common precepts, profess the evangelical counsels through the vows of obedience, chastity and poverty" (*Codex Iuris Canonici*, 1917, canon 487; the translation is ours). The current Code of Canon Law uses the category *institutes of consecrated life* to refer to a wide range of groups whose members profess the evangelical counsels. This category covers religious orders and congregations, secular institutes, and societies of apostolic life. (See *Code of Canon Law*, 1983, canons 573–746.)

everyday life through example and word, but are not called to give the official witness characteristic of members of institutes of consecrated life. In a technical sense, proper to theology and canon law, these lay faithful and diocesan priests are *secular*.* This applies to both the laity and priests of Opus Dei, who strive to be saints in and through the vicissitudes of their work or other activities and in living together with others.

Opus Dei has an institutional component that occupies a large part of our book. We will discuss demographic data and statistics; the forms of central, regional, and local governance; the collective diffusion of the Work's message; its corporate activities; the organic unity of its members within a specific, ecclesial, hierarchical structure; and the formative and evangelizing framework that inspires the mentality and actions of tens of thousands of men and women.†

Nonetheless, the life—and, therefore, the history—of most of the people of Opus Dei does not take place in institutional settings. Opus Dei's message of the call to holiness in the midst of the world is conveyed primarily by individual members and cooperators of the Work

---

* The teachings of Josemaría Escrivá present a secular way of life that unites, in thought and action, the sacred and profane realms. See Ana Marta González, "Mundo y condición humana en san Josemaría Escrivá: Claves cristianas para una filosofía de las ciencias sociales," *Romana* no. 65 (July–December 2017), pp. 368–390. In contrast to the meaning given to *secular* in the Church, in the writings of Escrivá, and in this book, *secular* in modern usage usually refers to realities and ways of life that are not related to spiritual and religious values. Obviously neither Opus Dei nor its members are "secular" in that sense.

† The demographic and statistical data kept in the General Archives of the Prelature of Opus Dei are quite incomplete until the 1980s. This is due to the fact that the registry of persons belonging to the Work and of cooperators was not centralized; it was in the hands of the regional governing bodies of the various countries. Every five years, the regions sent a tally to the central councils, particularly when a general congress of Opus Dei was held. Beginning in 1987, the directors of the Work provided the Holy See with the total number of members to be published in the *Annuario Pontificio*. At that time, improved computer systems helped to produce centralized and more accurate statistics. The demographic figures provided in this book come mainly from the acts of the general congresses of Opus Dei and from the archives of the general secretariat of the Work.

in a capillary way in their own professional and family environments. As a consequence, it is not easy to convey the living reality of Opus Dei's most important apostolate and its real impact in the Church and in civil society. Despite the difficulty, in chapter twenty-seven, at the end of Volume II, we attempt to explore this essential aspect.

Opus Dei has two sections, one for men and one for women. The two are united at the head, that is, in the prelate and his vicars in the different regions. On the other hand, they have separate governing bodies and economic management. The Work organizes formational activities like retreats and days of recollection separately for men and women, even in the case of married people. This will make it necessary to explore simultaneously the development and activities of both sections in each time and place, studying what is common to both and what is specific to one or the other, such as the priesthood among men and some forms of care of persons in the centers for women. In studying the evolution of the women's branch, we will pay particular attention to the impact on Opus Dei of the positive evolution of the role of women in the larger society and the growing social recognition of their equality with men, their leadership potential, and their specifically feminine contributions.

Because Opus Dei is made up of laypeople and priests, its structure mirrors the ordinary structure of the Church, rooted in the constitutional binomial between the ministerial priesthood and the common priesthood. We will need to analyze how the organic cooperation between the two arose and developed in the Work.

In addition to highlighting the institutional and hierarchical nature of Opus Dei, we will explore its familial and communitarian aspects. Although priests are an essential part of it, we will see that from a demographic and organizational point of view, and in terms of the scope of its message, the history of Opus Dei is, for the most part, a lay phenomenon.

This book has its roots in a course on the life of the Founder of Opus Dei taught by José Luis González Gullón at the Pontifical University of the Holy Cross (Rome) during the 2016–2017 academic year. While preparing the classes, he began to think about writing a book on the history of the institution founded by Escrivá. At that point, he invited John Coverdale to join the project. Then came a long process of searching for sources and of meetings in the two cities where we live (New York and Rome), as well as some trips to regions where Opus Dei has expanded the most, such as Argentina, Spain, the Philippines, and Mexico. González Gullón then wrote the history of Opus Dei during the years of Josemaría Escrivá and Javier Echevarría, and Coverdale wrote the period of Álvaro del Portillo. The two authors signed the entire book because we collaborated closely in writing the original drafts and each of us has thoroughly revised the other's text and translated it into our native language. However, the reader will find differences in the way we approach the story, since we come from different historiographic schools. We believe that this variety enriches the research.*

Between the death of Josemaría Escrivá in 1975 and his canonization in 2002, some members of Opus Dei published biographies of the Founder, mostly with hagiographic accents. Since the creation of the St. Josemaría Escrivá Historical Institute in 2001, numerous books and scientific articles about the Founder, the institution, and some of its members have appeared. Much of this research is limited to narrow areas and concentrates on the first three decades of the Work. Most of the books and articles deal with topics related to social, cultural, and political history, for example, the role played by members of the Work in Spanish public life.

Over the ninety years of Opus Dei's history, there have been important developments in the understanding, implementation, and explanation of the principal elements of its message, including awareness of divine filiation, the sanctification of work, the unity that should characterize a Christian's life, marriage as a human and divine vocation, and the spirit of service. We have attempted to reflect those

---

* The Spanish and English versions of this book are not exactly identical. The differences, although not many or substantial, go beyond what is usual in a translation because in preparing the two versions we have included explanations that seemed necessary or useful for the readers of one language but not the other. We consider both versions to be equally original and authentic and we each take full responsibility for both.

developments. The next steps—situating Opus Dei's charism in the theological, spiritual, and canonical context of the last hundred years, or elaborating its role within the various realities that make up the Church—are tasks that go beyond the scope of our book. To a large extent, they remain in the hands of theologians, canonists, and other specialists in these matters.*

Perhaps the main obstacle to the development of a richer literature on the history of Opus Dei lies in the fact that the General Archive of the Prelature of Opus Dei (AGP) is not yet open to the academic community. In this regard, we are grateful to Bishop Fernando Ocáriz, Prelate of Opus Dei, for accepting our research proposal and giving us access to the documentation. At the same time, we would like to express our hope that the process of cataloguing the collections will be completed soon, so that all interested researchers can have access to them.†

AGP is the most important archive for those who wish to know Opus Dei. It holds an enormous wealth of documents. In our case, we have used the primary sources that, in our opinion, were essential for a general history. For example, we read the minutes of the general congresses, the reports on visits of the directors of the Work to the regional organizations, the government notes, the documents on the

---

* From a theological and canonical point of view, two fundamental books are: Pedro Rodríguez, Fernando Ocáriz and José Luis Illanes, *El Opus Dei en la Iglesia*, 6th ed. (Madrid: Rialp, 2014); and Amadeo de Fuenmayor, Valentín Gómez-Iglesias, and José Luis Illanes, *El itinerario jurídico del Opus Dei: Historia y defensa de un carisma*, 4th ed. (Pamplona: EUNSA, 1990). On Opus Dei within the spiritual context of the twentieth century, we mention the three volumes of Ernst Burkhart and Javier López, *Vida cotidiana y santidad en la enseñanza de san Josemaría: Estudio de teología espiritual* (Madrid: Rialp, 2010–2013); and Antonio Aranda, *El hecho teológico y pastoral del Opus Dei: una indagación en las fuentes fundacionales* (Pamplona: EUNSA, 2020).

† A substantial portion of the AGP sources between 1928 and 1975 are catalogued. In these cases, the call number of the documents begins with the series, followed by three numbers that are, respectively, the *legajo*, the *carpeta*, and the *expediente*. From that year on, the documentation is in an intermediate file that, in the best of cases, only has series and *legajos*. We will cite the material according to the call numbers provided to us by AGP staff.

main corporate activities, and many personal testimonies. The quality and volume of these materials and the need not to extend the length of our book kept us from consulting other archives, with the exception of the Vatican Apostolic Archives (AAV), which has *fonds* (archive groups) available up to the year 1958. For the events of the last five decades we interviewed two hundred men and women from various countries.

Despite the length of this book, we suggest that it be read from beginning to end, so as to most clearly see the continuity and development of the various aspects that make up Opus Dei, such as formation, corporate activities, and the personal incarnation of the message of holiness.

This book has six chronological parts: four dedicated to the foundational stage and one each to the years in which Del Portillo and Echevarría governed Opus Dei. It concludes with a brief epilogue concerning the last five years. In synthesis, we can say that after eight years of initial development, Opus Dei found itself involved in two great collective dramas: the Spanish Civil War and then the Second World War. In the 1940s, it spread, initially in Spain and then to Europe and North America. Thanks to the pontifical approval of Opus Dei in 1950, the Work expanded to almost all the countries of America and a few in Africa and Asia. At the same time, it began important corporate activities in the field of education. The sixties and early seventies witnessed the multiplication of activities and a more extensive written exposition of the Work's spirit by its founder, both during and after the Second Vatican Council.

After the death of Escrivá in 1975, Del Portillo took on the responsibility of carrying forward the founding spirit and facing new challenges such as bringing to completion, with the Work's establishment as a personal prelature, its long quest for a satisfactory legal status, the beatification of the Founder, and the spread of the Work in countries with Christian minorities. With Javier Echevarría came a time of social transformation marked by the technological era that led the members of Opus Dei to seek more ways to radiate their spirituality in the Church and in the world.

Our exploration of Opus Dei's institutional evolution and the development of its apostolic undertakings can be somewhat repetitive because the message of Opus Dei is the same and its ways of acting are substantially similar across time. The basic structures of government and formation devised in the 1940s have evolved, but have not changed substantially. The issues involving relations with ecclesiastical authorities and other institutions in the Church were already present in the early days and remain important today. To keep repetition to a minimum, we have tried to explain concepts the first time they appear and refer back to those explanations when they reappear. Since this is a general history, we do not offer a bibliographical list at the end, which would be clearly incomplete.* The notes are at the end of the book, except for this introduction and the explanatory notes, which are at the foot of the page.

We are grateful to José Antonio Araña, Eduardo Baura, Rafael Domingo Oslé, Joseluís González, Andrew Hegarty, Marlies Kücking, Javier Marrodán, Juan Manuel Mora, Santiago de Pablo Contreras, Pablo Pérez López, Joseba Louzao, José Manuel Martín Quemada, Stefan Moszoro, María Eugenia Ossandón, Antón M. Pazos, Ana Sánchez de la Nieta, and Fernando Valenciano, who commented on the entire manuscript, and to people too numerous to name who read some chapters and sections; also to the two hundred historians, faithful of Opus Dei, and cooperators we interviewed. Their comments and suggestions contributed decisively to improving the book. We owe a special debt of gratitude to three great historians, our mentors Jesús Longares, Feliciano Montero, and Stanley Payne, for teaching us to ask good questions about the past in order to find answers that enlarge the future.

---

* With some exceptions, we have chosen to cite only the literature that makes direct reference to the history of Opus Dei. The website Biblioteca Virtual Josemaría Escrivá de Balaguer y Opus Dei offers exhaustive and updated bibliographical information on the Founder of the Work, his successors, the members of Opus Dei, and its institutional activities (*https://www.unav.edu/web/centro-de-estudios-josemaria-escriva/biblioteca-virtual/index*).

BACKGROUND

Josemaría Escrivá was born at the height of the *Belle Époque*, the period of Western European and American history that began in 1880 with the end of the Franco-Prussian war and lasted until the outbreak of the First World War in 1914. Those four decades were a period of great prosperity in Western Europe and North America. The economy benefited from rapid industrialization, growth of cities, and scientific and technological advances in fields as diverse as medicine, radio, aeronautics, and cinema. Impressionism, *Art Nouveau*, and cubism transformed the arts.

Philosophical positivism dominated the academic world. Optimism and the belief in progress were fed by scientific and technological developments. Confidence in increasing human capacity also colored the life of nations. The great powers expanded their colonial empires, moved by a desire to spread Western cultures throughout the world and, at the same time, to gain access to raw materials.

In the West, the transition from rural to industrial societies brought with it sharp social changes. The paradoxes and abuses of the liberal system were translated into inequalities and confrontation. Partially in reaction to this, socialism, communism, and anarchism grew exponentially, both in the world of thought and the world of political action.

Spain was trying to find its own identity. The loss of its colonial possessions in the Philippines, Cuba, and Puerto Rico (which Spaniards called the "disaster of 1898") convinced the country that it was no longer a superpower in the world of nations. The constitutional monarchy that had been established in 1874 showed signs of exhaustion and lack of political direction. Liberals and conservatives alternated in power based on *caciquismo*, the network of clients dominated by local political bosses referred to as "caciques," but the growth of mass political parties indicated that this system could not last. For this reason, the attempts at national renovation by the conservative Antonio Maura failed, as did those of his liberal counterpart, José Canalejas, who was assassinated by an anarchist in 1912.

Spanish society moved only slowly into the contemporary world. Sixty percent of the population was rural. Seventy-three percent was illiterate, and infant mortality was more than 1.5 percent. On the positive side, the cities were growing, as was the middle class, and life expectancy for adults reached fifty years.

Spain was a confessional country. At the beginning of the twentieth century the majority of the population was baptized and taught Catholic doctrine both in churches and schools. The church had a strong institutional presence throughout the country, from the largest cities to the smallest towns. There were 33,000 diocesan priests, 12,000 male religious, and 42,000 nuns. Twenty-five percent of primary education and 80 percent of secondary education was in the hands of religious institutions.

Although Catholicism was deeply rooted in social life, it suffered at times from clericalism and lack of personal reflection. Due both to the Church's teaching and the wider cultural background of the country, a large proportion of Catholics had a traditionalist mentality, favorable to a confessional state and contrary to liberal thought. They supported Pope Pius X's condemnation of modernism, an intellectual approach that eliminated the transcendent dimension of religious faith.

Section 1. Discovering his Calling

Josemaría Escrivá Albás was born in Barbastro, in the Spanish province of Huesca, on January 9, 1902. His father, José Escrivá Corzán, had been born in Fonz, in the province of Huesca, in 1867. The Escrivá family traced its roots to Balaguer, in the province of Lérida. His mother, Dolores Albás Blanc, was from Barbastro. Her ancestors came from Aínsa, Huesca. The couple had been married four years earlier, in 1898. They rented a house on Mayor Street, on the corner of the Plaza del Mercado. Their first child, Carmen, was born in 1899.*

Barbastro had only seven thousand inhabitants. Despite its small size, it had been a diocese for eight centuries. The economy was based on agriculture, particularly grain, wine, and oil. Store owners and small businessmen lived in close contact with their employees and day laborers. The political spectrum ranged from Carlists, who were traditionalists and supported the *ancien régime*, to republicans and socialists. The recreational and cultural scene was dominated by liberal thought. There were no obvious serious political or social conflicts in the town at the time.

Toward the end of the nineteenth century, José Escrivá and two partners created a business that sold cloth and chocolates. In 1902, when one of the partners withdrew and signed a noncompete agreement, José Escrivá formed a new business called *Juncosa y Escrivá*. At first the business prospered, and the Escrivá family was relatively well-off. As was common at the time for upper-middle-class families, they had four servants. José Escrivá's sense of Christian solidarity showed itself in the alms that he gave to needy people, his financial support of the Catholic Center of the city, and the religious conferences he organized for his employees.

Four days after his birth, Josemaría was baptized in his parish, the Cathedral of Barbastro. Shortly thereafter, on April 23, he was confirmed. In 1904, at the age of two, he suffered acute meningitis. Although the doctor was sure he would die, his mother prayed a novena to Our Lady of the Sacred Heart, promising that if the child recovered, she would make a pilgrimage to Our Lady of Torreciudad, some twenty kilometers from Barbastro. He recovered quickly, and

---

* An earlier version of this chapter was published as José Luis González Gullón, "La vocación de Josemaría Escrivá de Balaguer (1918–1928)," *Scripta Theologica* 50, no. 3 (2018), pp. 637–653. See Carlo Pioppi, "Infanzia e prima adolescenza di Josemaría Escrivá: Barbastro 1902–1915: Contesti, eventi biografici, stato delle ricerche e prospettive di approfondimento," *Studia et Documenta* 8 (2014), pp. 149–189; Andrés Vázquez de Prada, *The Founder of Opus Dei: The Life of Josemaría Escrivá*, vol. 1, *The Early Years* (Princeton NJ: Scepter, 1988), pp. 5–86.

in thanksgiving his mother carried him in her arms to Torreciudad, riding on horseback.

The Escrivá family was very close-knit. Josemaría learned from his parents to live with freedom and responsibility, and he acquired from them virtues such as hard work and order. They also taught him to pray in a simple, natural way. He later recalled, "Our Lord prepared things in such a way that my life was normal and ordinary without anything unusual. He had me born in a Christian home, as was common in my country, and gave me exemplary parents who lived and practiced their faith."[1]

In the following years the Escrivás had three daughters: María Asunción ("Chon") in 1905, María de los Dolores ("Lolita") in 1907, and María del Rosario in 1909. Death took the three of them, one after the other—Rosario at nine months of age, in 1910; Lolita at five, in 1912; and Chon at 8, in 1913.

Besides these painful events, Josemaría had a normal, happy childhood in which he gradually opened up to society and to the world. Between 1905 and 1908, he attended a nursery school run by the Daughters of Charity. From 1908 to 1915 he studied at a school run by the Piarist Fathers. In 1912, the year in which he began secondary school, he received his First Holy Communion, taking advantage of Pope Pius X's recent directives allowing children to receive Communion when they reached the age of reason. When he received Jesus in the Blessed Sacrament, Josemaría asked him for the grace never to commit a mortal sin.

Due to the difficult economic circumstances of the moment and to the fact that their former partner had not honored his noncompetition agreement, Juncosa y Escrivá faced an economic crisis. Juan Juncosa and José Escrivá sued their former partner. The trial court found in their favor in 1910. In 1912 the appeals court upheld the judgment but reduced the amount of compensation to which they were entitled. The Supreme Court rejected their appeal, and they had to pay the defendant's legal fees. Juncosa y Escrivá went bankrupt and eventually dissolved.[2]

The business's assets were not sufficient to cover its debts. Although he was not legally obliged to do so, Jose Escrivá decided to pay the creditors with his personal capital. His wife supported this decision, but some in-laws thought it was foolish because it left the family financially ruined. The Escrivás had to let their servants go and began to suffer want. Josemaría went through an inner crisis because of these economic difficulties coupled with the suffering caused by the early deaths of his sisters. Nonetheless, the Christian resignation of his parents in the face of adversity helped him to maintain his confidence in God and hope for the future.

In March 1915, José Escrivá found work as a clerk in a fabric store in Logroño called La Gran Ciudad de Londres. At the end of the summer, the family moved to Logroño, a city of twenty-four thousand inhabitants, where they knew no one.

Carmen enrolled in the School of Education, where she would graduate in 1921. Josemaría continued his high school studies in the public General and Technical Institute of Logroño. As was common at the time, in the afternoons he attended supplementary classes at a private school.

In late 1917 or early 1918, on a day of heavy snow, something happened which changed the course of Josemaría's life. "Suddenly seeing some Carmelite religious barefoot in the snow,"[3] he asked himself, "If others make such great sacrifices for God and for their neighbor, could I not offer him something?"[4] He began to think about becoming a priest, something that until then he had not considered.

He sought spiritual direction from a Carmelite, Fr. José Miguel de la Virgen del Carmen. He began to deepen his Christian life with, as he said, "daily communion purification, confession . . . and penance."[5] Three or four months later Fr. José Miguel proposed that he become a Carmelite. Josemaría meditated calmly on this proposal, but came to the conclusion that his path was that of a secular priest.

He rejected the idea that being a priest meant "having a career" or having a fixed place in the structure of the diocese. "That was not what God was asking of me, and I realized that. I did not want to be a parish priest in order to be a priest, a *"cura"* [parson] as people say in Spain. I had veneration for parish priests but that was not the kind of priesthood I wanted for me."[6] Deep inside he felt a different sort of call, both certain and indeterminate at the same time. Later he called these interior motions "inklings" (*barruntos*). That is to say, intuitions of God's calling him to a mission which was united to the priesthood. In his words, "I did not know what God wanted of me, but it was, evidently, a choice."[7] In this sense, being a priest seemed to be a necessary but insufficient condition for carrying out whatever it was God wanted. "Why did I become a priest? Because I thought that in that way it would be easier to fulfill something God wanted from me, although I did not know what it was."[8] Only the future would reveal what being a pastor in the Church would mean in his life. He intensified his prayer of petition. "The lights [I was asking for] did not come, but evidently, prayer was the way."[9] He was "convinced that God *wanted me for something*."[10] He repeated frequently two brief Latin phrases, praying to know God's designs: *Domine, ut videam!* (Lord, that I may see!) and *Domine, ut sit!* (Lord, let it be!).

When he told his father that he wanted to enter the seminary, José Escrivá wanted to make sure: "Have you thought about the sacrifice that the vocation to the priesthood entails?" Josemaría answered, "Just like you when you got married, I have only thought about Love."[11] Seeing that he was firm in his resolve, his father was moved to tears "because he had other possible plans, but he did not rebel."[12] He only advised him to study law at the same time as theology. (Until then, it had seemed that Josemaría might study architecture, law, or medicine). His father introduced him to the priest who was pastor and abbot of the collegial church of Logroño.

In 1918, Josemaría finished high school with good grades. During the summer he studied philosophy with a tutor, and in November he entered the seminary of Logroño. During the next two academic years he finished his studies through the first year of theology. On Sunday mornings he taught catechism to children. His seminary companions would recall him as being "responsible, a good student, cheerful, pleasant with everyone, somewhat reserved and pious."[13]

In Spain at that time, sons were expected to take care of the needs of the family. Josemaría thought that his family needed another son, and he asked God to send one although José Escrivá was fifty-one years old and Dolores Albás was forty-one. They had not had any children for nine years. On February 28, 1919, ten months after Josemaría has spoken to his father about his priestly vocation, Santiago Escrivá was born. Santiago's birth made an impression on Josemaría. He saw it as connected with his inklings and vocation to the priesthood. "My mother called me to tell me, 'You are going to have a new little brother or sister.' With this, I touched God's grace. I saw it as our Lord's doing, something I hadn't expected."[14]

Section 2. Priest and Jurist

At the end of the first decade of the twentieth century, Spain faced serious political and social difficulties. Thousands of soldiers were losing their lives in a colonial war in Spanish Morocco. The country needed political and institutional renewal. Social conflict was becoming more acute, fed by socialist and anarchist revolutionary ideologies and large-scale migration from rural areas to the larger cities.

In this context, Josemaría Escrivá moved to Zaragoza to continue his ecclesiastical studies. The capital of Aragon had about 150,000 inhabitants and was adding industrial activity to the traditional agriculture of the surrounding area. Two of his uncles lived in Zaragoza: Carlos Albás, who was a canon of the Cathedral of Zaragoza, and Mauricio Albás, who was raising a family there. Zaragoza offered many advantages over the small town of Calahorra where seminarians from the Rioja region normally finished their theological studies. Among other things, in Zaragoza he would be able to follow his father's advice about obtaining a law degree while finishing his ecclesiastical studies at the pontifical university.

Carlos Albás facilitated the transfer of his nephew to the seminary of St. Francis De Paul, where he was given a half scholarship. Escrivá immediately began classes in the Pontifical University of Saints Valero and Braulio, where he received the theological training typical of the era in Spain. He put off beginning his law studies until his fifth year of theology so as to be able to study both well.[15]

Escrivá continued to be convinced that God was calling him to something that would come in the future. By their very nature these inklings were clear in some respects and imprecise in others. As he said later, "I continued seeing, but without specifying what it was that the Lord wanted. I saw that the Lord wanted something from me. I asked, and continued asking."[16] Whenever possible, he went to the Chapel of the Virgin of the Pillar to ask for light about the will of God. He prayed to Our Lady an aspiration similar to the one that he often prayed to God: *Domina, ut sit!* (My Lady, let it be!). He backed up his supplications with phrases from the Gospels that at times he said aloud or even sang: *Ignem veni mittere in terram et quid volo nisi ut accendatur?* (I have come to set the earth on fire, and what do I want but that it burn?) And he replied, *Ecce ego quia vocasti me!* (Here I am, because you called me!).[17]

About the same time as he arrived in Zaragoza in 1920, Josemaría felt "moved to record haphazardly" in "loose notes" without any special order, different motions and events of his interior life.[18] He referred to some of these inspirations in which he sensed God's providence as "operative, because they dominated my will in such a way that I hardly had to make any effort."[19] They were ill-defined ideas. Some of them seemed to suggest a new foundation, but without anything concrete. On the other hand they clearly were founded on an intimate relationship with God, "something as beautiful as falling in love."[20] Years later, he would sum up this stage of his life in the following words: "I began to have inklings of Love, to realize that my heart was asking for something great and that it was love."[21] This interior rapture increased his desire to pray and to fulfill the will of God: "Truly, the Lord expanded my heart, making me capable of loving, of repenting, of serving, even despite my errors."[22]

Misunderstandings with the rector and one of the monitors of the seminary and the behavior of some seminarians led him to think that he had "mistaken the way."[23] During the summer of 1921, he sought spiritual direction from a priest in Logroño who, seeing his good dispositions, encouraged him to go forward despite these misgivings. He decided to do so and one year later, in September 1922, he received the tonsure, which officially made him a cleric. At the same time the Archbishop of Zaragoza, Cardinal Juan Soldevilla, named him monitor of the seminary.

The nationally prestigious Law School of the University of Zaragoza offered the possibility of being a "free student," which meant not being required to attend classes. Escrivá enrolled as a free student in 1923. Except for two preparatory exams, he did not attend classes or take exams until he finished his first theology degree, the *Licenciatura*, in June 1924. This approach and his lack of desire to "have a career" in the diocese upset his uncle Carlos, who wanted him to seek an ecclesiastical position as soon as possible. Escrivá "considered that his studies in the law school would make him more available for fulfilling God's will."[24] In this sense, he may have thought that having a law degree was related to his inklings. Later, his legal training would in fact help him situate Opus Dei within the Church's canonical structure.

On June 14, 1924, Josemaría was ordained a subdeacon. Five months later, on November 27, his father, José Escrivá, died suddenly in Logroño, leaving Josemaría the head of the family. His decision to move his family to Zaragoza led to a major confrontation with his uncle. Years earlier, Carlos Albás had not approved of his brother-in-law's using the family's money to pay off business debts. Now he did not want his impoverished sister, nephews, and niece to live in Zaragoza. He advised Josemaría to wait to be reunited with his family until he had been ordained a priest and had settled in the diocese. Josemaría's refusal to accept this advice led to an open break.

On December 20, 1924, Miguel de los Santos Díaz Gómara, auxiliary bishop of Zaragoza, ordained Escrivá a deacon. On March 28, 1925, he ordained him a priest. Two days later, Josemaría celebrated his First Mass in the Holy Chapel of the Pillar, in suffrage for his father. Very few people attended: his mother, his brother and sister, a few cousins, the family of a professor with whom he was friends, and a couple more guests. Conspicuous by their absence were his three priest-uncles: Fr. Teodoro Escrivá, Fr. Carlos Albás, and Fr. Vicente Albás. After taking off the vestments, the young priest began to cry, thinking of his father and of the problems that he had faced.

He spent the next month and a half in a nearby small town called Perdiguerra. There Josemaría took his first steps in the administration of the sacraments and in the spiritual direction of the parishioners. When he returned to Zaragoza, the diocesan officials did not give him any position in a parish or any other part of the pastoral structure of the diocese. He obtained a position as chaplain in the Jesuit church of St. Peter Nolasco. There he celebrated Mass each day and spent some time in the confessional. He spent the rest of the day attending law school classes and studying.

Escrivá found the academic world enriching, thanks in part to having a lay mentality that was not common among the clergy. For example, between one class and another he did not meet with priests or seminarians but rather talked with the lay students. He requested no privileges when it came to exams or attending class, and he did not "give sermons" when talking with his fellow students. For these reasons, some of them began to esteem and confide in him and even accompany him on the street, something they would not normally do with a priest.

His priestly activity put him in contact with some university students who belonged to the Sodality directed by the Jesuits. On Sundays, they taught Christian doctrine together to the children of indigent families in the Casablanca neighborhood on the outskirts of Zaragoza. Contact with the needy increased his desire to put his priesthood at the service of others.

For some time, and especially since his father's death, Josemaría had been thinking about the possibility of studying for a doctorate in law and becoming a law professor. He wanted to bring Catholic teaching to the academic environment because it seemed to him that his fellow students in the law school were a bit like "sheep without a shepherd."[25] The only law school in Spain that offered a doctorate was the Central University in Madrid. Furthermore his priest-friend and professor, José Pou de Foxá, advised him to build his life outside of Zaragoza since his uncle's hostility meant he had no future there.[26] Sometime around September 1926, Escrivá went to Madrid to gather information about doctoral studies there. In the meantime, he tried to earn some money to support his family by giving review classes in Roman law, canon law, history of law, and natural law in the Amado Institute, in Zaragoza.

In January 1927 he received his law degree from the University of Zaragoza. Two months later he made arrangements to begin a doctoral program in the Central University. After a brief stint filling in for a priest in the small town of Fombuena, Josemaría left Zaragoza.[27]

Notes

1. Meditation, February 14, 1964, quoted in Andrés Vázquez de Prada, *The Founder of Opus Dei: The Life of Josemaría Escrivá*, vol. 1, *The Early Years* (Princeton, NJ: Scepter, 1988), p. 5.

2. See AGP A.1, 12-1-1.

3. *Intimate Notes*, 1637b (April 10, 1932). This is Escrivá's oldest record of the incident of the footprints in the snow. We quote Josemaría Escrivá's *Intimate Notes* (*Apuntes íntimos*) from the critical-historical edition prepared by Pedro Rodríguez and found in AGP. For information on the content and scope of the *Intimate Notes*, see Josemaría Escrivá, *The Way: Critical-Historical Edition*, ed. Pedro Rodríguez (London, New York: Scepter, 2009), pp. 40–50. Pedro Rodríguez, "Apuntes íntimos (obra inédita)," in *Diccionario de san Josemaría Escrivá de Balaguer*, 3rd ed., ed. José Luis Illanes Maestre (Burgos: Monte Carmelo, 2015), pp. 131–135.

4. Phrase heard by Álvaro del Portillo and quoted in Andrés Vázquez de Prada, *The Founder of Opus Dei*, vol. 1, p. 96.

5. "A Divine Odyssey," (Meditation of February 14, 1964), in St. Josemaría Escrivá, *In Dialogue with the Lord* (London and New York: Scepter, 2018), 56.

6. "A Divine Odyssey," 57.

7. Notes from a meditation, March 19, 1975, quoted in Vázquez de Prada, *The Founder of Opus Dei*, vol. 1, p. 97. Escrivá understood that this was a divine calling. In his words, he prayed "for years, starting with that first year of my vocation in Logrono." *Intimate Notes*, 289 (September 17, 1931).

8. Quoted in *Crónica*, March 1975, p. 12, AGP Biblioteca, P01. On another occasion, he added, "Those inklings of love brought me to the priesthood." Meditation, October 2, 1968. Quoted in *Meditaciones* (Meditations), vol. 6, 306, AGP Biblioteca, P06.

9. Letter 32, n. 41, AGP A3, 94-2-3.

10. *Intimate Notes*, 289 (September 17, 1931).

11. Recollection of Luis Felipe Gómez Caballero, Gaztelueta (Bilbao), August 9, 1975, AGP A.5, 216-1-7.

12. "A Divine Odyssey," 57.

13. Jaime Toldrà, "Seminario Conciliar de Logroño," in *Diccionario de san Josemaría Escrivá de Balaguer*, p. 1143. See also Jaime Toldrà, *Josemaría Escrivá en Logroño (1915–1925)* (Madrid: Rialp, 2007).

14. "A Divine Odyssey," 56.

15. See Ramón Herrando Prat de la Riba, *Los años de seminario de Josemaría Escrivá en Zaragoza (1920–1925): El seminario de San Francisco de Paula* (Madrid: Rialp, 2002).

16. *Intimate Notes*, 179. Álvaro del Portillo transcribed these words of the Founder in 1968.

17. "One Second of October," in St. Josemaría Escrivá, *In Dialogue with the Lord*, 47.

18. *Intimate Notes*, 414 (November 24, 1931) and 306 (October 2, 1931).

19. "A Divine Odyssey," 57.

20. "Notes Taken at a Family Gathering," *Crónica*, May 1968, p. 48, AGP Biblioteca, P01.

21. "The Paths of God," in Escrivá, *In Dialogue with the Lord*, 194.

22. Letter 31, n. 3, AGP A.3, 94-2-2. Toward the end of his life he repeated this idea several times: "I had inklings of the love of God, but I did not know that it was so immense." *Meditaciones*, V, 117, AGP Biblioteca, P06.

23. *Intimate Notes*, 1748 (July 17, 1934).

24. Juan Francisco Baltar Rodríguez, "Los estudios de Derecho de san Josemaría en la Universidad de Zaragoza," *Studia et Documenta* 9 (2015), p. 231.

25. Recollections of Arsenio Górriz Monzón, Teruel, December 1975, AGP A.5, 218-1-8.

26. Recollections of Francisco Javier de Ayala (citing a conversation with Pou de Foxá), São Paulo, September 8, 1979, AGP A.5, 196-2-7. Ayala adds that Escrivá visited his uncle Carlos in the early 1940s and told him that he harbored no resentment for what had happened in the past.

27. See Pedro Rodríguez, "El doctorado de san Josemaría en la Universidad de Madrid," *Studia et Documenta* 2 (2008), pp. 13–103.

PART I

Foundation and Early Years
(1928–1939)

The **Treaty of Versailles** at the end of the First World War marked the end of the Austro-Hungarian and German Empires. The United Kingdom and France, the victors in the war, declared Germany and its allies culpable and imposed complete demilitarization on them. Although they created the League of Nations to mediate international disputes, they denied Germany membership. Meanwhile, the Bolshevik Revolution of 1917 overthrew the czarist regime in Russia and gave rise to the Union of Soviet Socialist Republics, an officially communist state. Under the direction first of Vladimir Lenin and afterward Joseph Stalin, the Soviet Union established a dictatorship of the proletariat that took the lives of millions of Russians and, later, of people from other countries.

In contrast, the Western countries with democratic systems experienced "the Roaring Twenties" as a period of scientific progress and economic growth based on industry and services. In the United States and Europe, the largest cities grew rapidly. Radio and telephone became widespread, and the well-to-do began to have automobiles and take the first commercial flights. Athletes and movie actors introduced new ways of life.

Economic prosperity ended, however, in October 1929 with the massive fall of the New York stock market. The subsequent crisis, the Great Depression, also affected Europe. Not until the second half of the thirties was President Franklin Roosevelt able to re-stimulate the American economy and society with a type of state interventionism that he called the "New Deal."

In Europe, some democratic-liberal systems entered into irremediable crisis. In 1922, Benito Mussolini proclaimed the Fascist regime in Italy. In 1933, Adolf Hitler established a National Socialist government in Germany. These totalitarian regimes proposed overcoming the cultural decadence of the West—the crisis of modernity—and in the case of the Nazis, the humiliation suffered in the Great War. Germany stunned other countries when it annexed Austria and the Czech Sudetenland in 1938, and then signed a nonaggression pact with the Soviet Union.

In the east, Mao Zedong created the short-lived Chinese Soviet Republic in 1931. Six years later, Japan invaded China, giving rise to a massive military conflict between the two countries. The menace of a new world conflict threatened the globe.

During this period there were three successive political systems in Spain. All three began with great hopes and ended with social conflict. The dictatorship of General Miguel Primo de Rivera began in 1923 with the backing of King Alfonse XIII. It ended in 1930 because it failed to renew political and social life. Lack of freedom under De Rivera provoked a strong reaction against the monarchy which had supported him. In April 1931, left-wing and centrist leaders proclaimed the Second Spanish Republic. From the beginning, the republic was challenged by lack of political agreement among its supporters, opposition from the right, intolerance, and growing violence. In July 1936, a group of generals launched a coup d'état. The rebels prevailed immediately in about half the country. But what had been intended to be a quick, relatively bloodless coup, degenerated into a three-year Civil War, marked especially by widespread, violent persecution of the Church. At the end of the conflict in April 1939, the victorious general, Francisco Franco, established an authoritarian personal regime.

The Pope of these decades was Pius XI. Elected in 1922, he managed the Vatican's diplomacy, with great prudence assisted by his secretaries of state, first Pietro Gasparri and then Eugenio Pacelli. In 1929 the Lateran Pacts with Mussolini's Italy recognized Vatican City as a sovereign state and established diplomatic relations between the Vatican and Italy. Pius XI criticized the dominant ideologies of the time. In March 1933, he published three encyclicals condemning German national socialist totalitarianism, Soviet communism, and Mexican revolutionary thought. He followed closely the repression of Catholics during the Cristero War in Mexico (1926–1929) and during the Spanish Civil War (1936–1939). He attempted to support the faithful on both sides.

The motto of Pius XI's pontificate was *Pax Christi in regno Christi* (The peace of Christ in the reign of Christ). He sought to develop a Christian society in the modern world, publishing numerous moral and social encyclicals and vigorously supported Catholic Action, defined as the participation of laypeople in the hierarchical apostolate of the Church. In the face of increasing secularization, the Pope called on lay men and women to collaborate in the creation of a social order with Christian roots. Under the direction of the bishops, laypeople would bring the gospel to the working and social environments in which the clergy were not present.

CHAPTER 1

The Foundation of the Work

Escrivá arrived in Madrid on April 20, 1927. He enrolled in doctoral classes at the Law School at the Central University and lived in a residence for priests from other dioceses. This residence was run by the Apostolic Ladies of the Sacred Heart of Jesus, a new religious congregation. A month after he began living there, the foundress of the Apostolic Ladies offered him the chaplaincy of the church of the Foundation for the Sick, the central house of the congregation and the site of various charitable activities. On June 1, 1927, Escrivá began his pastoral work there, which consisted in celebrating Mass and exposition of the Eucharist, hearing confessions, leading the Rosary. On weekends he heard the confessions of children from the low-tuition schools promoted by the Apostolic Ladies. Although it was not part of his official duties as chaplain, he frequently visited sick people in their homes to bring them Communion or hear their confession.[1]

Five months later, Escrivá was able to rent an apartment for himself and his family. To support his family, he began to teach Roman law and canon law in the Cicuéndez Academy, a private school that prepared students for the law school entrance exam and gave supplementary classes in some subjects. He taught class twice a week at least until 1931.[2]

Section 1. The Original Foundational Event

On September 30, 1928, Josemaría Escrivá went to the convent of the Vicentians on the northern outskirts of Madrid to make a retreat together with six other priests. On Tuesday, October 2, after celebrating Mass, he went to his room and began reading notes he had taken of ideas and events that he considered inspired by God and that reflected his inklings. Suddenly, in Escrivá's words, "Jesus wanted his Work to begin to take concrete form."[3] The young priest copied "with some unity the loose notes that till then he had taken,"[4] and "understood the beautiful but heavy load that the Lord in his inexplicable goodness had placed on his shoulders."[5]

What happened in that intense moment? The young priest received a supernatural grace. He had an "illumination about the whole Work,"[6] a "clear general idea of my mission"[7] that opened up an "immense apostolic panorama."[8] Deeply moved because he had just "seen clearly the Will of God"[9] for which he had prayed so much, he knelt down and gave thanks. Then he heard the bells of the parish of Our Lady of the Angels calling the faithful to Mass. Later he considered this a sign of the intercession of Holy Mary and of the angels in the foundational moment.

There is no definitive text on the content of the original vision of Opus Dei. Perhaps Escrivá preferred not to try to enclose in a single account a supernatural light and preferred to explain it with his example and word throughout his life. But he did make clear both orally and in writing that he had received the nucleus of a teaching, open to further development, that contained two inseparable dimensions: a message and an institution.

Escrivá received a Christian message that brought with it a mission: to proclaim the universal call to sanctity in secular environments. As he said many years later, he was called "to encourage people of every sector of society to desire holiness in the midst of the world."* This charism was for every place, time, and culture. It is directed in its fullness to ordinary Christians—lay men and women and secular priests—who are called together to discover in human and temporal realities a path that leads to the fullness of Christian life.[10]

---

* Josemaría Escrivá, *Conversations with Josemaría Escrivá* (New York: Scepter, 2002), 24. The quotation is from an interview carried out in 1967. Escrivá explained throughout his life that God calls all the baptized to sanctity. The place one occupies in the world does not modify, increase, or decrease the quality of the vocation: "Sanctity is not reserved for a privileged few. All the ways of the earth, every state in life, every profession, every honest task can be divine." *Conversations*, 26.

He also understood that there should be an institution whose members would incarnate and spread the message. It would be made up of male members—laymen and secular priests— who in time would become very numerous. They would all be united by the same vocational sense and by belonging to a spiritual family. They would carry out some practices of Christian piety and they would make an effort to seek sanctity and carry out Christian apostolate in the context of their own professional, family, and social life. Initially, he thought it would be limited to men.

This foundational light was deeply impressed in the head and in the heart of the Founder. Throughout his life he spoke about it with the certainty of someone who has been the witness of an event. Something similar occurred with later lights that completed the foundational message. He called them "knock down graces," because God's action within him was as evident as it was unexpected.[11]

Section 2. Initial Development

On October 2, 1928, the "gestational life," as Escrivá called it, "of the as yet unborn but very active Opus Dei began."[12] At the same time, "the first inspirations came to an end."[13] There followed thirteen months of "Our Lord's silence,"[14] in which "Jesus did not speak."[15] During this time, Escrivá dedicated himself to praying. He sought the intercession of Mercedes Reyna, one of the Apostolic Ladies, who died with fame of sanctity in January 1929.

The heart of Opus Dei's message, the universal call to sanctity or perfection, was already present in theology and in the magisterium of the time. In 1923, for example, Pius XI wrote in the encyclical *Rerum omnium* that "tending toward sanctity of life" was a "law that obliges everyone, without exception.*" Nonetheless, Escrivá's message

---

* Pius XI, *Rerum omnium*, AAS 15 (1923), p. 50. At the end of the nineteenth century and beginning of the twentieth century both individual intellectuals and institutions within the Church renewed theology and awakened Christian consciences. Among the great topics that they addressed were studies of the Bible and of the Fathers of the Church, liturgical renewal, and research on being and working within the Church and the mission of secular priests and laypeople. Among specialists in ascetical and mystical

was original in important aspects. He had received it in charismatic fashion and considered it a gift from God, not the fruit of his personal reflection. It was directed primarily to the secular members of the Church, to people immersed in ordinary life. It was transmitted by an institution whose members tried to incarnate it in their own lives. And finally, the Founder was certain that sanctity was not something theoretical but a reality that was possible for a great multitude of ordinary people.

Regarding the institution, Escrivá at first thought that there might already be one with the same goals. In his words, he had "the apparent humility of thinking that there might already be in the world things that were not different from what He was asking of me."[16] He adopted this attitude because Opus Dei was not his idea and because he did not want to be a founder. Later he asked his spiritual children to forgive him for what he considered his initial slowness in starting Opus Dei: "With a false humility, while I was trying to find the first souls, the first vocations, and to form them, I said to myself: there are too many foundations. Why do we need more? Isn't it possible that I will find already existing somewhere in the world this thing that the Lord wants? If it exists, it would be better to join it, to be an enlisted man rather than to found something, which could be pride."[17]

Escrivá sought information about different organizations in the Church that carried out activities with laypeople and secular priests and whose members lived a complete dedication to God without forming a traditional religious congregation. His investigation showed that there was nothing similar to what he had received in his heart. Sometimes the differences were institutional; for example the presence of women among their members. Other times the message was different.[18] In June 1929, the first person joined the newly founded institution, which still did not have a name but which we

---

theology, such as Adolphe-Alfred Tanquerey, Otto Zimmermann, and Crisógono de Jesús Sacramentado, there was a renewed interest in the topic of the calling of all Christians to seek sanctity, which had already been addressed by some spiritual authors such as St. Francis de Sales (1567–1622). See Vicente Bosch, *Llamados a ser santos: Historia contemporánea de una doctrina* (Madrid: Palabra, 2008), pp. 33–65.

will refer to as Opus Dei, the Work of God, or simply the Work. José (Pepe) Romeo was preparing to enter the School of Architecture in Madrid. Although at the time his home was in Zaragoza, he was staying in Madrid to take the entrance exams. Escrivá explained the Work to him, and Romeo said he was willing to accompany him. Some six months later, close to Christmas, Fr. Norberto Rodríguez, a diocesan priest from Astorga and the assistant chaplain of the Foundation for the Sick, asked Escrivá to let him join the Work.[19]

November 1929 saw the renewal of "the spiritual current of divine inspiration for the Work of God, sharpening and making more specific what he wanted. . . ."[20] At that moment, as Escrivá said, "the Lord's special, very concrete, help resumed, and I took notes."[21] These new interior motions helped Escrivá to develop the original light, which had been clear only in its nucleus.

On February 14, 1930, another decisive foundational event took place. Fr. Josemaría was celebrating Mass in the home of the mother of the foundress of the Apostolic Ladies. After Communion, he understood that there should also be women in Opus Dei. He later said: "I cannot say *that I saw*, but yes that *intellectually* I grasped what the Women's Section of Opus Dei had to be. Later I added other things, developing the intellectual vision."[22] From this moment on, the Work was structured as an ecclesial reality with a single head—the Founder—with two sections, one of men and the other of women, both with similar activities directed to spread its message. Escrivá also understood that he should not continue looking for an existing institution that embodied what he had seen in October 1928. God was calling him to open up a new path in the Church: "Without a doubt, it was necessary to found [something]," he explained later, commenting on what had happened on February 14, 1930.[23]

He spoke about the Work to people who were introduced to him or whom he met through spiritual direction, presenting to them a panorama of universal evangelization that consisted in bringing civil society to God in order to transform it from within. This task would be carried out by ordinary men and women who, through an intense life of prayer and personal penance, would proclaim God's truth in the ordinary circumstances of work, family, and social relations. The project was grandiose, but he asked for faith that the Work was divine. "The Lord founded his Work," he repeated.[24] He also asked people to have confidence in him as a witness of supernatural "lights" and "inspirations." For example, when a student told him that the project of the Work was beautiful but seemed to him an impossible dream, the priest responded: "Look, this is not an invention of mine. It is a voice from God."[25]

Some months later, he gave a name for the first time to the institution that he was developing. The idea came from his spiritual director, Fr. Valentín Sánchez Ruiz, who had been his confessor since July 1930. One day, Sánchez Ruiz asked him how "that work of God" was going. At the time the term "work" was a generic name to designate any pastoral or apostolic activity. Escrivá thought the name could be applied to a reality which, because it had been inspired, was properly a "Work of God."*

At first, Escrivá took note of spiritual considerations on loose pieces of paper. In mid-1930 he transcribed some 250 notes into notebooks. During the following decade he continued to use notebooks, eventually reaching a total of nine. He called them *Apuntes íntimos* (Intimate Notes), or *Catalinas* (Catherines) out of devotion to Catherine of Siena. In these writings, Escrivá took note of spiritual matters: reflections on his dealings with God and with people he knew; aspects of the spirit, aims, and activities of the Work; and possible legal structures for Opus Dei that would fit in the law and life of the Church.

The Founder saw the Work as having three goals: giving glory to God, leading men to Jesus through Mary under the guidance of the Pope, and making Christ reign effectively in society. He summarized them in three traditional Latin phrases: *Deo omnis Gloria* [To God

---

* See *Apuntes íntimos* (Intimate Notes), 1868 (June 14, 1948). After the Spanish Civil War, Escrivá, utilized the Latin translation of Work of God—Opus Dei—when he had to present the Work's statutes to the bishop of Madrid in Latin. He did not want the people who belonged to the Work to be referred to by a title, as is commonly the case with the members of religious orders and congregations, because the members of the Work were citizens like any other member of civil society.

be all the glory], *Omnes cum Petro ad Iesum per Mariam* [Everyone with Peter to Jesus through Mary], and *Regnare Christum volumus* [We want Christ to reign]. Although the Work was still tiny, as he contemplated it he saw something vast: "It will have a divine heart. It will give all the glory to God, and will affirm his kingdom forever," being effective and universal in its scope. "The Pentecost of the Work of God will come soon. . . . And the whole world will hear in its own language the ecstatic acclamations of the soldiers of the Great King: *Regnare Christum volumus.*"[26]

He indicated that the spirit and essential content of the Work could be summed up in three aspects of Christian life: prayer (*Oratio*), mortification and penance (*Expiatio*), and apostolic action (*Actio*). They would lead the members to move in the world with the motto "God and Daring!" He added to this triad what he defined as the loves of a child of God: Jesus, Mary, and the Pope.[27]

Thinking about the legal structure of the institution, he could find nothing in canon law that combined a full self-giving to God with complete secularity. He considered for a while the military orders, created during the Crusades to care for and defend the pilgrims that went to the holy land, but later he abandoned that solution. Similarly, for a time he thought that the best canonical expression for the two sections of the Work might be a pious union or association of faithful to which a fraternity of secular priests might be joined. He was quite clear that the members would be ordinary Christians. For that reason, he thought that they would not use insignias, habits, or other external signs of their dedication, and that they would work in civil institutions like public schools and would claim no privileges in social life because of their membership in Opus Dei.[28]

The Founder also sketched out in the 1930s some possible organizational schemes. The Work would be made up of two sections, one for men and the other for women, which would carry out their activities in parallel, united in the head. He indicated that there would be married and single members, both priests and laymen, and outlined the type of formation they would receive. The principal apostolate of the members would be personal, that is to say that each one would spread the universal call to sanctity in his or her place of work and social relations. Nonetheless, the Work would have some corporate activities. They would be civil (as opposed to ecclesiastical) in character, directed by people who were professionals in the field, and subject to each country's civil legislation. They would be carried out in residences, hospitals, and retreat houses. Among those whom they would try to reach would be intellectuals, journalists, doctors, industrialists, and professionals in the entertainment sector.[29]

Escrivá realized that his plans were "just germs which may be no more like the complete reality than an egg is like the arrogant chicken who breaks out of it." He wrote in summer 1930, "I am astonished seeing what God does. I never thought about these works that the Lord is inspiring and the way they become more concrete. At the beginning one sees clearly only a vague idea. Afterwards He produces from those blurry shadows something well-defined, precise and viable. He! For all his glory." In this way he distinguished the goals and spirit of the Work (that had been defined in the foundational moment) from its legal structure and government and from the organization of the apostolate. The latter would develop over time as experience was acquired. He was not particularly worried about the lack of solutions to particular issues because he was confident that God would illuminate him "in his own time."[30]

Throughout his life, Escrivá always felt free to change the plan of the members' practices of piety, to modify ways of expressing things if the meaning of words changed, to re-elaborate the methods the Work used to offer Christian formation, and to adjust the structure of corporative and personal activities. Escrivá was familiar with the way other institutions in the Church lived the gospel and he freely adopted traditional terminology and practices of devotion. When it came to the spirit of the Work, however, he considered it inviolate. Since the nature of Work had a charismatic underpinning, he tried, above all in his prayer, to find ways to explain the underlying theology. From the beginning he rejected offers to join the Work or its activities to other institutions in the Church. The charismatic origin of Opus Dei worked against possible fusion with—or even alliances with—other institutions, which he thought would lead to a loss of the initial vision.

Section 3. New Lights and First Followers

Escrivá's confessor, Fr. Sánchez Ruiz, confirmed his conviction that Opus Dei should take its first steps in Madrid, the city which "has been my Damascus, because the scales fell from the eyes of my soul there" and it was there that "I received my mission."[31] For this reason he renewed the permission he had received from the bishops of Zaragoza and Madrid to live in the Spanish capital. He put off until 1935 finishing the coursework for his doctorate and continued working on his doctoral thesis, which was the official reason for his residing in Madrid. He sought, although unsuccessfully, a pastoral occupation that would be more stable both legally and economically. For instance, he took steps to become a military chaplain or a cathedral canon or to enter the diplomatic corps.

Escrivá did not have family money, influential contacts, or social prestige. He was a priest from outside the diocese who found himself in Madrid for academic reasons and lived with his family, which had very few resources. Years later he summed up his situation in a few words: I had only "my 26 years of age, the grace of God and good humor."[32] This phrase highlights some crucial elements: youth, which permitted him to spread his message during a long period, special assistance from God, and a cheerful character joined to a magnanimous heart.

Gradually the number of people with whom he was in contact grew. He tried to intensify his dealings both with friends he had made recently and those from the more distant past, like Isidoro Zorzano, with whom he had studied in high school in Logrono and who was currently working in Malaga for Andalusian Railways. On August 24, 1930, Zorzano passed through Madrid and in providential fashion met Escrivá on the street. The Founder explained the Work to him, and that same day Zorzano asked to become a member.[33]

He frequently took walks with Pepe Romeo and his friends, or accompanied them to El Sotanillo, a café that specialized in hot chocolate, close to the Alcalá Gate. He talked with them about all kinds of topics except politics, which he preferred not to discuss. Some of these young men, like the medical student Adolfo Gómez Ruiz or the painter José Muñoz Aycuens, joined Opus Dei. He also got to know more diocesan priests. Two of them, Sebastián Cirac and Lino Vea-Murguía, said they wanted to accompany him in the Work. In a broader sense, he spread the message of the Work when he spoke with working men and artisans who came to the doctrinal activities organized by the Foundation for the Sick. For example, in February 1930 he preached to workers in a mission held in the Capilla del Obispo, near the parish of St. Andrew.[34]

When he thought that a particular person could understand and live the spirit of the Work, he invited him to pray about whether this might be his Christian path. He was confident that if Divine Providence had given him a charism, it would also give him the people and the means needed to carry it out. At the same time, he did everything he could personally, beginning with intense prayer and mortification. He did not, however, carry out promotional activities or publish explanations of Opus Dei in magazines or periodicals. He thought that the message should be spread in conversations among friends. As he described the situation, "The Work grew on the inside, not yet born, in gestation. There was only personal apostolate."[35]

The first steps of the Work took place in a difficult political situation. In April 1931, a group of Spanish politicians proclaimed the Second Republic. (Recall there had been a First Republic at the end of the nineteenth century.) King Alfonse XIII went into exile to avoid a civil war. A few weeks later, the cardinal primate of Spain published a pastoral letter in which he criticized the new form of government and its secularist policies. In reaction, on May 11 there was a "burning of convents." Groups of socialist and anarchist union members sacked and burned convents and churches, primarily of religious orders. In Madrid ten were destroyed. Escrivá hurriedly removed the Eucharist from the chapel of the Foundation for the Sick and looked for a safe place for his family to live.

The Founder tried to find a new position outside the Foundation for the Sick, because he needed more time to dedicate to the development of Opus Dei. In addition, he felt he should not make use of the confessional at the foundation to look for vocations of women to Opus Dei, because it was the motherhouse of the Apostolic Ladies. Finally, he had had a falling out with the superiors of the Apostolic Ladies because they had not supported his attempt to promote the cause of canonization of a member of the congregation, Mercedes Reyna.

He found a new position in summer 1931. The cloistered monastery of Recollect Augustinians, which formed part of the Patronato of St. Elizabeth, needed a chaplain. The official position had been abolished by the Second Republic, so it was unstable from a legal point of view and carried no salary, but it would give him more free time for the Work and make it easier for him to remain in Madrid. He took the position, but did so reluctantly because it meant that his family would suffer want for some months.

When he left the Foundation for the Sick, he shifted from making frequent visits to the homes of poor sick people to meeting with patients in the hospitals. In Spain at the time, hospitals were places of last resort for those who could not afford a private clinic. Most were overcrowded, understaffed, and dirty.

Escrivá volunteered regularly in the Provincial Hospital of Madrid on Sunday afternoons, and often went to other hospitals either alone or accompanied by students and priest friends. In addition to providing spiritual care, he often washed the patients, cut their nails, and offered other small services. He observed, as he wrote, that "my priestly heart" expanded among the sick.[36] He asked the patients he visited for prayers and to offer their sufferings to God so that the Work might open up a path for itself in the Church and society.

Escrivá's interior world was growing, and the general idea he had received of Opus Dei was becoming sharper. On August 7, while he celebrated Mass in the Foundation for the Sick, he understood in a new way Christ's words "And I, when I am lifted up from the earth, will draw all men to myself" (Jn 12:32). He understood that a Christian becomes identified with Christ and makes him present in the world through the activities that he carries out. As he noted that day, "I understood that it would be the men and women of God who would lift up the cross with the doctrines of Christ to the summit of all human activity. . . . And I saw the Lord triumph, attracting to Himself all things."[37] In this way, work appeared as the material that sanctifies the "men and women of God," as the instrument with which they sanctify themselves and sanctify others. This teaching is a key to understanding the spirit of Opus Dei, which "hinges upon ordinary work, professional work carried out in the midst of the world."[38]

These events were intertwined again with the complex political situation in Spain. Escrivá suffered because of the attacks on and criticism of the members and the institutions of the Church. In October 1931, the Spanish Parliament approved the articles of the new Republican Constitution, which established separation of church and state, subordinated the religious orders to the state, and prohibited them from teaching in high schools. The Society of Jesus, which had educated a large part of the Catholic elite of the country, was dissolved.

In the fall of 1931, the Founder received additional inspirations that were strongly Christocentric in nature. On October 16, while in a streetcar, he suddenly felt "the Lords' action which made blossom in my heart and on my lips, with the strength of something absolutely necessary, this tender invocation: *Abba! Pater!*"[39] For a while, he lost the sense of space and time because he saw himself flooded with the joy of being and knowing that he was a son of God. From that moment on, he indicated that the foundation of the spirit of Opus Dei is the sense of divine filiation.

He practiced devotion to the Merciful Love of Jesus, a specific form of devotion to the Sacred Heart, and lived the "way of spiritual childhood" that he had admired in the Apostolic Lady Mercedes Reyna, whose motto had been "to hide and disappear."[40] Escrivá felt God's fatherly presence in his life and saw himself as a child in God's hands. In this spiritual climate, one day during the novena to the Immaculate Conception in 1931, he wrote at a single sitting a pamphlet that he entitled *Holy Rosary*. The attractively written text invites the reader to accompany the narrator in each one of the scenes of the Rosary. The contemplation of Jesus, Mary, Joseph, and the other personages of the gospel pours itself out in affectionate phrases and resolutions to improve our Christian life. The Founder ran the manuscript off on a primitive mimeograph machine and distributed it to people with whom he was in contact.[41]

In 1932, Escrivá dug deeply into a book entitled *10 Day Devotion to the Holy Spirit*. The author, Francisca Javiera del Valle, was a simple woman who had been a seamstress, but the meditation she wrote had great spiritual depth. He also made a resolution to read Thérèse of Lisieux's *Story of a Soul*. During the summer, he put together a booklet made up of notes he had taken, mostly from his *Apuntes íntimos*. He ran them off on a mimeograph machine and gave them the title *Consideraciones Espirituales* (Spiritual Considerations). The pamphlet consisted of 246 thoughts designed to lead the reader up an inclined plane to consider God's call and our response.[42]

During the 1931–1932 academic year, he met more or less regularly with various groups of people: students, the majority of whom were friends of Pepe Romeo; professional men and workers who volunteered in the Provincial Hospital; women who were hospital patients or young professionals he had gotten to know in the confessional at St. Elizabeth's; and diocesan priests whom he had contacted directly or through Lino Vea-Murguía.

Starting on February 22, 1932, he held a formative activity for the priests every Monday. Five came to the first meeting. He wanted them to make their own the spirit of the Work and to help him transmit it to laypeople. The majority of these priests had a good background in spiritual life and showed some social concern. They were not parish priests but rather chaplains of convents of nuns or hospitals. This gave them the ability and the time to take care of pastoral and formative activities of Opus Dei.[43]

Josemaría met many difficulties in his apostolate with women. When he started working at the St. Elizabeth Foundation, he began to give spiritual direction to some young women who lived in the area and came there for confession. On February 14, 1932, one of them, Carmen Cuervo, joined the Work. She spoke several languages and held a relatively high position in the bureaucracy where she had worked for many years. Little by little, the Founder explained to her the spirit of Opus Dei. He was confident that, once she assimilated it, she would play a key role in spreading it to other women. In the following months four more women joined Opus Dei: two who were chronically sick (María Ignacia García Escobar and Antonia Sierra) and two who lived near St. Elizabeth (Modesta Cabeza and Hermógenes García Ruiz). Later, another three joined. Cuervo, however, could not assimilate the message of the Work and drifted away from the Founder, and García Escobar soon died of tuberculosis.[44]

During the summer of 1932, two events momentarily slowed the growth of Opus Dei. The priest who seemed to understand the Work best, José María Somoano, was poisoned to death on July 16 out of hatred for the faith. On August 10, Pepe Romeo and some of his friends who supported a return to a non-parliamentary monarchy took part in an unsuccessful coup d'état headed by José Sanjurjo. Most of them were sent to jail or to exile, dispersing the group of students whom the Founder knew. (Escrivá had not been involved in their political activities.)[45]

After four years, Opus Dei was advancing only slowly and with difficulty. Escrivá had little to rely on whether in terms of money or people who followed him. But, as he saw it, the success of a supernatural enterprise cannot be measured the same way as a human undertaking. He was transmitting a Christian message with the conviction that he was fulfilling the will of God, "an imperative command of Christ."[46] If he was going to remind others of the call to sanctity, first he had to live it himself. He thought that, in some way, the success or failure of the Work depended on his own personal search for sanctity. Consulting his confessor about a demanding list of mortifications, he said, "Don't hesitate to approve it. Consider that God is asking this of me and, furthermore I need to be a saint and the father, teacher, and guide of saints."[47]

Notes

1. See Julio González-Simancas y Lacasa, "San Josemaría entre los enfermos de Madrid (1927–1931)," *Studia et Documenta* 2 (2008), pp. 147–203; and Julio Montero and Javier Cervera Gil, "Madrid en los años treinta: Ambiente social, político, cultural y religioso," *Studia et Documenta* 3 (2009), pp. 13–39.

2. See Constantino Ánchel, "Actividad docente de san Josemaría: el Instituto Amado y la Academia Cicuéndez," *Studia et Documenta* 3 (2009), pp. 307–333.

3. *Intimate Notes*, 331 (October 15, 1931). Escrivá used the expression "Work of God" beginning in 1930. From 1928 to 1930 he didn't use any name to define the reality to which he was giving life.

4. *Intimate Notes*, 306 (October 2, 1931).

5. *Intimate Notes*, 306 (October 2, 1931). Unless indicated to the contrary, all italics in quoted texts are in the original. Escrivá's 1928 notes have not been preserved. The first volume of the *Intimate Notes* begins in March 1930. For that reason, Escrivá's texts related to the foundation date from then or later. See the introductory material in Escrivá, *The Way: Critical-Historical Edition*, pp. 40–41.

6. *Intimate Notes*, 306. These words are a marginal note added by Escrivá in 1968 in the course of revising, with Álvaro del Portillo, the *Intimate Notes*, making additions and corrections.

7. *Intimate Notes*, 179. Del Portillo transcribed these words of the Founder in the summer of 1968.

8. Letter from Josemaría Escrivá de Balaguer to José María Hernández Garnica, Rome, December 29, 1948, AGP A.3.4, 260-1, 480129-2. The Founder is recalling the events of October 2, 1928.

9. *Intimate Notes*, 978b (April 10, 1933).

10. This book distinguishes with some frequency between secular Christians and consecrated religious. We use the term *religious* to designate a person who forms part of a religious order or congregation, not in its generic sense of someone who believes in God. In the ecclesiastical legislation of the time, "the religious state or stable form of life in common" involved not only fulling the commandments but also "professing the evangelical counsels through vows of obedience, chastity and poverty." *Code of Canon Law*, 1917, canon 487. (Unless otherwise indicated, translations from other languages are the authors'.) With the public profession of vows or the evangelical counsels, the religious embrace a state or condition of life traditionally referred to as the *state of perfection*, and

they separate themselves in greater or lesser degree from secular realities—*contemptus mundi* (contempt of the world)—in order to give testimony to the fact that man's end is God, not created things. It was commonly held that the free public profession of the three vows facilitated the fullness of communion with God, because the religious was obliged to tend to perfection not only in conscience but also legally. For this reason the religious or consecrated life was presented as the paradigm of Christian sanctity. It was not denied that a secular person could achieve perfection through the fulfillment of the commandments and precepts of the law of God, but it would be in a lesser degree than that of consecrated persons, and it was more difficult because the world was seen as an obstacle. See José Luis Illanes, "Apuntes para una reflexión teológica sobre el itinerario jurídico del Opus Dei," *Studia et Documenta* 10 (2016), pp. 327–362.

During the twentieth century the Magisterium and theological thought gradually abandoned the idea that the degree of sanctity depends on one's state in life. Pope Pius XII affirmed in 1939 that "God does not call his children to the state of perfection but he invites all of them to perfection in their state." General Audience of June 12, 1939, in *Discorsi e radiomessaggi di Sua Santità Pío XII*, vol. 1 (Vatican City: Tip. Poliglotta Vaticana, 1940), p. 414. The message that Escrivá received in 1928 moved along these lines. He told lay men and women and priests immersed in secular realities that God invited them to "the ordinary done with perfection" (Letter 1, n. 12, AGP A.3, 91-1-3). He insisted that their "ordinary life, which appeared nothing special, could be a means to achieve sanctity. There is no need to abandon one's own state" (Letter 1, n. 2). Spreading this message was the aim of the institution which he was founding: "The Work was born to help those Christians who, through their family, their friendships, their ordinary work, their aspirations, form part of the very texture of civil society, to understand that their life, just as it is, can be an opportunity for meeting Christ. That it is a way of holiness and apostolate." Josemaría Escrivá, *Conversations with Josemaría Escrivá* (New York: Scepter, 2002), 60. On the relationship between secular life and consecrated life, see Ernst Burkhart and Javier López, *Vida cotidiana y santidad en la enseñanza de san Josemaría: Estudio de teología espiritual*, vol. 1 (Madrid: Rialp, 2010), pp. 213–239.

11. On the theological, canonical, and historical significance of the foundation of Opus Dei, see Antonio Aranda, *El bullir de la Sangre de Cristo: Estudio sobre el cristocentrismo del beato Josemaría Escrivá* (Madrid: Rialp, 2000); Carlos José Errázuriz M., "Reflexiones sobre la unidad esencial entre el carisma

del Opus Dei y su dimensión institucional constitutiva," *Ius Ecclesiae* 31, no. 1 (2019), pp. 289–302; José Luis Illanes Maestre, "Datos para la comprensión histórico-espiritual de una fecha," *Anuario de Historia de la Iglesia* 11 (2002), pp. 655–697; Gonzalo Redondo, "El 2 de octubre de 1928 en el contexto de la historia cultural contemporánea," *Anuario de Historia de la Iglesia* 11 (2002), pp. 699–741; and Pedro Rodríguez, *Opus Dei: Estructura y Misión. Su realidad eclesiológica* (Madrid: Cristiandad 2001).

12. *Intimate Notes*, 179. These words of the Founder were transcribed by Álvaro del Portillo in 1968. See also John F. Coverdale, *Uncommon Faith: The Early Years of Opus Dei (1928–1943)*, 2nd ed. (New York: Scepter, 2002); and José Luis González Gullón, *DYA: La Academia y Residencia en la historia del Opus Dei (1933–1939)*, 4th ed. (Madrid: Rialp, 2016), pp. 39–56.

13. *Intimate Notes*, 179 (March 22, 1931).

14. *Intimate Notes*, 475b (December 12, 1931).

15. *Intimate Notes*, 475b (December 12, 1931).

16. Meditation, February 14,1964, quoted in Vázquez de Prada, *The Founder of Opus Dei*, vol. 1, p. 318.

17. *Intimate Notes*, 1869 (June 14,1948). Years later, he added that he had spent that time "as if in a stupor. It was the Lord who led me and who rescued me [from that state]." Letter 15, n. 5, AGP A.3, 93-1-4.

18. In the AGP there are more than forty clippings of articles published between 1920 and 1933 about different Catholic institutions (pious unions, third orders, and associations) and about schools, congresses, and religious publishing houses in Spain, the United States, France, Holland, Hungary, Italy, and Poland. Escrivá put them together with the help of José Romeo. AGP A.1, 6-4-1; A.3,179-1-5; and A.3, 179-1-6.

19. See José Romeo Rivera, autobiographical note (early 1935), AGP A.2, 34-3-10. In 1935, Romeo left Opus Dei because of psychological problems. That same year, Rodríguez left because he could not acknowledge the Founder's leadership. See González Gullón, *DYA*, pp. 32, 37, and 294–300.

20. *Intimate Notes*, 179 (March 22, 1931).

21. *Intimate Notes*, 179. These words of the Founder were transcribed by Álvaro del Portillo in 1968.

22. *Intimate Notes*, 1871 (June 14, 1948). See also Francisca R. Quiroga, "14 de febrero de 1930: la transmisión de un acontecimiento y un mensaje," *Studia et Documenta* 3 (2009), pp. 163–189.

23. *Intimate Notes*, 1872 (June 14, 1948).

24. *Intimate Notes*, 306. This phrase was added by Escrivá in 1968.

25. Recollections of Pedro Rocamora Valls (Madrid, November 12, 1977), AGP A.5, 241-1-5.

26. *Intimate Notes*, 290 (September, 1931), and 240 (August 24, 1930). In 1931 he wrote: "The effective reign of Christ, all the glory to God, souls." *Intimate Notes*, 171 (March 10, 1931).

27. See AGP A.3, 87-06-1.

28. See AGP A.3, 175-9-1.

29. AGP A.3, 175-9-1.

30. *Intimate Notes*, 14 (March 13, 1930), 65 (June 16, 1930), and 60 (June 16, 1930).

31. *Intimate Notes*, 993 (March 30, 1933).

32. Letter 13, no. 11, AGP A.3, 92-6-2.

33. See José Miguel Pero-Sanz Elorz, *Isidoro Zorzano Ledesma: Ingeniero industrial (Buenos Aires, 1902–Madrid, 1943)* (Madrid: Palabra, 2009).

34. He wrote in 1968 that he considered that the diffusion of Opus Dei would be in time a "great catechesis." *Intimate Notes*, 548. This phrase is a marginal note added by Escrivá in 1968. Similarly, he described the apostolate of the Work as "a sea without shores." Letter 15, no. 6, AGP A.3, 93-1-4.

35. *Intimate Notes*, 164. This phrase is a marginal note inserted by Escrivá in 1968.

36. *Intimate Notes*, 731d (May 20, 1932).

37. *Intimate Notes*, 217 (August 7, 1931).

38. Josemaría Escrivá, *Christ is Passing By* (Princeton: Scepter 1974), 45. Escrivá's initial ideas about the sanctification of work are related to this foundational event. There are other references in his *Intimate Notes*: For example, "Work sanctifies, and obliges everyone" (970b, March 28, 1933). For Escrivá "professional work" means the ordinary work someone carries out to make a living. It is not restricted to "the professions" like law and medicine. We use the phrase with the same broad meaning.

39. Letter 29, no. 60, AGP A.3-94-1-5.

40. Escrivá completed the phrase with a Christological addition and took it as the motto of his own life: "To hide and disappear is my thing. May only Jesus

shine." Letter to the members of the Work, December 28, 1975, AGP A.3.4, 309-2, 751228.

The idea of the "way" or "little way" of spiritual childhood is taken from St. Thérèse of Lisieux. See Federico M. Requena, "San Josemaría Escrivá de Balaguer y la devoción al Amor Misericordioso (1927–1935)," *Studia et Documenta* 3 (2009), pp. 139–174.

41. See Josemaría Escrivá de Balaguer, *Santo Rosario: Edición crítico-histórica*, ed. Pedro Rodríguez, Constantino Ánchel, and Javier Sesé (Madrid: Rialp, 2010); and José Luis Illanes, "Obra escrita y predicación de san Josemaría Escrivá de Balaguer," *Studia et Documenta* 3 (2009), pp. 203–276.

42. See Escrivá, *The Way: Critical Historical Edition*, pp. 28–30.

43. See José Luis González Gullón and Jaume Aurell, "Josemaría Escrivá en los años treinta: los sacerdotes amigos," *Studia et Documenta* 3 (2009), pp. 41–106.

44. Escobar died on September 13, 1933. See José Miguel Cejas, *La paz y la alegría: María Ignacia García Escobar en los comienzos del Opus Dei, 1896–1933* (Madrid: Rialp, 2001); and Gloria Toranzo, "Los comienzos del apostolado del Opus Dei entre mujeres (1930–1939)," *Studia et Documenta* 7 (2013), pp. 15–93.

45. See González Gullón, *DYA*, pp. 60–64. Another participant in the failed coup attempt, Luis Gordon, a young businessman who had recently joined Opus Dei, escaped being sent to jail or exile, but he died in November from pneumonia. See Pedro Pablo Ortúñez Goicolea and Luis Gordon Beguer, "Luis Gordon Picardo. Un empresario en los primeros años del Opus Dei (1898–1932)," *Studia et Documenta* 3 (2009), 107–138; and José Miguel Cejas, *José María Somoano en los comienzos del Opus Dei* (Madrid: Rialp, 1995).

46. *Intimate Notes*, 1076 (November 6, 1933).

47. *Intimate Notes*, 1725 (June 22, 1933).

CHAPTER 2

The DYA Academy-Residence

The thinkers of the Enlightenment, taking their cue from the Greco-Roman period, used the term *intellectuals* to designate a minority who give rise to culture and science. Intellectuals, they thought, understand society as a whole, dictate the laws that govern peoples, and influence the thought and behavior of the other citizens. In nineteenth-century France, intellectuals were writers closely linked to liberalism and deeply concerned about the destiny of their country. As the twentieth century wore on, the term *intellectual* came to be applied in Spain to the wider group of those who take part in the university community, whether as professors, students, or graduates. Escrivá used the term in this broader sense, and we will use it in the same way, although at times we will simply refer to college graduates where Escrivá talks about intellectuals.

The Church formed intellectuals to carry Christian doctrine to society. The hierarchy encouraged students and graduates to be involved in Catholic Action and other organizations. It also moved them to be united in political parties and to be involved in Catholic publications. These efforts on the part of the hierarchy had little success in the academic world. Western culture in both Europe and North America had banished the discussion of God from the public sphere and from intellectual life. The dominant philosophies were immanentist (theorizing an abstract spirit or mind that permeates the world), and theology, which had played such a central role in the thought of the great masters of the Middle Ages, was reserved to confessional universities. Many professors maintained that faith and reason were clearly two autonomous spheres which could not come into contact with each other.

Escrivá felt the desire to spread the gospel in the academic world. In 1927, speaking to a priest-friend, "he talked about the need to do apostolate with intellectuals as well, because, he added, they are like the snowcapped peaks. When the snow melts the water runs down and makes fruitful the valleys."[1] Faced with the "rebellion of the intellectuals," he noted, other intellectuals are needed "to respond with a decisive 'I will serve! I will serve you, O, God.'"[2]

Opus Dei had not arisen in opposition to the cultural currents of the moment, whether the secularist approach of the *Institución Libre de Enseñanza* (The Free Institution of Education), the atheism of the Socialists, or the narrowness of integralist Catholics who tended to reject most recent social, political, and economic developments. Nor did it propose to solve the problem of the scant influence of Catholic intellectuals in Spanish or international society. The charism that gave rise to it was an invitation to identify one's life with that of Jesus Christ.

Escrivá understood that the Work would give a Christian orientation to the head and heart of those who approached its apostolates. Then each of them would bring Christ's teaching to their place of work, whether important or not, and to the rest of their social relations.[3] Spiritually united to Jesus Christ and conscious of being children of God, the members of Opus Dei would give the witness of an upright life and professional prestige without pretending to be what they were not: official representatives of the Church.

From mid-1932 on, the Founder gave priority to explaining the Work to intellectuals, people who, as he sometimes said repeating a phrase of a friend of his, were "the aristocracy of intelligence" because they searched for coherence between faith and reason.[4] He thought that beginning with intellectuals was the most effective way of reaching all sectors of society.

For professors, this came down to trying to achieve the highest possible academic status, whether at a university or a high school. In his first conversation with the priest who would be his confessor, Fr. Sánchez Ruiz, SJ, back in 1930, Fr. Sánchez "spoke to him about the need [for Catholics] to become professors, etc., and the Father, who had not dared to bring up the subject, said: 'that is precisely what I came to talk to you about.'"⁵ Escrivá encouraged college students to consider a university teaching career "while making clear that the Work does not act [in this field] and that it is a question of individuals acting with full personal liberty who try to become professors."⁶ Talking to university students, many of whom were destined to play an important role in society in the future, he encouraged them to study seriously: "We won't pardon someone who could be a luminary and isn't."⁷

At the same time he explained that the message of the Work was for all men and women in all times and places. He commented that "we are interested in 100 of every 100 souls" and "our vocation is not that of professors but of saints."* For this reason, he stayed in touch with diocesan priests, with professional people, and with workers.

Section 1. The Beginning of the St. Raphael Work

In June 1932 Escrivá thought about creating a Catholic student association as a way of promoting his activity. Within a few weeks, however, he decided that it was more in accord with the spirit of the Work that each person receive Christian formation in his personal capacity, not as a member of an association. Receiving Christian formation in the spirit of Opus Dei would not imply joining an institution.

In October, the Founder made a retreat at the Carmelite convent in Segovia. On Thursday, October 6, while praying near the tomb of St. John of the Cross, he received an interior inspiration. He would structure the apostolates of Opus Dei into three works, each under

---

* Josemaría Escrivá, *Furrow* (London/New York: Scepter, 1987), 183, and note of Juan Jiménez Vargas, paraphrasing something Escrivá said in 1943, AGP E.2.2, 171-2-2. He insisted particularly in the '30s and '40s on the idea of beginning with intellectuals in order to reach everyone. For example, in 1940 the bishop of Barcelona commented "the University is only a starting point." Relación del viaje a Barcelona, March 31 to April 2, 1940, AGP A.2, 47-2-2. This way of spreading Opus Dei's message continues to this day. Its statutes specify that "the Prelature tries with all its strength to lead people of all social conditions and statuses in civil society, and in the first place those who are called intellectuals, to adhere with their whole heart to the precepts of Christ our Lord." *Codex iuris particularis Operis Dei*, 1982, no.2 §2.

the patronage of an archangel: the Work of St. Raphael, for the Christian formation of young people; the Work of St. Michael, for those who had received a calling to live celibacy in the midst of the world; and the Work of St. Gabriel, for married persons and single persons not called to celibacy. He soon also entrusted them to the patronage of the apostles St. John, St. Peter, and St. Paul, respectively.

At the end of 1932, he met Juan Jiménez Vargas, a medical student. Like many other people his age, he had grown up in the faith, held traditional ideas, and belonged to a number of religious, political, and athletic associations. After several sessions of spiritual direction, on January 4, 1933, Jiménez Vargas asked to be admitted as a member of Opus Dei. Two weeks later, on January 21, along with two friends from the medical school, he attended a class of Christian formation given by the Founder. The class was held in the Porta Coeli Asylum for abandoned children. The next day, Jiménez Vargas and several of his friends taught catechism in a school for poor children in the northern part of Madrid. In Escrivá's mind, these two activities constituted the beginning of the Work of St. Raphael.

The Escrivá family continued to be very short of money. Fr. Josemaría took out a bank loan to be able to rent an apartment for his family in Martínez Campos Street. Although the apartment was small, unlike the previous apartment, it did permit him to meet with persons who wanted to talk about their spiritual life, mostly students. Sometimes his mother invited the students for a snack. Before they went home in the evening, the Founder commented briefly on the Gospel passage read at Mass that day.

In the spring of 1933, Escrivá proposed to his first followers in the Work that they have a daily program of practices of Christian piety. He referred to them as "norms" or as a "plan of life." This program, which took up about two hours a day, was similar to what was generally suggested to secular priests and devout laypeople. It included mental prayer, Mass and Communion, a visit to the Blessed Sacrament, praying of the Rosary, spiritual reading, and examinations of conscience. Each one would carry it out at times compatible with his professional and social obligations.

The apostolate with students was growing. There were nine regulars for the class of Christian formation in Porta Coeli, and a slightly larger number came to see him at his home. He thought the time had come to find Opus Dei a locale of its own. During the summer of 1932 he had already sought advice from some priests he knew, like Fr. Pedro Poveda, the founder of the Teresian Institute. Finally, he decided to open a university academy, a type of institution for whose services there was a market in Spain. High schools did not sufficiently prepare students for the entrance exams required by the universities, so many students took prep courses at academies. Once at the university, even very good students often felt the need for supplementary instruction in certain subjects, which they also sought at academies. The academy Escrivá had in mind would offer Christian formation as well as these traditional professional services, and have a good library. At the base of the project lay the idea of academic excellence for those dedicated to teaching.

Academies of this sort would be, in the Founder's words, "a means for incorporating intellectuals into a secular apostolate, and an instrument for forming members of the Work who hoped to become professors. Although the Work would inform the spirit of those who directed the academies, the academies would *never be an end* of Opus Dei."[8]

The students who came to the academy would draw closer to the faith by learning more about Catholic doctrine, and would in their turn transmit it to their friends. The academy itself, and the apostolate of the students who studied there would, however, have a secular, character. This was a novel idea. In Spain there was a sharp distinction between Catholic and public education at the primary and high school level. All universities were public. Escrivá saw his message directed to Catholics who worked in state-run educational centers and other secular institutions. His friend Fr. Pedro Poveda supported this idea, but few other devout Catholics did. Most considered that it was better for Catholics who took their faith seriously to be united in confessional schools and in explicitly Catholic media and political organizations.

In November 1933, after a long search, the members found a small apartment at 33 Luchana Street. They sought appropriate licenses, contracted professors, and furnished the apartment. At Christmastime, the Founder told them that the academy would be called DYA. The initials referred to the two principal subjects that would be taught there: law (*derecho*) and architecture (*arquitectura*). For the members of the Work, however, the initials would also be the abbreviation of the phrase *Dios y Audacia* (God and Daring).

The DYA Academy opened its doors on January 15, 1934. Escrivá named Ricardo Fernández Vallespín its director. He was studying the last year of architecture and had just joined Opus Dei. The rent was paid by two members of the Work, Isidoro Zorzano and José María González Barredo, and some of their friends.

The academic activities of DYA got off to a slow start because it had opened when the school year was already well-begun and there was no time to really advertise it. Fernández Vallespín taught a preparatory course for the entrance exam of the architecture school. Other professors taught Latin and Christian apologetics. On the other hand, the transmission of the spirit of the Work grew at an accelerated pace, especially in spring 1934. About a hundred students were in contact one way or another with the activities organized in the academy. Thirty attended the classes of Christian formation, and seven joined Opus Dei.

The college students who went to the academy came from Catholic families and had studied Christian doctrine in their parishes and in high schools run by religious orders. This could be seen in their way of thinking and acting. Many of them received the sacraments regularly and lived other practices of Christian piety. They studied in a number of different schools, including medicine, law, architecture, and engineering, and they belonged to different student and political associations. Some wanted Spain to become a monarchy again, while others accepted the Republic as long as it was respectful of the Church.

In spiritual direction, Fr. Josemaría explained to them individually the message of Opus Dei. Various group activities helped improve their Christian life: classes of formation, monthly days of recollection (organized in the nearby Redemptorist Church), teaching catechism to children who were preparing for their First Communion, and visiting the sick. To help them practice mental prayer, Escrivá gave them classic books of spirituality such as Luis de la Palma's *The Sacred Passion* and his own *Holy Rosary* and *Spiritual Considerations*, which by then had grown to more than four hundred points.

The Founder met one-on-one at the academy with each of the members of the Work to give them spiritual direction. They met once a week as a group for what he at first called *emendatio* and later the Brief Circle. The goal of the circle was to help them grasp, with practical examples, the spirit of Opus Dei. He told them, for example, that their life was rooted in union with God. He stressed that they were free to form their own opinions in questions of politics and culture on which the Church had not taken a stand. And he pointed out that because of the secular rather than clerical character of Opus Dei, they should live their dedication to God naturally and with sobriety, without altering their way of dressing or speaking.

By the spring of 1934, nine women had joined Opus Dei. For a few months Escrivá met with them as a group to explain the whole spirit of Opus Dei, but this experiment promptly came to an end because one of the families objected. It seems the problem lay in the fact that in the social and cultural environment of Spain at the time it was difficult to understand that a woman could have a vocation to celibacy in the midst of the world. Celibacy of women was thought of as something proper to religious congregations, whether cloistered or dedicated to teaching or care of the sick. Because of this difficulty, and because he thought he needed to concentrate more on the pastoral care of the larger group of men, the Founder asked Fr. Lino Vea-Murguía to give formational talks to the women members and, along with Fr. Norberto Rodríguez, to hear their confessions. The women met as a group to sew clothing for needy families and children.

The Founder's sense of paternity grew during this time. On March 11, 1934, he told the members of the Work that he would prefer to be addressed as "Father" rather than as "Don" Josemaría, because that term defined his mission in Opus Dei. He also asked them to be concerned for each other with affection, because forming a spiritual Christian family was an essential characteristic of the spirit of Opus Dei.

At this time, he wrote two documents directed to his spiritual children. Both of them contained permanent doctrinal elements, which reflected foundational inspirations, and circumstantial elements, which reflected the state of the Work at the moment and might serve as experience for the future. He entitled the first one *Instruction on the Supernatural Spirit of the Work of God*, dated March 19, 1934. He pointed out that Opus Dei was something desired by God, that God called each person to the Work, and that the response of those chosen ought to be full of enthusiasm and love, ready for any sacrifice. He also indicated that, because of its charismatic origin, the Work would never merge with Catholic Action or any other institution.[9]

The second document was titled *Instruction on the Way of Doing Proselytism*, dated April 1, 1934.* There the Founder reflected on the nature of the vocation to Opus Dei and on how best to explain it to those who might have that vocation.

---

* In the 1930s, the term "proselytism" did not have its current negative connotation of trying to win people over by forcing their consciences and abusing their freedom. Escrivá understood it as announcing Christ, incorporating new faithful to the Church, and concern to bring one's friends and acquaintances to Opus Dei, all with full freedom and without any sort of coercion. See Josemaría Escrivá de Balaguer, *The Way: A Critical-Historical Edition*, ed. Pedro Rodríguez (London, New York: Scepter, 2009), pp. 892–893 n4; and Congregation for the Doctrine of the Faith, "Doctrinal Note on Some Aspects of Evangelization. December 3, 2007, n49. *http://www.vatican.va/ roman_curia/congregations/cfaith/documents/rc_con_cfaith_doc_20071203_nota-evangelizzazione_en.html*. In the face of the negative connotations which the term later acquired, Escrivá's second successor as the head of Opus Dei, Bishop Javier Echevarría, suggested using other words that would express the original positive content. See General Note, 104/16 (December 6, 2016), AGP E.1.3 and Q.1.3.

Section 2. The DYA Residence

No sooner had they begun the academy in January 1934 than Escrivá told the first members of the Work that he wanted to open a student residence in October, at the beginning of the next academic year. Because a number of members of the Work, beginning with the Founder, would live there, it would be easier to offer Christian doctrine and to explain the content of Opus Dei in more systematic fashion. And, they could have a chapel—which he preferred to call an oratory, because it was a place for personal prayer.

During summer 1934, they found three apartments at 50 Ferraz Street, not far from the new campus of the university then under construction in the northeast part of the capital. On September 12, the director of the future residence, Ricardo Fernández Vallespín, signed the rental contract.

The members of the Work studied the regulations of other residences and wrote one for the DYA residence. It began: "This residence gives students an effective religious, professional, and physical education."[10] They hired an administrator and four other people to work in the residence: two waiters, a cook, and an errand boy. They bought the linen for the future twenty-five residents on credit. Since they had no money to buy furniture, they decided to ask each resident to pay in advance the first month's rent. But since they had had no time to advertise, when the academic year began in October they had only one resident. This was the beginning of a year plagued with economic problems.

Escrivá asked his mother and siblings to donate to the DYA residence part of the proceeds from the sale of some land that they had inherited in Fonz in the province of Huesca. The family agreed despite the fact that they had no other property. The Founder also asked for donations from wealthy people in Madrid. Looking for help from heaven, in December 1934 he named as intercessor for the economic needs of the Work St. Nicholas of Bari, a fourth-century bishop to whom people prayed for financial questions because he had taken care of the poor in his diocese

Things got so bad that on February 21, 1935, Fr. Lino Vea-Murguía told Escrivá he should shut the residence because there was no way to pay the debts. The Founder asked the opinion of the Council of the Work, a consultative body which helped him govern Opus Dei. It had three members who lived in Madrid (Juan Jiménez Vargas, Ricardo Fernández Vallespín, and Manuel Sainz de los Terreros) and two who lived outside the capital (Isidoro Zorzano and José María González Barredo). Despite the difficult economic situation, they all favored continuing the DYA project.

For the moment, they gave up the apartment that had been rented for the academy, which they squeezed into the two remaining apartments of the residence.[11] This measure saved DYA from failure. In addition, Escrivá received money from his family's sale of land, and they found some additional residents, which increased their income.

This event demonstrated that the priests to whom Escrivá had been explaining the message of Opus Dei since February 1932 did not believe the Work would go forward, perhaps because they lacked confidence in him as Founder or did not fully accept the Work's supernatural origin. For this reason, he suspended the weekly formative meetings for diocesan priests, although he maintained his personal friendship with each of them. He concluded that in the future the priests of Opus Dei would have to come from the ranks of its lay members.

As the months went by, a growing number of young men came to the residence to study, to pray before the Blessed Sacrament, to attend classes of Christian formation, to help teach catechism to children, or to visit poor people, whom Escrivá called "Our Lady's poor." During the academic year more than 150 men, including both students and recent graduates, attended some formative activity in the residence. About half of them attended the St. Raphael classes and seven asked to join Opus Dei. When summer arrived, two more asked for admission: Álvaro del Portillo and José María Hernández Garnica. Both of them were studying engineering.[12]

On January 9, 1935, the Founder finished a new document titled *Instruction on the Work of St. Raphael*. The *Instruction* stresses the spiritual but at the same time familial character of the Work of St. Raphael, designed to lead young people to serve others and above all to encounter Christ. "If you do not make the boys men of prayer, you will have wasted your time"[13]

The academic year 1935–1936 began well. All the beds in the residence were taken from the beginning, so there were no economic problems. The residence was building up its own identity and reputation with cultural get-togethers, celebrations of feast days and birthdays, and academic and sporting activities. An unusual characteristic was a prohibition on talking about politics in collective gatherings in the residence. Because of the tense political situation of the country, passions were running high, and the Founder didn't want anyone to feel inhibited because of his personal opinions. Some of the members of Opus Dei who had been particularly active in politics, like Jiménez Vargas, reduced their political activities in order to dedicate more time to the spread of Opus Dei.

DYA was the "showcase" Escrivá used to explain the Work to ecclesiastical authorities. Because Christian doctrine was taught there, he frequently sent information about DYA to the bishop of Madrid, Leopoldo Eijo Garay, through the vicar general, Msgr. Francisco Morán. Morán did not understand the secular character of the Work, which he thought would end up becoming a religious congregation. Nonetheless, he supported Escrivá because he was one of the few priests carrying on any significant pastoral work with university students. It was Morán who facilitated Escrivá's being named rector of the Foundation of St. Elizabeth in December 1934. At this time. diocesan officials agreed with Escrivá that, since the Work was just beginning, it was too soon to think about legal approvals.

In giving Christian formation at DYA, Escrivá stressed dealing with God. He told the students that they could not be content with a merely cultural religion. Their relationship with God needed to be personal, face-to-face. As concrete forms of piety he suggested spending some time in prayer before the Blessed Sacrament, attending weekday Mass, and praying the Rosary.

He placed as much stress on study as on dealing with God, something which caught the young men's attention. This was their professional work. They had a "serious obligation," a moral duty, to attend class, to study, to learn their subjects well, and prepare for the exams. They would sanctify themselves and make God present in their lives through their studies. He added that the best way of bringing the gospel to the academic world was being a good student. He lamented the fact that some Catholic students who could be influential in the university and in society dedicated themselves to unrelated apostolic activities that prevented them from fulfilling their professional duties.

> Consider how *the enemies of the Christian idea help each other* in their profession. With more or less intellectual foundation (oftentimes with less) they are present at the peak of intellectual activities. By contrast, the talent of many outstanding young Catholics goes to waste. They are led to neglect cultural work and to waste their time as secretaries or presidents of boards and meetings and carrying out propaganda. Today it's a question of giving a talk. Tomorrow writing an article. These things are fine, but they contribute nothing to their professional formation.[14]

Finally, he stressed friendship and openness to others. If people came to DYA because someone invited them, they came back because of friendship. Friends invited their friends to get to know Escrivá because he was an attractive personality, and he created a pleasant and cheerful atmosphere which made it easy to confide in him. The Founder said that a Christian cannot limit his contacts to those who are closest to him nor form closed groups. The gospel message was meant for their friends and acquaintances from work and from the social circles they moved in. He also encouraged them to take special care of needy and underprivileged people, particularly children and the sick.

These three elements—relationship with God, study, and friendship—were not entirely new for the young Catholics who heard Escrivá talk about them. The original factor was that these elements could fill their lives with meaning and that God called them to "materialize their spiritual life," avoiding "a "double life. On one side, an interior life, a life of relation with God; and on the other, a separate and distinct professional, social and family life, full of small earthly realities."[15]

Escrivá invited those who seemed interested to join Opus Dei. He was looking for men and women who would undertake to live celibacy. He wanted to form a group of persons whom God had called to this specific path and who would be available to extend Opus Dei and direct its activities. Once this first nucleus (the Work of St. Michael) had been formed, Opus Dei would spread to all sorts of people, married and single, from all social environments.

Until 1934 incorporation into Opus Dei was purely verbal. Then one of the priests who was in the Work commented that people ought to manifest their incorporation in some more tangible way. Escrivá adopted a two-pronged solution. Actual incorporation into Opus Dei would take place in a brief ceremony that included a declaration of giving oneself entirely to God, but without sacred bonds. This would be done in three steps: admission, oblation or temporary incorporation, and fidelity or definitive incorporation.* In a separate act, each member would express his spiritual bond by taking private vows of poverty, chastity, and obedience, lived in accord with the spirit of Opus Dei. This procedure, which reflected the theological and canonical tradition of the time, did not affect the secularity of the members of the Work. They would oblige themselves before God to live these virtues in the midst of ordinary life.[16]

DYA also had some activities for those who had already graduated from the university, including some married men. Starting in 1934 the "Friends of DYA" came to the residence on Saturday afternoons for meetings in which they took turns giving a talk about their

---

* The names were taken from the academic and civil world of the moment. In choosing them, Escrivá wanted to avoid the terminology used in religious orders, which called these three steps novitiate, temporary profession, and perpetual profession. See *Intimate Notes*, 278 (October 11, 1931).

specialty. In the 1935–1936 academic year, a not-for-profit organization called Sociedad de Colaboración Intelectual (SOCIN, Society for Intellectual Collaboration) was formed under Spanish law to be the legal sponsor of the cultural and formative activities of DYA. The twenty-some members of this society met weekly in the residence. Escrivá viewed this as the first of the many activities that the Work of St. Gabriel would carry on.

The environment of DYA reflected some characteristics of the family style of Opus Dei. Many Sundays Escrivá preached a meditation to the members of the Work, who then had breakfast together and met for an explanation of some aspect of the spirit of Opus Dei. For example, he told them that the fullness of Christian life, which in their case involved full self-giving to God in the midst of the world and immersed in everyday realities, was the same as it was in apostolic times. He described it in a letter as "*living the virtues* of poverty, chastity and obedience, passing unnoticed, and being leaven."[17] In another moment, he referred to the members of the Work as "apostles in dress shirts," men who live "fully the life of the first Christians, struggling in the world, against the world, with the world's arms, finding among those fully . . . immersed in university life, God's champions, who will re-Christianize universal thought."[18]

In the February 1936 elections, the Popular Front coalition, made up of left Republicans, Socialists, Communists, and Anarchists won by a small margin, due at least in part to electoral fraud.[19] Social unrest became widespread. In Madrid the extreme Right and Left fought each other. Acts of violence and assassinations became frequent. One of the DYA residents, Alberto Ortega, was arrested and subjected to a political trial. He was sentenced to twenty-five years in prison for the presumed assassination of a policeman. Escrivá urged his friends to visit him in prison, but in the residence to continue the policy of not talking about politics in group meetings.

By the spring of 1936 there were twenty-one male members of the Work. Most of them had come in contact with Opus Dei after hearing about it for the first time at the DYA residence. There were only five women because the Founder still had not found a woman to act as the director and because they did not have any adequate place of their own. Although the numbers were still small, Escrivá thought the time had arrived to begin in other cities. He prayed fervently for this intention and asked other people to pray for it. He prepared two groups of men to open student residences in Valencia and Paris in the fall. In Madrid the members of the Work were searching for a new facility for DYA because the one at 50 Ferraz Street was too small.

Isidoro Zorzano and other members of the Work had created in late 1935 a foundation to support the cultural and professional formation of students by providing buildings. Fomento de Estudios Superiorers (FES) purchased in June 1936 a building at 16 Ferraz Street to house the residence. It cost 400,000 pesetas. During the first half of July the members of the Work moved DYA's furniture to the new location.

This marked the end of the 1935–1936 academic year in which 190 people had attended at least one formational activity in DYA. Twenty-six were residents, 144 were students who lived with their relatives or in boarding houses, and twenty-three were recent graduates. They belonged to many different Catholic organizations, especially Catholic Action, as well as to academic and athletic associations. Some were active members of different political parties that respected the rights of the Church, and others had no particular political position. None of them sensed that the country was about to fall into the abyss.

Notes

1. Recollection of Fidel Gómez Colomo, Madrid, October 15, 1975, AGP A.5, 216-1-8.

2. *Intimate Notes*, 89 (October 2, 1930). See also Ethel Tolansky, "The Dynamic Role of the Intellectual in the Message of Blessed Josemaría," in *Figli di Dio nella Chiesa: Riflessioni sul messaggio di San Josemaría Escrivá. Aspetti culturali ed ecclesiastici*, ed. Fernando de Andrés (Roma: EDUSC, 2004), pp. 237–249.

3. In 1935 he wrote that "men, like fish have to be caught by their head, by their intelligence." Escrivá, *The Way: Critical Historical Edition*, p. 1033

4. *Instrucción sobre el modo de hacer el proselitismo* (April 1, 1934), no. 63. AGP A.3, 89-2-1; *Estatutos* (Statutes) (1941), "Espíritu," n. 25. AGP L.1.1, 1-3-3.

5. *Diario de Luchana*, September 8, 1934, p. 175. AGP A.2, 7-2-1. Something similar occurred in the summer of 1930, when Escrivá told Fr. Sánchez that he was thinking of talking to Isidoro Zorzano about the Work. The Jesuit encouraged him: "Give him the big picture. Talk to him about professorships." *Intimate Notes*, 84 (August 25, 1930).

6. Recollection of Juan Jiménez Vargas. Madrid, February 22, 1985. AGP A.5, 221-1-2.

7. *Intimate Notes*, 234 (July 19, 1931).

8. "Academia" (n.d.). AGP A.3, 174-1-6. The words we have quoted in italics are in capital letters and underlined in the original.

9. See Luis Cano, "Instrucciones (obra inédita)," in *Diccionario de san Josemaría Escrivá de Balaguer*, pp. 650–652. The original versions of the three instructions dated February 19, 1934; March 1, 1934; and January 9, 1935; were written on the dates they bear. As we will see, the Founder had them privately printed in book form in the 1960s and in preparing them for publication added some ideas.

10. AGP A.2, 7-3-1 and A.2, 41-2-2.

11. On the members and the activity of the Council of the Work before the Spanish Civil War, see González Gullón, *DYA*, pp. 284–286, 297–299, and 396–397. John Coverdale, "José María González Barredo: An American Pioneer," *Studia et Documenta* 10 (2016), pp. 23–44; José Luis González Gullón and Mariano Galazzi, "Ricardo Fernández Vallespín: Sacerdote y arquitecto (1910–1988)," *Studia et Documenta* 10 (2016), pp. 45–96; Francisco Ponz and Onésimo Díaz, "Juan Jiménez Vargas (1913–1997)," *Studia et Documenta* 5 (2011), pp. 229–260.

12. See José Carlos Martín de la Hoz, *Roturando los caminos: Perfil biográfico de D. José María Hernández Garnica* (Madrid: Palabra, 2012); and Javier Medina Bayo, *Álvaro del Portillo: Un hombre fiel* (Madrid: Rialp, 2012).

13. *Instrucción sobre la obra de San Rafael* (*Instruction on the Work of St. Raphael*) (January 9, 1935), 49. AGP A.3, 89-3-1.

14. *Instruction on the Work of St. Raphael* (January 9, 1935), 40. AGP A.3, 89-3-1. Escrivá seems to be describing some of the activities of Catholic Action at the time.

15. Josemaría Escrivá de Balaguer, *Conversaciones con Mons. Escrivá de Balaguer*, edición crítico-histórica (Madrid: Rialp, 2012), 114 (phrases taken from a 1967 homily).

16. They took vows because, together with the reception of the sacraments, it was the way that people in the Church expressed self-giving to God. Escrivá used it "to help the people who joined Opus Dei to become more aware of what they were committing themselves to." Amadeo de Fuenmayor, Valentín Gómez-Iglesias, and José Luis Illanes, *El itinerario jurídico del Opus Dei. Historia y defensa de un carisma*, 4th ed. (Pamplona: EUNSA, 1990), 77.

17. Letter from Josemaría Escrivá to Ángel Basterra, SJ, Madrid, February 28, 1936. AGP A.3.4, 253-4, 360228-1.

18. Letter from Josemaría Escrivá to Ángel Basterra, SJ, Madrid, April 25, 1936. AGP A.3.4, 253-4, 360425-1. This bellicose language was typical of ascetical writing at the time.

19. See Manuel Álvarez Tardío and Roberto Villa García, *1936: Fraude y violencia en las elecciones del Frente Popular* (Barcelona: Espasa, 2017).

CHAPTER 3

The Spanish Civil War

On **July 17 and 18, 1936,** part of the Spanish army executed a coup d'état. Their stated objective was to reestablish the rule of law, the territorial unity of the country, and public order, all of which had suffered during the first half of 1936. The uprising prevailed in some regions but not others, and the country was divided into two, half under governmental control and half controlled by the rebellious officers.[1]

Section 1. Republican Spain

In the days immediately prior to the military uprising, the Founder and the members of the Work who lived in Madrid were preparing the new DYA residence at 16 Ferraz Street. Directly across the street was the Montana Barracks, which would be the principal stronghold of the uprising in Madrid. On Monday, July 20, army units loyal to the government, police, and groups of militia assaulted the barracks. After their victory, Madrid was completely in Republican hands.

The government handed out arms to the members of the parties and unions that formed the Popular Front coalition. This unleashed a revolution led by socialist, communist, and anarchist militia units. Their common goal was to suppress or kill wealthy people, members of the clergy, and military personnel who did not support the Republic, and confiscate their property. Revolutionary committees and tribunals interrogated and assassinated thousands of people without any real trial. Three hundred and six diocesan priests and 398 religious priests were assassinated in Madrid, almost all of them between July and November 1936. They constituted one-third of the two thousand priests who lived in Madrid.

In the face of this brutal, systematic repression, the Founder and members of the Work took refuge in their relatives' homes. Belonging to Opus Dei was not a cause of danger, since outside Catholic environments at the University of Madrid the institution was not publicly known. To be a priest, to be known as Catholic, or to be considered an opponent of the Popular Front, however, were sufficient motives to be detained or even assassinated.

During the first three months of the war, Escrivá hid in eight homes of friends and relatives of the Work's members. He moved frequently from one place to another because militia units were constantly searching for people they considered enemies of the revolutionary movement. He was accompanied in all of these moves by Juan Jiménez Vargas, who had set as a goal for himself saving the Founder's life.

On October 7, Jiménez Vargas took Escrivá to a small, private psychiatric asylum. It was safer than the homes of friends and relatives, but it isolated the Founder from the rest of his spiritual children and forced him to behave as if he were mentally ill.

The other members of the Work who were in Madrid remained in their own homes or with friends. Over time, militia units discovered and jailed four of them: José María Hernández Garnica, Juan Jiménez Vargas, Álvaro del Portillo, and Manuel Sainz de los Terreros.

November 1936 marked a turning point in the Civil War. General Francisco Franco had led his troops to the western edge of Madrid. If he succeeded in capturing the city, it would be a definitive victory for the "Nationalist" band. After three weeks of intense combat, however, the Republican Army, aided by fighters from other countries in the "international brigades," threw back the attack. Franco stabilized the Madrid front and turned his attention to the northern part of the peninsula.

November also represented the high point of violence in the Republican rearguard. Some 2,500 prisoners were taken out of the jails of Madrid and shot in Paracuellos del Jarama, a village east of the city. In reaction to the criticism this aroused in international public opinion, the government took back control of the prisons from the militia units and entrusted them to official prison guards. It also released prisoners who had not committed any crime. Three members of the Work, Jiménez Vargas, Sainz de los Tereros, and Del Portillo, were set free in January 1937. Hernández Garnica was sentenced to eight months in prison because they found a right-wing party handbill in his home.

Until November, the Founder and members of the Work had hidden out in the hope that the war would end soon, but stabilization of the Madrid front suggested that the conflict might last a long time. The situation in the Republican zone did not permit Opus Dei to develop further. Although assassinations for religious motives diminished sharply from December 1936 on, all public worship remained prohibited, priests continued to live in hiding, the faithful could not receive the sacraments, and many churches were destroyed. By contrast, in the Nationalist zone, the church was permitted to operate freely. For these reasons, Escrivá decided that he and the other members of the Work should flee to the other side.

The diplomatic corps accredited in Spain was granting asylum to people who felt they might be persecuted. By early 1937, there were more than ten thousand refugees in embassies in Madrid, an unprecedented occurrence in international diplomacy. The head of the various diplomatic missions negotiated the evacuation of refugees from their embassies with the Republican government. Argentina, for example, evacuated some three hundred Argentine citizens. The members of the Work decided to see if they could be diplomatically evacuated. Prerequisite for that was gaining asylum in an embassy or consulate.

Thanks to a friend, in February 1937 José María González Barredo won entrance to the consulate of Honduras located in downtown Madrid, in the Castellana Promenade. He was joined somewhat later by Escrivá and his brother Santiago, Álvaro del Portillo, Juan Jiménez Vargas, and Eduardo Alastrué. Another member of the Work, Vincente Rodríguez Casado, took refuge in the Norwegian legation.

Their stay in the counsulate of Honduras lasted longer than they expected. Because Zorzano had been born in Argentina, he enjoyed a certain degree of security and did not feel he needed to seek refuge. He remained in his family's apartment throughout the war. The refugees in the Honduran consulate suffered greatly because of overcrowding and insufficient food. Thirty people were living in the consul's residence, which had been designed for one or two families at most. In May, the situation of the members of the Work improved somewhat when the consul gave them a separate room, although it was very small. There, the Founder celebrated Mass, preached meditations, and encouraged them to maintain their faith and hope.[2]

Because the government censored the mail, Escrivá sent his letters to Miguel Fisac, who was hiding with his family, through Miguel's sister Dolores. Even though he had never met her, in his first letter the Founder invited her to join Opus Dei. After praying about it for some time, in August she replied that she was ready to do so. She was the only woman to join Opus Dei in the Republican zone during the Civil War.[3]

During the time he spent in the consulate, Escrivá insisted on three efforts: trying to be evacuated through diplomatic channels; claiming from the Republican government payment for the damage that an anarchist committee had done to the DYA residence; and praying that his mother and sister might take care of the housekeeping at the DYA residence when the war ended. Escrivá sought the advice of those who accompanied him in the consulate on these concerns, especially Juan Jiménez Vargas, whom he considered his probable successor. They were unsuccessful in achieving the first two objectives, despite the fact that Zorzano worked very hard at them.

Eventually, the Republic of Honduras recognized the Franco regime. This put an end to any hope that the consulate might be able to get them out of Spain. Zorzano's efforts to include the Founder and the members of the Work in the evacuation plans of other embassies also failed. In the face of these difficulties, Escrivá decided they should try to get to the Nationalist zone on their own, and that he would be the last to leave Madrid.

In late summer of 1937, Escrivá, his brother Santiago, and Juan Jiménez Vargas left the Hounduran consulate with counterfeit identification documents from the Popular Front. Once back on the streets of Madrid, Escrivá carried on clandestine pastoral activities with the members of the Work and their friends. He even preached an unusual retreat to five young men. Each of the meditations on aspects of the life of Jesus Christ was held in a different apartment to avoid possible detection.

At the beginning of October 1937, Jiménez Vargas convinced the Founder that he should leave the Republican zone as soon as possible, although some members of the Work might not be able to join him. Escrivá, Jiménez Vargas, José Maria Albareda, Pedro Casciaro, Francico Botella, Miguel Fisac, Manuel Sainz de los Terreros, and Tomás Alvira met in Barcelona at the beginning of November. The only one who did not belong to the Work was Alvira. The Founder had told him that because he had a vocation to marriage he could not join Opus Dei until it was able to admit married people.

The group fled Republican Spain through the Pyrenees Mountains, which separate the Iberian Peninsula from France. The expedition went by bus from Barcelona to Peramola, a town in the northern part of the province of Lérida. They spent the night of November 21 in a building attached to a church that had been sacked by militia units. Escrivá suffered great distress because he thought that God's will might be for him to remain in the Republican zone until the last of the members of the Work had escaped. The following morning, torn by uncertainty, he departed from his usual rule of conduct and asked for a sign from heaven. Concretely, he thought about "a flower or other wooden decoration from the destroyed altar pieces."[4] He went back into the church and found a gilded wooden rose on the floor in a spot where he had been the day before without seeing anything. He was filled with joy because he understood that God was indicating that he should keep going forward.

After several days of waiting hidden in a hut, hired guides took them out of the Republican zone. Over five nights they hiked fifty-three miles (eighty-seven kilometers), climbing a total of nineteen thousand feet (five thousand eight hundred meters). On December 2 they reached the Principality of Andorra, a tiny country situated between Spain and France. They were forced to stay there a few days by snow that blocked the mountain pass to France. As soon as they could make it to southern France, they went by bus to Nationalist Spain, stopping briefly in Lourdes, where Escrivá celebrated Mass.

Isidoro Zorzano, enjoyed some freedom of motion because he had been born in Argentina. Other members of the Work as well as relatives including Escrivá's mother, brother, and sister, remained in the Republican zone until the end of the war. They suffered from lack of food and heat, especially during the painful final months of the conflict.

Section 2. In the Rebel Zone

The situation of the members of the Work changed radically when they reached the Nationalist zone. Almost all of them, including the Founder, had been very close to suffering a violent death in the Republican zone. In the Nationalist zone, there was freedom of worship, the bishops were openly present, and the Franco regime was officially confessional. The Holy See granted diplomatic recognition to the Franco government in May 1938. Like the majority of Spanish Catholics, the members of the Work wanted the rebel army to win, if for no other reason than that it would mean freedom for the Church and permit spreading the message of Opus Dei.

Escrivá and his companions reached the Nationalist zone on December 11, 1937. The young members of the Work were immediately incorporated into the army. Escrivá first went to Pamplona, where the bishop invited him to rest for a few days. He took advantage of his stay in the bishop's palace to make a retreat entirely on his own. On January 8, 1938, he moved to Burgos. The city was the capital of Franco's Spain, and a number of administrative departments were located there. Because of its geographic position and the fact it was a communications hub, Burgos seemed the best place for reorganizing Opus Dei's activities. The former students of DYA, almost all of whom were now in the army, could see Escrivá there when they were on leave.

During the early days of his stay in Burgos, the Founder wrote a circular letter to the members of Opus Dei dated January 9, 1938. He assured them of his spiritual closeness and underlined a few ideas:

cultivating a relationship with God through the fulfillment of their plan of life, growing in affection for the Work, and bringing their friends closer to God.⁵

Although he would have liked a house or apartment which would permit him to have guests, Escrivá had to settle for a small room in a boardinghouse. He was accompanied by José Maria Albareda, Pedro Casciaro, and Francisco Botella. The person who had most helped him to that point, Juan Jiménez Vargas, was stationed at the warfront in Teruel, more than two hundred miles (three hundred twenty kilometers) away. Because he was a doctor caring for the wounded, he did not even get any leaves.

With the permission of the bishop of Burgos, Escrivá resumed his priestly ministry. In a letter to the bishop of Madrid, Escrivá informed him that he was "fulfilling my particular vocation, carrying on apostolate with university students and professors."⁶ He also went to Salamanca to visit the vicar general of Madrid, Francisco Morán.

The people who lived with him, especially Casciaro and Botella, saw that he lived an intense spirit of penance, with disciplines, fasting, and long periods without drinking water. They were also concerned about an illness he suffered for several weeks, with fever, sore throat, and spitting up blood. They feared that he might have tuberculosis, but the doctor assured him it was chronic sore throat. What they did not see was the richness of his prayer. Escrivá revealed some of that in letters to Jimenez Vargas. In June 1938, for instance, he told him: "I have made a great discovery, the most holy wound in my Lord's right hand. That's where I spend the whole day, kissing and adoring. How loveable is the humanity of our God! Ask him to give me real love for him. That will purify all of my other affections."⁷

Escrivá was able to obtain a safe-conduct pass, which permitted him to move within the Nationalist zone to see people. One by one, he visited his children in Opus Dei, met with former DYA residents, corresponded with people all over the Nationalist zone, and sent out a homemade newsletter. Despite the problems of censorship in the Republican zone, he corresponded with the members of the Work and his family in Madrid. He explained Opus Dei to bishops who passed through Burgos or when he visited their diocese. All of this was preparation for the expansion of the Work at the end of the war.

In Burgos, Amparo Rodríguez Casado, whose brother Vicente was a young member of the Work, asked to become a member herself. Together with her mother she helped the Founder by sewing vestments and altar linens which would be needed in the oratories of the Work after the war. This was a common activity among pious women at the time, and Amparo and her mother were joined by several other women. Escrivá gave them classes of Christian formation which, according to Amparo, "dealt with interior life and practical ways to improve our personal conduct." For example, he told them that in social life they should act "with naturalness, being well-dressed and in style, with modesty but without overdoing it."

The Founder reworked his book *Spiritual Considerations*, adding new points to reach a total of 999, a number he chose in honor of the Blessed Trinity. He changed the name of the book to *Camino* [*The Way*]. He also wrote a dissertation for his doctorate in law, a project that had been long-delayed by the foundation of the Work and the outbreak of the Civil War. The topic was the exempt jurisdiction enjoyed for centuries by the abbesses of the cloistered Monastery of Las Huelgas Reales, located just outside Burgos. In August and September he preached a retreat to nuns and another to priests from the Diocese of Vitoria. At the end of September he made his own retreat in the Silos monastery.

On October 12, Escrivá had the joy of seeing Álvaro del Portillo, Eduardo Alastrué, and Vicente Rodríguez Casado. These three members of the Work had enlisted in the Republican Army in Madrid two months earlier and providentially had been assigned to the same unit on the front line. They crossed the line, arrived in the Nationalist zone, and made their way to Burgos. For several months Del Portillo was assigned to a camp near Burgos for training. Escrivá took advantage of the situation to talk with him at length about the Work. In one of his letters to him at this time he called him "*Saxum*" [Rock] because he saw him as a firm support for the expansion of the Work.

The Founder wanted to return to Madrid as soon as possible, to resume the activities interrupted by the war. While waiting, he diligently collected things that would be useful in Madrid, including the altar linens for the future oratory that Rodríguez Casado and her friends were sewing. A friend gave him a tabernacle. With the help of Albareda he wrote to professors in various European countries asking for donations of books for the library of the DYA residence. He stored up food to bring with him for the members of the Work and his family who were suffering from hunger in Madrid.

In November 1938, the Nationalist Army won an important battle along the banks of the lower Ebro River. The Republic was exhausted and appeared to have definitively lost the war from a military point of view. The biggest remaining question was whether the Republic would surrender unconditionally, as Franco demanded, or hold out for a negotiated peace.

On January 9, 1939, Escrivá wrote a new circular letter to the members of Opus Dei, summing up their current situation and looking forward to the future. He said that the word "optimism" summed up his thoughts, and encouraged them to remain united. "I see only one important obstacle: your lack of *filiation* and your lack of *fraternity*, if that should ever happen in our family."[8] A few weeks later, on March 24, he wrote a third circular letter. With their return to Madrid now imminent, he insisted that they be cheerful because the moment had arrived to begin again and to expand to other countries. "Sow, for I assure you in the name of the Lord of the ripe grain, that there will be a harvest. But sow generously. . . . If we do that, the world [is ours]!"[9]

Escrivá entered Madrid on March 28, 1939, in the back of a military truck. He was the first priest wearing a cassock that many people had seen since the beginning of the war three years earlier. People kissed the crucifix he carried in his hand. He immediately went to see his mother, brother, and sister, and the members of the Work who were in the city.

Four days later the Civil War came to an end. The moment had arrived to rebuild a country destroyed by three years of armed conflict.

Three hundred thousand people had died. Two hundred fifty thousand were in prison or concentration camps, and five hundred thousand had been forced into exile. The Catholic Church had recovered freedom of worship but also needed to rebuild its structures damaged by the loss of so many clergy and buildings. The demand for pastoral services in the parishes, and in educational, charitable, and social activities run by the Church, was great.

The Founder dreamed of extending the message he had received, but a decade later Opus Dei remained very small: a total of only fourteen members and Escrivá himself. Two members had died (Jacinto Valentín and José María Isasa) and seven others had left during the Civil War. But those who remained had been toughened by the terrible trial of the Civil War, and they were ready to fulfill their mission. There were twelve men: Isidoro Zorzano, Juan Jiménez Vargas, José María González Barredo, Ricardo Fernández Vallespín, Álvaro del Portillo, José María Hernández Garnica, Pedro Casciaro, Francisco Botella, Eduardo Alastrué, Vicente Rodríguez Casado, Miguel Fisac, and Rafael Calvo Serer. The Founder was left with only two women: Dolores Fisac and Amparo Rodríguez Casado, both of whom had joined Opus Dei during the Civil War. There were another forty or fifty students and young professional men who had received spiritual direction and a larger group of friends and acquaintances. The DYA residence had been destroyed by artillery fire. In some ways, these were the assets and liabilities of the fledgling Church institution preparing to begin a new page in its history.

Notes

1. For information about the members of Opus Dei who figure prominently in this chapter, see Constantino Ánchel, "Francisco Botella Raduán: los años junto a san Josemaría," *Studia et Documenta* 10 (2016), pp. 141–194; Pedro Casciaro, *Soñad y os quedaréis cortos*, 16th ed. (Madrid: Rialp, 2011); John Coverdale, *La fundación del Opus Dei* (Barcelona: Ariel, 2002), pp. 167–234; José Luis González Gullón, *Escondidos: El Opus Dei en la zona republicana durante*

la Guerra Civil española (1936–1939), (Madrid: Rialp, 2018); José Carlos Martín de la Hoz, "Mons. Pedro Casciaro Ramírez (1915-1995)," *Studia et Documenta* 10 (2016), pp. 97–140; Luis Martínez Ferrer, "Vicente Rodríguez Casado: niñez, juventud y primeros años (1918–1940)," *Studia et Documenta* 10 (2016), pp. 195-260; Pablo Pérez López, "San Josemaría y José María Albareda (1935-1939)," *Studia et Documenta* 6 (2012), pp. 13–66; Pablo Pérez López, "Burgos", in *Diccionario de san Josemaría Escrivá de Balaguer*, pp. 169–174; Jesús Sevilla Lozano, *Miguel Fisac: Arquitecto de Dios o del "Diablo"?* (Madrid: Nueva Utopía, 2014); and Andrés Vázquez de Prada, *The Founder of Opus Dei*, vol. 2, *God and Daring* (New York: Scepter, 2002).

2. For a brief summary of the meditations see José Luis González Gullón, *Escondidos*, pp. 209–218.

3. See Yolanda Cagigas Ocejo, "Cartas de Josemaría Escrivá de Balaguer a Dolores Fisac (21 de mayo de 1937–16 de noviembre de 1937)," *Studia et Documenta* 4 (2010), pp. 375–409.

4. *Intimate Notes*, 1440 (December 22, 1937).

5. The text of the letter has been published in Alfredo Méndiz, "Tres cartas circulares del fundador del Opus Dei (Burgos, 1938–1939)," *Studia et Documenta* 9 (2015), pp. 353–377.

6. Letter from Josemaría Escrivá de Balaguer to Leopoldo Eijo Garay, Burgos, January 10, 1938, AGP A.3.4, 254-5, 380110-1.

7. Letter from Josemaría Escrivá de Balaguer to Juan Jiménez Vargas, June 6, 1938, AGP A.3.4, 255-3, 380606-1.

8. *Carta circular* (Circular Letter), Burgos, January 9, 1939, AGP A.3.4, 256-2.

9. Circular Letter, Burgos, March 24, 1939, AGP A.3.4, 256-2.

PART II

Approvals and Initial Expansion
(1939–1950)

The 1940s is among the most tragic decades in human history. On September 1, 1939, Hitler's army invaded Poland. France and the British Empire immediately declared war on Germany. Two weeks later the Soviet army invaded Eastern Poland. The Second World War began. After two years of victories, in 1942 the Axis powers (Germany, Japan, and Italy) lost decisive battles at Soviet Stalingrad, in North Africa, and at sea. By 1943, the invasion of Italy and American triumphs in the Pacific had tipped the balance in favor of the Allies. The following year, they liberated France and Germany as Russian armies drove into Eastern Europe. On May 8, 1945, Germany surrendered unconditionally. After the Russian invasion of Manchuria and the use of atomic bombs on Hiroshima and Nagasaki, Japan surrendered on August 15, ending the war.

At the 1945 conferences at Yalta and Potsdam, the Soviet Union, the United Kingdom, and the United States reached agreements about the destiny of Europe and the Far East. They also created the United Nations as an intergovernmental organization to promote peace and international cooperation. In 1948, the General Assembly of the United Nations approved the Universal Declaration of the Rights of Man. The document recognized individual rights of freedom, thought, religion, movement, education, and an adequate standard of living.

The world was divided into two great geopolitical spheres of influence. On one hand was the Western bloc, led by the United States, which gave economic and political aid through the Marshall Plan (1947) and established a military alliance (NATO) in 1949. On the other was the Eastern bloc, made up of countries with communist regimes in the orbit of the Soviet Union.

The Pope during these years was Pius XII. Immediately after his election in March 1939, he tried to avoid a new international conflict. Once the World War broke out, he established systems to help people persecuted by the Axis powers, especially Jews and advocates of democracy. He worked to reestablish peace through the nuncios, then suffered through the Nazi occupation of Rome from September 1943 to June 1944.

Both during and after the war, Pius XII worked for the establishment of a new social order that would assure peaceful relations among nations. He envisioned something that would respect the political decisions of individuals and of peoples but also rest on the moral norms given by God to mankind. According to the Pope, this meant that the moral law should serve as a support for the liberal democratic system. He called for the so-called "popular" democracies of the communist countries to modify their policies and give primacy to people rather than to the system.

In Spain, the civil war gave way to the nationalist and authoritarian regime of General Francisco Franco. He invoked traditional cultural and social principles such as political, territorial, and religious unity and authority in the exercise of power. He rejected communism, freemasonry, and liberal democracy. To ensure political unity, he established a single party known as the Falange. The army stood as the guarantor of territorial unity against separatism or even significant autonomy in Catalonia and the Basque country. The Church was the principal support of moral unity in society. It supported Franco because during the years of armed conflict he had protected it against revolutionary repression.

Franco was both head of state and head of government. He was advised by a Council of Ministers. The Spanish Cortes collaborated in formulating legislation, although it had no ability to limit Franco's authority. Most people active in political life belonged to one of the factions that had supported the rebellion in 1936: Falangist, Carlist monarchists, and monarchists who supported the Bourbons. They created political minorities that fought with each other for control of society, from politics to culture and education.

Although sympathetic to Italy and Germany, because they had supported him during the Civil War, Franco declared neutrality at the beginning of the Second World War, even though he allowed the Axis limited use of Spanish ports. In June 1940, when an Axis victory seemed likely, Spain shifted to "non-belligerence" and began to give more help to the totalitarian dictatorships. It did not enter the war both because the Civil War had left it in such poor economic condition, and because it needed the food and petroleum that were reaching it from the United States and England. In June 1941, however, Spain applauded the invasion of the Soviet Union by German troops, touting it as part of the struggle against communism. Franco sent more than forty thousand Spanish volunteers to fight in Russia. Spanish propaganda presented this as a new crusade, but the Holy See rejected that characterization.[1]

Spain returned to neutrality in October 1943 in response to Allied victories, but the winners of the war penalized the Franco regime because it had given diplomatic and economic support to the Axis countries. At the Potsdam Conference in the summer of 1945, they prohibited Spain's membership in the United Nations. The veto would last a decade. In December 1946, the United Nations condemned Spain as a philo-fascist regime, and many countries withdrew their ambassadors. Juan de Borbón, claimant to the throne, asked for the reestablishment of a constitutional monarchy. With his habitual pragmatism, Franco gradually toned down the Falangist character of the regime and adopted less rigid approaches. At the same time, he approved a set of Fundamental Laws that recognized him as lifelong leader, stressed the confessional character of the state, and established mechanisms for some slight political representation by representatives of families, municipal governments, and vertical syndicates, government sponsored groups that purported to represent areas of the economy, and included both owners and workers. Spanish society accepted this unusual regime, in some cases willingly and in others because there were no other options.

During its early years, the Franco regime was strongly totalitarian. Economic self-sufficiency and protectionism dominated the political economy of a country destroyed by civil war and with no prospect of outside help. Government entities controlled the world of labor and the prices for consumer goods. They built major infrastructure projects and started government-controlled businesses like Renfe (railroads) and the National Industrial Institute. These attempts to rebuild the economy progressed very slowly because the country was extraordinarily poor. The population suffered famine, and foodstuffs were rationed until 1952. Some two hundred thousand people died of malnutrition between 1940 and 1945.

The regime strongly repressed communism, socialism, anarchism, and freemasonry, which it considered responsible for the Second Republic and the Civil War. Thirty thousand people were executed between 1939 and 1945. Immediately after the end of the Civil War, there were 270,000 political prisoners. The number declined gradually to 44,000 in 1945. Repression made itself felt in culture, education, and art as well as politics. Society clearly distinguished between the victors and the vanquished, and there was widespread abuse of power and favoritism. Only with time, and with the guarantee that they would not be tried, did some outstanding exiled intellectuals such as Gregorio Marañón and José Ortega y Gasset return to Spain. Even they were not able to express their ideas in public, however, since no political or cultural dissent was permitted. Others preferred to remain in exile rather than return to an authoritarian country.

The Falange tried to control all parts of society from business to the world of labor and unions, and from politics to culture and education. For example, at the universities, only one student organization, the *Sindicato de Estudiantes Univesitarios*, controlled by the Falange, was permitted, and starting in 1943 membership was obligatory. Press and the radio were censored and served largely as organs of government propaganda.

Many Catholics collaborated actively with the regime in the hope of creating a new society whose legislation and way of life would reflect Christian values. There was tension between some Catholics groups and the regime, partly due to its totalitarian tendencies. Franco, for instance, insisted on having a voice in the naming of bishops. He suppressed various Catholic associations and replaced others with state-controlled equivalents. He did not hesitate to censure Church documents such as Pope Pius XII's April 1939 request for clemency for the losers in the Civil War or Cardinal Isidro Gomá's pastoral letter urging that those who had persecuted the Church be pardoned.

The Church in Spain flourished in the years after 1939. Many people attended Mass and other devotions. Religious orders regained control of primary and secondary schools. There was an explosion of vocations to the priesthood and the religious life, and many laypeople joined Catholic organizations. In addition to the ordinary life of the parishes, there were many spiritual retreats, missions, and *Cursillos de Cristiandad* through the Cursillo Movement. Many students joined Young Catholic Action and other organizations that sponsored religious and social activities. Large numbers of university students decided to give their life to God and entered the seminary or the novitiate, while others aspired to form Christian families.

Notes

1. The Founder of Opus Dei was aware of the problems raised by both National Socialism and Communism before the Second World War and publicly criticized those regimes. (See Vázquez de Prada, *The Founder of Opus Dei*, vol. 2, pp. 285–286). Silverio Palafox was the only member of Opus Dei to fight in the so-called Blue Division. Juan Jiménez Vargas, Miguel Fisac, and Eduardo Alatrué also volunteered, after consulting the bishop of Madrid, but were not accepted. (The authors owe this information to Onésimo Díaz).

Escrivá rejected all forms of nationalism and respected the political opinions of others. The case of Juan Bautista Torello, who joined Opus Dei in Barcelona in the Catalan region of Spain, is significant: "1941 witnessed great nationalist exaltation among the members of the Falange. The walls and façades of buildings in Barcelona were full of patriotic graffiti: 'If you are Spanish, speak Spanish!' Or similar things like: 'Spaniard, speak the language of the Empire!' In a long conversation that Juan Bautista had with don Josemaría, he told him he belonged to an organization for the defense of Catalan culture. The police consider[ed] it a clandestine anti-Franco organization since speaking Catalan was prohibited. The Founder insisted on the freedom that he enjoyed in this regard. It was up to him to decide, and nobody in the Work would ask him about it." Vázquez de Prada, *The Founder of Opus Dei*, vol. 2, p. 282–283.

CHAPTER 4

Growth of the Men's Branch

Arriving in Madrid in March 1939, Escrivá and the other members of the Work faced the difficulties poverty brought with it, but were enthusiastic about beginning a new era in which the Church could act freely and the message of Opus Dei could reach new people and environments.

The Founder's *Apuntes íntimos* and other writings from the 1930s contained practical guidelines for immediate action as well as passages that reflected or clarified core aspects of the spirit of the Work. Although he did not attempt to make a long-term strategic plan, for the period right after the war, he established a number of priorities including reestablishing the governing structure of Opus Dei, opening student residences, explaining the Work's spirit to students and recent graduates, and resuming activities with women.

Since he had only a dozen people and they had little experience, the governmental structure the Founder established was very simple. He named the twenty-five-year-old Álvaro del Portillo, who was studying third-year engineering, General Secretary and Economic Administrator of the Work. At the student residence in Madrid, Juan Jiménez Vargas was the director, Isidoro Zorzano the administrator, and Ricardo Fernández Vallespín the legal representative. Francisco Botella and Vincente Rodríguez Casado would focus on activities with students (the Work of St. Raphael). José Maria Albareda would take care of the Sociedad de Colaboración Intelectual (SOCOIN), which organized activities for recent graduates and professional men within the Work of St. Gabriel. As time went by, the Founder delegated more responsibilities. He met periodically with Del Portillo, Jimenez Vargas, and Albareda to review how things were going.[1]

Escrivá continued dedicating himself personally to forming the members of the Work both in groups (in the brief circles, meditations, and days of recollection) and in individual sessions of spiritual direction. He also asked several members who had belonged to the Work for a longer time, such as Jimenez Vargas and Del Portillo, to help him in the spiritual accompaniment of younger members. They did so through informal conversations based on fraternity and friendship, in which they oriented the first steps of new vocations by means of spiritual and apostolic advice. It was a novelty for a layman to do this. The ordinary practice was that members of religious orders or diocesan priests directed and shaped the Christian life of the faithful. The Founder generally did not hear the confessions of the members. Rather he suggested that they go to confession with priests whom he knew. This made it possible for him to talk with them about spiritual matters without involving the sacramental seal of confession.

Escrivá also had to spend some time on personal tasks not directly related with Opus Dei. He finished writing his doctoral thesis and defended it at the Central University of Madrid in December 1939. No copy survives, but it was probably some two hundred pages long, as was the norm at the time. The title was "Historical Canonical Study of the Ecclesiastical Jurisdiction *Nullius dioecesis* of the Abbess of Las Huelgas of Burgos." At the suggestion of the bishop of Madrid, in 1940/41 he taught a course on general and professional ethics for journalists in a government-sponsored program for journalists in Madrid. At the petition of the Minister of Education, he served for a few months as a member of the National Council of Education. In February 1942, he received a written canonical appointment as rector of St. Elizabeth and was incardinated in the Diocese of Madrid.[2]

Section 1. From Madrid to the Provinces

The first corporate activity of the Work after the Civil War was a student residence. Since the building on Ferraz Street had been destroyed by artillery fire, in the summer of 1939 they rented three apartments at 6 Jenner Street. In two apartments on the fourth floor they put the oratory, bedrooms for some thirty-five students, a study room and a living room. In a single apartment on the first floor they put the dining room, the kitchen, and rooms for the Founder, his mother, and his brother and sister.[3]

Escrivá informed the diocese that he was once again doing pastoral activities with students and asked for permission to have an oratory in the residence. On September 2, 1939, he had his first face-to-face interview with Bishop Eijo Garay. It lasted five hours. From then on they were in close contact through personal meetings in the bishop's palace, as well as by mail and telephone. Bishop Eijo gave Escrivá his unconditional support. He thought that he was a man of God and that Opus Dei would contribute to the renewal of the Church.

The Jenner residence was similar to DYA. The students spent most of their time studying and attending classes, but they also organized cultural, charitable, and athletic activities. Escrivá's priestly work focused on preaching and celebrating the sacraments. His spiritual children focused on teaching doctrine. For example, for some time, Vicente Rodríguez Casado and José Maria Hernández Garnica gave the classes of Christian formation for the St. Raphael Work.

In June and September 1939, Escrivá preached retreats for university students in Valencia. Several of those who attended joined Opus Dei—among others, Amadeo de Fuenmayor, José Manuel Casas Torres, and José Orlandis. In September, Rafael Calvo Serer rented an apartment on Samaniego Street in Valencia. It was so small they called it El Cubil (the cubby-hole). Calvo directed the house and gave classes on Christian life. A year later they moved to a place big enough for sixteen residents. They called it the Samaniego Residence.

Prior to the Civil War, Escrivá had thought of opening residences as the first step in beginning in a new city. After the war, they usually began with periodic visits to the new city to meet people and encourage them to live a more intense Christian life. The Founder thought of these trips as similar to those "the apostles made when they started churches in new cities. They let them act independently and supported them with letters and frequent visits."[4]

Starting in November 1939, the young men of the Work made weekend trips from Madrid to Barcelona, Salamanca, Valladolid, and Zaragoza to meet students. Some traveled frequently, others less so because of the demands of their classes or military obligations. After finishing work or classes at midday on Saturday, they took a train or bus, returning Sunday night or in the early hours of Monday. Several students in each of these cities joined Opus Dei. The one exception was Salamanca, where it seemed harder to convey the message of the Work.

Escrivá asked the travelers to prepare a plan for the trip, to pray for the people they were going to meet and for the bishop of the diocese, and to offer to God the discomfort they experienced. Once they arrived, they asked the people they already knew to introduce them to their friends. The explanation they gave of Opus Dei followed a set plan. They invited them to study or carry out their professional work well, to maintain a personal relationship with God, and to cultivate friendship. At the end of each trip, to facilitate continuity, they prepared a brief overall report and a card with information about each of the students and professional men they had met.[5]

The members of the Work explained to those they met that they were not trying to form a new association. "Here we don't say, 'We belong to such and such an association,' but rather 'We study this or that.'" Each member received Christian formation personally or in small groups. They wanted to transmit a Christian spirit to the university "by studying a lot and helping each other as brothers. Our apostolate is confidential, from one friend to another."[6]

On April 23, 1940, they opened an apartment on Montero Calvo Street in Valladolid, provided by the father of Teodoro Ruiz, who had just joined Opus Dei. Like the first apartment in Valencia, it was very small, so they called it "The Corner." Pedro Casciaro decorated it. In June, Amadeo de Fuenmayor, Rafael Termes, and others found an apartment in Barcelona which they ironically called El Palau (The Palace). None of them yet held a degree, so the lease was signed by a doctor-friend, Alfons Balcells. In the afternoon, students came to study, to pray, to receive Christian formation, and for informal get-togethers.[7]

The Way was an important tool for explaining Opus Dei. The first edition of 2,500 copies came out in September 1939. It had an attractive modern cover and 999 spiritual maxims. Its direct style impressed students, who found some of its topics novel, including working with human and supernatural perfection for love of God, the virtues needed by laypeople, marriage as a vocation, and professional prestige as a means of apostolate. The Founder himself and the members of Opus Dei distributed copies to bookstores in the places they visited.

From March 17 to March 24, 1940, thirty-three members of Opus Dei from Barcelona, Madrid, Valencia, Valladolid, and Zaragoza attended a "study week" in the Jenner residence. The Founder preached and spoke personally with each one. He explained in detail the spirit of Opus Dei so that all the members would have a clear sense of their universal mission and know how to carry it out in practice. Álvaro del Portillo and Juan Jiménez Vargas gave classes about the spirit and activity of Opus Dei. The participants visited some of the places where the Work had begun, including the Porta Coeli Asylum and the buildings on Ferraz Street that had housed DYA.[8]

During the summer of 1942, more Study Weeks were held. Twenty-eight young men attended the first in mid-August, and twenty-four the second at the beginning of September. Most were from Madrid, but some of them came from new places like Bilbao, San Sebastián, and Murcia. These activities strengthened the bonds of family life in Opus Dei based on friendship and a shared Christian ideal. To underline the need to be united in intentions and affections, the Founder told them about the Forty Martyrs of Sebaste who died together in a frozen lake in fourth-century Turkey while their executioners promised to save anyone who would renounce his faith.

By the end of the 1939/40 academic year, Opus Dei had two centers in Madrid, the Jenner student residence and a large apartment on Martínez Campos Street where a number of members who had already graduated from the university lived, among them the architect Ricardo Fernández Vallespín and two high school teachers, José María Gonzalez Barredo and José María Albareda. Members of the Work had traveled more than seventy times to a total of eleven Spanish cities. In Valencia, Barcelona, and Valladolid they had rented apartments in which they meet with people. Many students and young professional men in a number of Spanish cities had heard about Opus Dei. Seventy of them asked to be admitted.

At the beginning of the academic year 1940/41, they rented a house in Madrid to serve as the headquarters of Opus Dei and a student residence. It was a three-story building with a semi-basement on the corner of Diego de León and Lagasca Street. Escrivá and his family, Álvaro del Portillo, and a number of other members of the Work moved there despite the fact that the building had been damaged during the Spanish Civil War and that they did not have enough money to turn on the heat.[9]

In the fall of 1941, Diego de León became a center of studies, a residence in which members of the Work who were studying at the university also took two years of classes of Christian formation in apologetics, philosophy, Latin, and public speaking, as well as receiving detailed instruction in the spirit of Opus Dei. The first year there were sixteen students. Many of the theology classes were given by José María Bueno Monreal, a professor in the seminary of Madrid. Escrivá gave meditations and spent much time in get-togethers and other informal meetings with the students. Some of the early members such as Álvaro del Portillo and Juan Jiménez gave formation classes. The Founder asked several friends of his who belonged to religious orders, such as the Augustinian José López Ortiz and the Dominican José Manuel Aguilar, to hear the students' confessions and celebrate Mass and benediction in the house.

The growth of the number of members who had finished their studies led to acquiring apartments on Nuñez Balboa Street and Villanueva Street as centers for the "older" members (whose average

age was less than thirty).* Among the residents of Villanueva were Álvaro del Portillo and Isidoro Zorzano.

In the summer of 1943 the Jenner residence lost its lease because the owner needed the apartments for his family. The members of the Work rented three houses on Moncloa Avenue. That fall, the new Moncloa residence opened with some fifty residents, although it could accommodate up to a hundred. In November, an apartment on Españoleto Street took the place of the one on Nuñez de Balboa Street, which was too small. In Barcelona they rented a larger house. Among the residents were two physicians, Juan Jiménez Vargas and Alfons Balcells, so they called the center La Clínica (The Clinic).

Section 2. Opus Dei Becomes a Pious Union

A year and a half after the end of the Civil War, the Work was relatively well-known in a number of Spanish universities. Some 120 people belonged to Opus Dei, and many more students had heard its message of sanctity in the midst of the world through professional work. Its activities grew gradually on the basis of friendship. Escrivá wanted the members to act in this discreet manner so as not to interfere with other Catholic associations and so as not to be mistaken for a religious order. He personally took care of relations with the bishops

---

* The word *center* designates in Opus Dei two closely related realities. It is a unit of Opus Dei's local government, established by the authorities of Opus Dei to take care of apostolic activities. It also refers to a locale used for the apostolate of Opus Dei, usually a house or apartment, owned by a not-for-profit corporation or similar civil entity that takes care of its economic and technical aspects. A center in the first (legal) sense need not necessarily have a locale of its own. The centers in the second (physical) sense often serve as residences for some numerary members, and are used as a place to give formation to members and other people and to take care of activities of Opus Dei. See *Codex iuris particularis Operis Dei*, 1982, no. 8, section 1, and no. 166. Members of the Work are assigned to a center in the first sense, taking into account their personal circumstances and the needs of the apostolate. The current Statutes of the Prelature provide that before canonical erection of a center which carries on corporate activities, the vicar of Opus Dei must request the *venia* of the local bishop. See *Codex iuris particularis Operis Dei*, 1982, no. 177, section 1.

of the cities in which there were members. Before opening a center, he asked the local bishop for his *venia* or permission to have an oratory.[10]

Some priests and members of religious orders were critical of Opus Dei's message or behavior. To help them understand that the hierarchy supported Opus Dei, in March 1940 Bishop Eijo Garay suggested that Escrivá ask for canonical approval. This would be the first time that the Founder would ask ecclesiastical authorities for a legal approval of his charism of people who "have to sanctify themselves in the world, in the heart of society, wherever they may be, in their professional work (not excluding positions in the public administration) without changing state and without being a new link in the evolution of religious life."[11] The legal question was complex and required prudence because, as he confided to his children, it was "difficult to make something new fit in the canonical norms."[12] After seeking advice from the diocesan expert on canon law, Fr. José María Bueno Monreal, he decided to seek a provisional solution, respectful of the essence and spirit of the Work and open to future change.

The Founder decided that within the possibilities offered by the Code of Canon Law, the best solution was to ask that Opus Dei be approved as an association of laypeople, specifically what was then called a pious union and today would be called an association of the faithful. He wrote the required documents and discussed them with Bueno Monreal, Albareda, Del Portillo, Fernández Vallespín, Hernández Garnica, and Jiménez Vargas. After translating the documents into Latin, as was customary at the time, he asked Bishop Eijo Garay to approve Opus Dei but without erecting it canonically since this was a temporary solution.

On March 19, 1941, the bishop approved Opus Dei as a pious union with statutes made up of six documents (Regulations, Governance, *Ordo*, Customs, Spirit, and Ceremonies). The approval covered the goals of Opus Dei, its governmental structure and internal organization, the classes of members, its way of transmitting its message, and the interplay of corporate and personal activities.

Opus Dei defined itself as a "Catholic Association of men and women, living in the midst of the world, who seek Christian perfection through the sanctification of ordinary work. Persuaded that man has been created '*ut operaretur*' [to work] (Gen 2:15), the members of Opus Dei are obliged not to abandon their professional work or other equivalent activity, even though they may enjoy high economic or social status." To achieve this goal, they oblige themselves to "live an interior life of prayer and sacrifice according to the regime and spirit approved by the Holy Church, and to carry out their professional and social activities with the greatest rectitude."[13]

The members of Opus Dei were lay men and women who gave themselves completely to God in celibacy in the midst of the world. "The members of Opus Dei are not religious, but their way of living, fully given to Jesus Christ, is not different in its essence from the religious life because they commit themselves definitively to seek perfection. Their vocation is of total self-giving, but in the world, in the heart of earthly realities."[14] This showed that the approval was necessarily provisional, since Opus Dei asked its members for a commitment to God that went much further than merely belonging to an association of the faithful.

The 1941 statutes provided for different categories of members. The terms that the 1941 statutes used are still used today, but their meanings have changed. In 1941, the members who undertook to live celibacy were described as "Supernumeraries," and only those of them who would dedicate themselves to internal tasks of direction were called "Numeraries." The members could be incorporated into Opus Dei for a fixed period by the "Oblation" or for life by the "Fidelity." People related to Opus Dei but not technically members could be either single or married. They were labeled as "Inscribed." The reason why married people could not yet be members of the Work was that Church law at the time made no provision for complete dedication to God with a specific vocation without celibacy. Furthermore the Founder wanted first to form a group of celibate men and women that would be available to expand the Work. Looking to the future, the statutes mentioned without further explanation those who "undertake ecclesiastical studies and become priests" dedicated "specially to the spiritual formation of the other members."*

The system of government for men and women would be the same but separate. Their activities would also be similar but separate, although the women would also take care of the administration of the houses of both sections as a specific apostolic task.† The statutes specify that all the members of the Work "form a family with supernatural ties. Therefore, when three or more members live together, they are said to live as a family." Their homes are characterized by "the tone and environment of a Christian family." They have the tenor of "the aristocracy of intelligence (among the men) and great refinement in mutual dealings."‡

The Association would be directed by its President, who would be called Father. He would be advised by a Senate made up of the Secretary General, three assistant secretaries, and at least one delegate from each territory. The General Administrator would advise the Father and Senate on economic questions and would audit, steer, and oversee the Association's accounting and the economic activity of the members.[15] The Women's "Advisory" would have the same functions as the men's Senate. Alongside these central organisms of government, there would be territorial Commissions and Advisories to

---

* *Estatutos* (Statutes) (1941), "Régimen," art. 4. As we will see, from 1947 on the celibate members were called "numeraries" and the term "supernumerary" was used for members who were married or likely to get married. The term "inscribed member" began to be used for numerary members dedicated to institutional tasks.

† See chapter 5, section 2 ("The Administration").

‡ *Statutes* (1941), "Espiritu," arts. 19, 24, and 25. Although at the time few women went to college (see chapter 5), the Founder wanted the message of the Work to contribute to the promotion of women in all environments, from the worlds of agriculture and domestic service to the universities and the liberal professions. See Mercedes Montero, "Mujer y Universidad en España (1910–1936): Contexto histórico del punto 946 de *Camino*," *Studia et Documenta* 6 (2012), pp. 211–234. Following the Founder's usage, the word Administration (with a capital A) means in this book the people who organize and direct the household work of the centers of Opus Dei, especially the care of the oratory, cleaning, food preparation, laundry, and the door. It is also used to refer to the tasks involved and to the areas of the building dedicated to them.

improve the formation of the members. In each territory there would be a center of studies for men and another for women, which would offer instruction in Christian doctrine and in the spirit of the Work.

Regarding the apostolate of the Association, the statutes foresaw that individual members "would exercise an apostolate of friendship and confidence among the best people in their environment." This would take place across the entire social spectrum. "By opening themselves up like a fan, the members avoid forming groups." They would work primarily in the civil, as opposed to confessional, sphere: "The members ordinarily exercise their apostolate from positions within the public administration [including public schools and universities]" and "more generally management positions."[16]

The discussion of institutional activities in the statutes reflects the reality of Opus Dei at the moment: On the men's side, six centers, approximately one hundred members, almost all college students or recent graduates. On the women's side, ten members, almost all quite young, and as yet no center. The statutes described the men's Work of St. Raphael as directed to college students. The Work of St. Raphael among women was described as having "as its immediate goal forming good mothers of Christian families," both in the agrarian world and in the cities. The St. Gabriel Work gives Christian formation to the collaborators of the Work so that they might expand the apostolate by "spreading themselves out in the various sectors of society." The statutes added that women connected with Opus Dei would carry out an "apostolate of written and oral information through publishing houses, book stores, etc., but especially through a quiet but effective apostolate through private conversations without show."*

All of the members were celibate and, with the exception of the Founder, were lay men or women. Priests and married people would come later. In March 1941, almost all the male members were students or worked in the academic world or in the liberal professions and dedicated part of their time to taking care of Opus Dei's activities and centers. They belonged to the upper middle class of Spanish

---

* *Statutes* (1941), "Régimen", art. 12, §1; art. 13, §1; art. 12, §§ 2 and 3.

society, and their social life was the same as that of their colleagues, although as a manifestation of sobriety they did not ordinarily go to the movies or the theater. They used a small cilice two hours a day and a cord discipline once a week as a penance. They kept an account of their expenses and handed it in each month. Any earnings that exceeded their personal expenses they used for the activities of Opus Dei. They were completely secular, but had a deep awareness of having given themselves completely to God.

Section 3. In the University World

After the Civil War, Spain needed to find new cultural and social leaders and to rebuild all aspects of society including intellectual life. In November 1939, the government created the Consejo Superior de Investigaciones Científicas (CSIC) [Higher Council for Scientific Research] to promote research in Spain. In the upcoming years, the CSIC was a leading force in Spanish intellectual and scientific life. It funded and helped organize conferences, granted scholarships and financed study and research at foreign institutions, and sponsored the publication of journals. Its first director was a member of Opus Dei, José María Albareda, a professor of agricultural sciences. His appointment may have been due to the fact that, in addition to having excellent academic credentials, he was a personal friend of the minister of education, José Ibáñez Martín. As head of the CSIC, he contributed to the growth of research in Spain and laid the foundations for a solid academic institution.[17]

Some other members of Opus held positions at CSIC research centers or received scholarships to study and carry out research abroad, but they were relatively few. Of the 177 grants for study abroad awarded by the CSIC in 1945, for example, five went to members of Opus Dei. To the extent that the grants made it possible for members of Opus Dei to go to other countries, they also contributed to the Work's international expansion.

During the war, many professors had died, been purged, or gone into exile, so there was an urgent need to fill vacant university chairs.

Between 1939 and 1945, 179 new *catedráticos* [chaired full professors] were appointed. Professorships were awarded on the basis of *oposiciones*, grueling six-part competitive exams carried out publically before panels of five professors. Not many publications were required beyond the doctoral thesis, so it was possible to win a professorship shortly after receiving a PhD. In many cases, the new professors were under thirty years of age.

A *catedrático* was a government employee who held his position for life, enjoyed social prestige, and could influence society. Not surprisingly, a number of religious and political groups made it a corporate goal to have as many as possible of their members win professorships. At the confessional level, the National Catholic Association of Propagandists was especially important. It had been formed to prepare select Catholics for action in public life so they could spread Catholic principles by directing politics and culture in official institutions. The group had only about five hundred members at the end of the Civil War, but it was highly successful. Thirty-four of its members won university professorships in the first five years of the 1940s. Furthermore, until the mid-1950s, Franco drew his ministers of education from its ranks.

In the political sphere, the Falangists would have liked to win university chairs as a way to influence culture, but only a small number succeeded, perhaps because they focused more on propaganda and organizational structures than on education and culture. Other groups were also represented among the *catedráticos*. Some were associated with the Alfonsine monarchical tradition. They generally focused on the vision of Spanish history offered before the Civil War by Menéndez Pelayo and Ramiro de Maeztu, and on the sociopolitical program of *Acción Española*, a journal published during the Second Republic. A small number of professors were traditionalists—supporters of an authoritarian monarchy, a confessional state, and a single "Catholic" answer even to political and other questions on which the Church did not have an official position.

Although Escrivá continued offering spiritual care to people from diverse social groups, including tradesmen and domestic workers, most of the men who joined Opus during the 1940s were university students or recent graduates. As an institution, Opus Dei continued to believe that starting with the educated was an effective way to bring Christ's message to the entire society. Specifically, the Founder encouraged the Work's members to reach out with their message of holiness in the midst of the world to those who felt called to work professionally in public administration, education at its various levels, and the media. Concretely, in June 1940, he spoke with Del Portillo, Albareda, Fernández Vallespín, and Jiménez Vargas about the high number of university professorships that were open and about encouraging people of the Work to consider trying to win one.[18]

José María Albareda was the first member of the Work to obtain a university chair. In November 1940 he was appointed *catedrático* in the School of Pharmacy of the University of Madrid. During the next five years, fifteen members of Opus Dei—among others, Rafael Calvo Serer, Antonio Fontán, Amadeo de Fuenmayor, Juan Jiménez Vargas, Francisco Ponz, and Vicente Rodríguez Casado—won university chairs. This was 8.3 percent of the total number of chairs filled since 1939. Like the rest of their colleagues, they became professors by winning in an *oposicion* after training in state or foreign centers. Many of them joined or created research centers and periodicals that gave them a platform for publicizing their theories. They were all united by the desire to promote a cultural order with Christian roots. But in other areas they differed, sometimes sharply. Politically some were Monarchists, others Falangists, and some unaffiliated.

Some heads of the Spanish Falange and Falangist university professors with a "doctrinaire secularist mentality"[19] spread the rumor that Opus Dei had an institutional objective of controlling higher education and the state. They also accused it of fostering favoritism in the awarding of CSIC chairs, jobs, and scholarships. As the only legally permitted party and because it embraced an authoritarian and corporatist model, the Falange took offense when it encountered people, especially professors, who refused to accept its programs and ideas. It accused them of being contrary to "the national spirit."

Specifically, some Falangists said that Opus Dei was a secret institution that had infiltrated the officially sanctioned organization of university students to seize the centers of power and then distort the essence of the national-syndicalist state.

In the summer of 1941, Opus Dei was denounced before the Special Tribunal for the Repression of Freemasonry for practicing clandestine activities and for de-Christianizing youth. The few people from the Work with positions in the Falange, such as Eduardo Alastrué, Miguel Fisac, and Juan Jiménez Vargas, could not prevent the accusation, but the tribunal dismissed the case in late 1942 or early 1943.

In January 1942, the Spanish Falange Information Delegation, led by David Jato, drew up a *Confidential Report on the Secret Organization Opus Dei*. The report claimed that the Work's purpose was "the conquest of power through cultural entities, and manipulating the teaching staff of the university and of all kinds of academic centers."[20] It added that through Albareda and other intellectuals, the Work controlled both the CSIC and the panels that administered the *oposiciones* through which professorships were awarded. Finally, it accused Opus Dei of being clandestine and internationalist, in opposition to the principles of the National Movement. This attack on the Work fizzled out after the bishop of Madrid told the head of the Falangist trade union, "I sponsor and authorize all the works of piety and apostolate in my diocese, but I specially love Opus Dei. I would put my hand in the fire for it."[21]

The fact that members of Opus Dei continued to sign up for *oposiciones* for professorships provoked the Falange to launch another attack in June 1943. A new report claimed that Opus Dei was a secret organization and that the CSIC was the cover it used to hide its desire to control government positions and to monopolize Spanish culture. It claimed that the minister of education, Ibáñez Martín, had left the university in Albareda's hands and, therefore, in those of Opus Dei. A few months later, a third Falangist report returned to the idea that Opus Dei proposed "to achieve the conquest of power through cultural entities, manipulating the university faculty."[22]

In mid-1945, the fifteen professors who belonged to the Work represented 6.2 percent of its total membership of 243 (223 men and 20 women). This small but significant percentage was due to the fact that at the time a disproportionately large portion of the members were connected to the academic world. The percentage of members who were professors declined sharply as members began to work in a broader range of fields and to live more frequently outside Spain. Thus, in 1951, of the total membership, only 0.77 percent were professors. Looked at another way, in 1951, 23 of the total of 614 Spanish professors belonged to the Work (3.7 percent)[23]

The political and cultural vicissitudes of the Franco regime should not have affected Opus Dei, which had as a corporate plan the international dissemination of holiness in the secular sphere. But the Falangist accusation that Opus Dei wanted to lead the regime and that it acted as a conspiracy left a lasting mark. It also adversely affected the careers of some Spanish members.[24]

Section 4. Opposition within the Church

The first two decades of Opus Dei's life coincided with a vigorous debate within the Church on the organization of the secular apostolate. The Founder had already encountered some lack of understanding of his message and activity in the 1930s, but in the summer of 1940 he began to suffer a serious problem in the Work's apostolate with students.

It all started when two young members of the Jesuit-led Sodality of Our Lady, Salvador Canals and Álvaro del Amo, who had decided to enter the Jesuit novitiate, changed their minds and joined Opus Dei. Fr. Ángel Carrillo, a fiery-tempered young Jesuit, the director of the sodality and former spiritual director of Canals and Del Amo, reacted harshly. He commented that Escrivá might be excommunicated for his ideas about the Christian life and that the activities carried out at the Jenner residence were suspect. When he heard about this, Escrivá requested a meeting with Fr. Carrillo. They agreed to tell each other about criticism of the other that came to their attention, but in the end nothing came of the meeting.

In December of that year, during a novena to the Immaculate Conception for young members of the Barcelona Sodality, Fr. Carrillo criticized Escrivá's book *The Way*. Three months later, in February 1941, Fr. Manuel Vergés, SJ, director of the Barcelona Sodality, said in a speech that Escrivá's approach to vocation in the midst of the world might be heretical and charged him with recruiting sodality members. When the people associated with the Work did not react, Fr. Vergés expelled from the sodality Ramón Guardans, Juan Bautista Torelló, Raimundo Pániker, Rafael Escolá, Jorge Brosa, and Alfons Balcells for going to the Opus Dei center. (They were all members of the Work except Balcells.) One more member of the sodality, Laureano López Rodó, voluntarily left. Anonymous writings appeared alleging that Opus Dei prohibited its members from telling their spiritual directors about their membership and from attending spiritual exercises. Jesuits visited several families to tell them that their children's association with Opus Dei put them in danger of eternal damnation.[25]

The accusations of Carrillo and the Jesuits of Barcelona spread through the Spanish provinces of the Society of Jesus and then through other religious orders and among the diocesan clergy. The president of the Youth of Catholic Action, Manuel Aparici, commented that Opus Dei used young people for its own purposes. After speaking with people who knew the Work, however, he retracted his accusation. The same happened with some members of various religious orders. A Dominican who had launched some attacks against the Work in Valencia, for example, changed his attitude after talking with Pedro Casciaro, the director of the Samaniego residence.

Escrivá thought that the situation had been created by people who had acted in good faith and, therefore, that the Work was suffering "opposition from good people."[26] He begged the members to "keep quiet, work, forgive, smile and pray, and suffer with joy."[27] He asked them to love the Jesuits, reminding them that for years he had used ideas from St. Ignatius' *Spiritual Exercises* in his preaching, and he recommended that they read the saint's classic biography written by one of his companions.

Bishop Eijo of Madrid encouraged Escrivá and defended him openly. When Abbot Aureli Escarré of the Montserrat monastery consulted him about the Work, the bishop replied that he had known it since its foundation and that he had approved it recently in an effort to stop the attacks on it. "Believe me, Rev. Abbot," he wrote, "from its inception and in all its steps and works, the *Opus* is truly *Dei* [the Work is truly of God]."[28]

Both personally and in writing, the Founder explained to various church officials what Opus Dei was and what activities it carried out. He wrote to Fr. Carrillo asking him to stop what he characterized as his "campaign" against the Work, and in the spring and summer of 1941 he visited the Jesuit provincials in Spain and met twice with the nuncio, Bishop Gaetano Cicognani. At the nuncio's request, he gave him a copy of the statutes approved by the bishop of Madrid in March, and explained that his message consisted of renewing the call to secular holiness "as a way to serve the Holy Church and not to dominate anything."[29] He also said that "deep down all this is simply a question of vocations," starting with those of Canals and del Amo.[30]

Attacks on the Work were concentrated in Madrid and Barcelona, but had some repercussions in Valencia, Valladolid, and Zaragoza. Some critics called it a Masonic society that stole vocations from the religious orders.

Escrivá asked some of the older members, including Álvaro del Portillo and José María Albareda, to help him explain to ecclesiastical and civil authorities the Work's aims and to show them the approval received from the bishop of Madrid. With the younger members, however, he preferred not to talk about the events so as not to create a feeling of victimhood within Opus Dei or distract them from their work and activities.

There were three primary reasons why some people found it hard to understand Opus Dei and its activities. The first was theological. According to a centuries-old mentality, the perfection of the Christian life, perfect holiness, could be achieved only in the religious state. Dedicating oneself to the realities of the world and enjoying prestige and professional competence while earning money and possessing the goods of the earth was seen as incompatible with the highest degree of sanctity. That Opus Dei urged people to seek Christian perfection in the secular realm was for many incomprehensible. They believed, as Fr. Carrillo put it, that "a layman in a jacket and pants cannot, simply cannot, be a man of total dedication."[31]

A second factor behind the attacks was the fact that the Work attracted some outstanding students from well-known Catholic families who had belonged to Catholic organizations, especially the Jesuit-sponsored sodality. Some of them had even been considering joining a religious order. When they learned about Opus Dei, they sometimes distanced themselves from the Catholic organizations they had belonged to and from the priests from whom they had sought spiritual guidance.

The third factor was the novelty of the way in which the lay members of Opus Dei lived and moved in society. They did not hide their membership in the Work, but they did not advertise their activities and preferred to explain its message one-on-one to fellow students and other friends. They did not wear external signs of their membership such as the medals and insignia typically worn by members of religious associations in Spain at the time. They did not generally meet in public places, but in private homes. Escrivá saw this way of acting as appropriate to lay men and women, not as secretive. Critics, however, saw it as indicative that Opus Dei was a secret society. Some of them branded the Work a "white mafia" or a "Christian Freemasonry." In Franco's Spain, this was a damning accusation.

In July 1941, the bishop of Barcelona authorized the members of the Work to meet at the center they had opened on Balmes Street. In addition, he reassured the civil governor, who was about to confiscate the premises because he had been told that they were the headquarters of a Masonic group. Meanwhile, the nuncio requested reports from diocesan bishops and the Jesuits. The bishops of Madrid, Barcelona, Vitoria, Pamplona, Zaragoza, Valencia, León, Toledo, and Valladolid gave favorable opinions. In the following months, the nuncio sent to

Rome several dispatches with the reports received. Personally, he was favorable to the new institution, although he expressed reservations about complete surrender to God in the midst of the world without the ecclesiastical discipline to which members of religious orders were subject. He was also troubled by the way members of the Work combined a hidden life and the collective humility of not boasting about corporate successes with the search for professional excellence.[32]

Escrivá was told that the Jesuits were going to file a complaint against Opus Dei with the Holy See. At the time it did not make sense for him to go to Rome, as there was no formal accusation, the Work was already approved in the diocese of Madrid, and travel was difficult in the midst of World War II. He did, however, ask José Orlandis and Salvador Canals to move to Rome in the fall of 1942 to continue their professional studies and to establish contacts in order to make the Work known to people from the Vatican Curia and the diplomatic corps.[33]

The favorable attitude of the nuncio and of most Spanish bishops and subsequent approvals of Opus Dei by the Holy See eventually led to an improvement in the intra-ecclesial vision of the Work. The events we have just summarized did, however, leave their mark. They had some positive repercussions in that the Spanish Catholic community had come directly or indirectly to know about Opus Dei and its founder. The events also helped the members learn to explain its message better. On the other hand, so many hoaxes and half-truths made many people think of Opus Dei as an organization that sought the conquest of the state and created tension within the Church.[34]

Notes

1. See *Diario de la residencia de Jenner* (Diary of the Jenner Residence), September 4, 1939, p. 33r; October 10, 1939, pp. 39v and 40r; October 29, 1939, p. 46r; November 12, 1939; p. 50v, AGP A.2, 11-1-1. Assignments varied to meet the needs of the moment. For instance, in April Justo Martí became assistant director of the Jenner Residence, José Maria Hernández Garnica took charge of the Work of St. Raphael with the help of Vicente Rodríguez Casado,

and Franciso Botella began working in the Society for Intellectual Collaboration. See *Diary of the Jenner Residence*, April 9, 1940, p. 13r; April 17, 1940; p. 15r and 15v.

2. See Pablo Pérez López, "Josemaría Escrivá de Balaguer, profesor de Ética para periodistas: Madrid 1941," *Studia et Documenta* 3 (2009), pp. 335–368; Beatriz Comella Gutiérrez, *Josemaría Escrivá de Balaguer en el Real Patronato de Santa Isabel de Madrid (1931–1945)* (Madrid: Rialp, 2010), p. 238. Escrivá served as rector of St. Elizabeth until December 1945.

3. See Onésimo Díaz, *Posguerra* (Madrid: Rialp, 2018).

4. *Relación del viaje a Valencia*, May 26, 1940, AGP A.2, 48-1-2.

5. See "Advertencias para los viajes," February 1940, February 1941, and November 1944, AGP A.2, 47-1.

6. Report from Francisco Ponz (n.d.), AGP A.2, 47-1-4. In this report, written in 1940 or 1941, Ponz said, in exaggerated fashion, "We're tired of seeing what happens to intelligent students in many Catholic associations. If one of them is studying Law, they have him give a talk about the liver. They flatter him and destroy his humility. They have him give more talks and lead meetings. He doesn't study and barely passes his exams. He graduates without knowing his subject well and contents himself with earning a modest salary. Someone who could have been an outstanding professor ends up a mediocrity, while the enemies of the church occupy the University." Turning to the Christian formation given by the members of the Work, he clarified: "We do all this with a supernatural aim. We are not politicians, but we do want countries to be governed by a religious, Catholic spirit. Like the first Christians, we will combine professional work with apostolate. And we will fish for men." Another member of the Work observed, "Precisely the possibility of following Jesus Christ without becoming 'official Catholics' was one of the attractive features of the vocation to Opus Dei for many people." José Orlandis, *Años de juventud en el Opus Dei* (Madrid: Rialp, 1993), p. 105.

7. See Francesc Castells i Puig, "Barcelona 1939–1940: los viajes para establecer el primer centro del Opus Dei," *Studia et Documenta* 8 (2014), pp. 91–210.

8. See AGP E.2.2, 171-1-1 a 171-1-4.

9. Over the years, the center was called Donadío, Lagasca, and eventually Diego de León. We will always refer to it as Diego de León. See Santiago Martínez Sánchez, "Diego de León, Centro de Estudios," in *Diccionario de san Josemaría Escrivá de Balaguer*, pp. 332–334.

10. For this whole section, see Fuenmayor, Gómez-Iglesias, and Illanes, pp. 85–139.

11. Handwritten report of Josemaría Escrivá de Balaguer, January 9, 1943, AGP L.1.1, 1-3-8.

12. *Diary of the Jenner Residence*, April 19, 1939, p. 28r, AGP A.2, 11-1-1; *Diary of the Jenner Residence*, May 28, 1940, p. 23v; June 7, 1940, p. 25r, AGP A.2, 11-1-2.

13. *Statutes* (1941), "Reglamento," art. 1. This and the following quotes are taken from the original found in AGP L.1.1, 1-3-4.

14. *Statutes* (1941), "Espíritu," arts. 1 and 3.

15. *Statutes* (1941), "Ordo," art. 16, section 2. The task of the Administrators in Opus Dei has these two aspects. They assure the proper use of institutional assets and try to help the members be detached from material goods, especially in using their earnings.

16. *Statutes* (1941), "Espíritu", arts. 7 and 27; "Régimen," art. 1, section 2, and "Espíritu," art. 28.

17. See María Rosario de Felipe, ed., *Homenaje a D. José María Albareda en el centenario de su nacimiento* (Madrid: Consejo Superior de Investigaciones Científicas, 2002); Pablo Pérez López, "José María Albareda en los comienzos del Consejo Superior de Investigaciones Científicas (1936–1949),", in Francisco Javier Caspistegui and Ignacio Peiró Martín, eds., *Jesús Longares Alonso: el maestro que sabía escuchar* (Pamplona: EUNSA, 2016), pp. 203–229.

18. See *Diary of the Jenner Residence*, June 19, 1940, p. 28, AGP A.2, 11-1-2.

19. José Orlandis, *Años de juventud*, p. 179.

20. "Informe confidencial sobre la organización secreta Opus Dei." January 16, 1942, AGP M.2.4, 117-3-3. See also Onésimo Díaz, "Falange versus Opus Dei: Política y religión en la posguerra española (1939–1945)," *Hispania Sacra* 142 (2018), pp. 671–680; and Onésimo Díaz, *Expansión. El desarrollo del Opus Dei entre los años 1940 y 1945* (Madrid: Rialp, 2020), pp. 344–355.

21. Report of interview of Bishop Eijo Garay with Valcárcel and Eduardo [Alastrué], Madrid, March 10, 1942, AGP M.2.4, 115-03-02.

22. Copy of the report dated February 24, 1944, AGP M.2.4, 125-1-5; see also copy of the report dated June 2, 1943, AGP M.2.4, 125-1-2.

23. See Díaz, *Expansión*, pp. 238–52.

24. For example, in 1947, the minister of foreign affairs, Alberto Martín Artajo, "prohibited admitting to the Diplomatic Corps members of Opus Dei even if they had won the *oposición*. Against all fairness, that order was fulfilled in several cases." Alvaro del Portillo with Cesare Cavalleri, *40 Years With a Saint: Blessed Alvaro del Portillo on Saint Josemaría Escrivá* (New York: Scepter, 2016), p. 44.

25. See Alfons Balcells, *Memoria ingenua: Primeros pasos del Opus Dei en Cataluña* (Madrid: Rialp, 2009); Vázquez de Prada, *The Founder of Opus Dei*, vol. 2, pp. 315–324 and 392–393

26. *Intimate Notes*, 1622 (September 14, 1940).

27. Letter 13, no. 77, AGP A.3, 92-6-2. Although the phrase is from later years, it sums up the Founder's thought and action during the 1940s.

28. Letter from Leopoldo Eijo y Garay to Aurelio María Escarré Jané, OSB, May 25, 1941, cited in Vázquez de Prada, *The Founder of Opus Dei*, vol. 2, p. 357–358.

29. Report on interview between Josemaría Escrivá and Gaetano Cicognani, May 24, 1941, AGP M.2.4, 136-5-5.

30. Report on interview between Josemaría Escrivá and Gaetano Cicognani, June 10, 1941, AGP M.2.4, 136-5-5.

31. Handwritten account of José María González Vallés, March 27, 1945, AGP M.2.4, 127-4-1.

32. The reports of various Spanish bishops, Jesuits, and religious are found in AAV, *Arch. Nunz. Madrid*, 1305, fasc. 4. Gaetano Cicogani sent them, together with his opinion, to the Holy See in dispatches dated October 15 and November 21, 1941 (see AAV, *Arch. Nunz. Madrid*, 1305, fasc. 4). See Francisca Colomer Pellicer, "Un informe del arzobispo de Valencia sobre el Opus Dei para la nunciatura de Madrid (1941)," *Studia et Documenta* 7 (2013), pp. 403–430.

33. See Fernando Crovetto, "Los primeros pasos del Opus Dei en Italia. Epistolario entre Roma y Madrid (noviembre 1942–febrero 1943)," *Studia et Documenta* 11 (2017), pp. 267–314.

34. See AGP M.2.4, 116; Jaume Aurell Cardona, "La formación de un gran relato sobre el Opus Dei," *Studia et Documenta* 6 (2012), pp. 242–250.

CHAPTER 5

Development of the Women's Branch

At the end of the Civil War, Spanish society viewed women primarily as mothers and wives. Legislation viewed as protecting women relegated them to the private sphere. Women under twenty-five could not leave their parents' home without permission. Husbands were the legal guardians of their wives and had complete control of the family's assets. In 1939, women made up only eight percent of the working population.

What limited tendencies existed to give women a larger role in society were confined mostly to Catholic organizations and the Women's Section of the Spanish Falange. Membership in Catholic groups offered women a very limited sphere of action, often confined to organized charity, but it was a way of establishing social relations outside the domestic sphere. Young women with an entrepreneurial mentality found a meeting place in some Catholic Action groups where they could not only receive religious formation but also discuss possible forms of public action for women.

Section 1. At the "Third Attempt"

In the spring of 1939, Escrivá met in Madrid with the two women who had joined Opus Dei before the Civil War, Hermógenes García and Ramona Sánchez. Although they had good will, he realized that they had not captured the secular spirit of the Work and would not be able to help spread its message. He suggested that their true vocation was as religious sisters and put them in contact with appropriate religious institutions.

The two women who joined the Work during the Civil War, Ampáro Rodríguez and Dolores Fisac, lived outside Madrid, but went regularly to the capital to talk to the Founder. There they met Escrivá's mother, Dolores Albás, and his sister, Carmen Escrivá de Balaguer, who helped Josemaría in his formative activities with women. Amparo Rodríguez introduced Fr. Josemaría to María Jesús Hereza, a medical student who belonged to Catholic Action. After speaking with Fr. Josemaría for some time, she joined Opus Dei in July 1940. Around this time three other women also joined Opus Dei: Juan Jiménez Vargas' sister Dolores, and Concepción and Laura Fernández del Amo.[1]

These young women had been introduced to Escrivá by their brothers or by priests who knew Escrivá well. They belonged to Catholic Action and in some cases held office in it. They worked as secretaries, teachers, and nurses. Opus Dei's message impressed them because it went beyond the organization of a few confessional activities and constituted an invitation to holiness through a personal relationship with God and a professional job well done.

Escrivá, accompanied by his mother and sister, met with the members of the women's branch in the part of the Jenner residence where his family lived. He encouraged them to follow the plan of life and gave them classes in Christian formation and the spirit of the Work. Dolores Albás and Carmen Escrivá accompanied the young women in the meetings. Sometimes, they would do a little meditation with *The Way* or comment on the text of the Gospel of the day. They also set up a home workshop for making liturgical vestments and learned some household tasks.

In September 1940, ten girls attended a retreat preached by Escrivá at the convent of the Mothers of Reparation in Madrid. Escrivá suggested that they go to confession with another priest so he would not have to worry about the sacramental seal of confession in dealing with them outside the confessional. In his preaching, he particularly insisted that God's call was forever, since a number of the young women had commented that they lacked constancy and commitment.

Shortly thereafter, the Founder moved to the new Diego de León center with his family. His mother and sister took charge of the center's household management. Fr. Josemaría was concerned about the lack of time necessary to form his spiritual daughters. To facilitate meeting with them, he rented an apartment in Castelló Street. On November 6, 1940, he blessed the apartment. But the experiment lasted only a month. The Founder decided to close it because the doorman asked too many questions, people in the neighborhood were scandalized at a priest's meeting women in an apartment, and the girls wasted their time in frivolous conversations and showed little practical interest in the development of the Work.

Despite these setbacks, during the following months Escrivá gave a training course in the Diego de León service area. Six of the young women who attended took the step of being formally admitted to the Work on February 14, 1941. A few weeks later, on April 22, Dolores Albás, who was sixty-four years old, died of pneumonia in the arms of Dolores Fisac. That day, her son was preaching a retreat to priests in the diocese of Lérida. He returned immediately to Madrid and before the body of his mother who was being waked in the Diego de León center, he said in tears, "My God, what have you done? You take everything from me. You take everything from me. I thought that my mother was very much needed by these daughters of mine, but you leave me with nothing, with nothing!"[2]

The year 1941 marked a turning point in the history of the women's branch. With the sole exception of Lola Fisac, all the young women who had joined the Work until then eventually left. That spring, however, three young women, who lived in the provinces, joined: Narcisa (Nisa) González Guzmán from León, and Encarnación Ortega and Enriqueta (Enrica) Botella from Valencia. They would persevere, and the Founder was able to rely on them because they took seriously the challenge of spreading Opus Dei. Although the invitation to holiness gave them a certain amount of vertigo, it also attracted them. According to Encarnación Ortega, "I was very afraid that God would ask me to launch into something that seemed wonderful, that suited me completely, but that demanded everything of me."[3] For the Founder, this "third attempt"—the two previous attempts had been those of 1930–1936 and 1937–1941—made the Work among women a reality.

At Escrivá's suggestion the women who lived outside Madrid wrote frequently to each other as well as to those living in the capital. Their letters were full of enthusiasm and a desire to support Escrivá's projects, to share the same ideals, and to dream of future developments. The Founder assured them that in a short time there would be women of the Work in all kinds of professions. On one occasion, he talked with Ortega and González Guzmán about the many activities women of the Work would carry out both corporately and individually: "Farm schools for peasant women; professional training centers; university residences; activities in the world of fashion; maternity homes in cities throughout the world; lending libraries to bring healthy and formative reading to the most remote towns; bookstores; and, most importantly, the personal apostolate of each of the members, which cannot be recorded or measured."[4]

Twelve women, including members of the Work and friends, attended a retreat the Founder preached in Diego de León in August 1941. They still had not been able to open a center in Madrid. Amparo Rodríguez Casado had contracted tuberculosis and both Dolores Fisac and Enrica Botella had to stay home to take care of their families. For the time being, only the thirty-four-year-old Narcisa González had been able to obtain her parents' permission to move to the capital.

During the 1941/42 school year, Dolores Jiménez Vargas worked with Carmen Escrivá overseeing the housekeeping of the Diego de León center. Concepción Fernández del Amo took care of the Jenner residence. The Founder, who traveled regularly to Valencia to meet with his spiritual daughters and sons there, asked Enrica Botella and Encarnación Ortega to manage the housekeeping at the Samaniego residence. They oversaw the work of the housekeepers, prepared menus, and made liturgical linens and vestments. They also gave Christian formation to the employees and fulfilled pious customs with them, praying the Rosary and carrying out other acts of piety.

Fr. Josemaría suggested that, since the members of the women's branch were too few to take care of everything, they should focus on the important things and ask God to multiply their time. Things, he assured them, would get better. They should not lose sight of the fact that they were called to transform the world, to bring Christ's teaching to all environments. At the same time, he stressed that Opus Dei's success did not depend on brilliant personalities but on women and men who would sacrifice themselves for God in ordinary, everyday tasks. Despite the smallness of the beginnings, the early women trusted the Founder. His proposals went beyond the prevailing mentality and were attractive. They felt they were pioneers.

On July 16, 1942, the first women's center opened on Jorge Manrique Street in Madrid. Narcisa González Guzmán, Concepción Fernández del Amo, Encarnación Ortega, and Visitación Alvira were the first residents. Escrivá reminded them, as he also did the men, that their dedication to God in Opus Dei was complete and that it required them to live an intelligent and free obedience. They should be simple and let the directors know clearly what was happening to them, even if it was something unpleasant, never being afraid of the directors. Joy would fill their lives as a consequence of their relationship with God and their concern for others. He taught them to grow in naturalness and common sense, without being carried away by euphoria or pessimism. Their enthusiasm for doing Opus Dei had to be channeled into daily life, weaving together dealings with God, work, constancy in their tasks, relationships with friends and acquaintances, and the desire to contribute to the Work's being a Christian family.

In November 1944, the women of Opus Dei opened Los Rosales, a house on the outskirts of Madrid, in the town of Villaviciosa de Odón. A year later, it became the first center of studies for women of the Work.

Section 2. The Administration

From the beginning, Josemaría Escrivá thought about the possible legal structure of the Work, the activities it would carry out, and the members who would form part of the institution. He foresaw that the professional work of some members would be to take care of the centers and the people who lived in them, so that the houses of the Work would be Christian homes. Those who dedicated themselves professionally to homemaking within the Work would be as much a part of Opus Dei as the others. Thinking about them, he wrote: "They must understand well the beauty of their profession before God, however lowly it may be. Instill in them the heroism of doing the little things of each day with perfection, as if the salvation of the world depended on each one of them."[5]

Opus Dei's experience in this area began at the DYA residence. The all-male housekeeping staff comprised an administrator and four other employees: a cook, two servants who took care of cleaning and serving the table, and an errand boy. The Founder tried to give a professional tone to their work. The servants, for example, wore uniforms and received training in how to serve the table, receive visitors who came to the door, and clean the house. In contrast to the common practice of the time, they were not expected to be available whenever needed but had fixed schedules. In addition, the Founder offered them classes in Christian doctrine to improve their spiritual life. He hoped that some of the staff members might eventually feel called by God to join Opus Dei.

DYA's Administration worked relatively well, although it did encounter some problems in returning laundry on time and maintaining order in the kitchen and dining room. Escrivá was troubled, not so much by these specific shortcomings as by his sense that despite everyone's goodwill, he had not been able to create a Christian family atmosphere in the residence.

In the spring of 1937, in the Honduran consulate, the Founder pondered how he could improve the Administration once the Civil War was over. Moved by the desire to establish in the centers of

Opus Dei an atmosphere like that of his parents' home, he decided to ask his mother and sister for help. He prayed and asked the members of the Work to pray. Before escaping from Madrid and crossing over into the Nationalist zone, he spoke to his mother who agreed to help. From then on, the men and women of the Work called Escrivá's mother "Grandmother" and his sister "Aunt Carmen," because they understood that this was really their place in Opus Dei.[6]

Fr. Josemaría asked his mother and sister to help him explain to the women of the Work how they could take over the domestic care of the centers. This momentous change in the history of Opus Dei modified the pre-Civil War practice of having the Administration of the men's centers made up of men, and the presumption that the Administration of women's centers would be made up of women. Now women would take care of all the centers, with an administrator in charge of each house. Dolores and Carmen would teach them how to create a Christian family atmosphere through work that united feminine spirit and professionalism.

In Spain at the time, work in the home was considered a humble task that did not require special abilities or training, although it was not thought of as degrading and carried no social stigma. Those who were especially good at cooking, cleaning, and sewing were recognized and adequately paid. Many women, particularly those from rural areas, saw domestic service as a good way of entering the world of paid work, which allowed them to improve their economic and social situation.

Escrivá saw in domestic work not only a way for people from economically and socially poor environments to advance humanly and financially, but also a marvelous human and divine vocation on a par with every other vocation: a call to identify oneself with Christ in and through work—in this case, work in the home. In contrast with the prevailing tendencies in Western culture, he believed that a correct understanding of human nature showed that full-time homemaking could lead to full human development. He was also convinced that women had a special characteristic contribution to make in caring for persons and helping them to develop as well-rounded human beings. He thought that the way the Administration created a family atmosphere in the centers of the Work could serve as a model for married people.

When the Jenner residence opened in the summer of 1939, Escrivá's mother and sister moved to the Administration area and collaborated with him in developing the Work among women, both university students and domestic workers. His mother, who was sixty-two years old, spent much of her time sewing and making linens for the oratory. Carmen, who was forty-one years old, took responsibility for cooking, cleaning, and buying groceries. She supervised a cook and three domestic workers, or servants, as they were then called in Spain.

Each of the new centers opened in the post-Civil War period added to the amount of domestic services required. Escrivá asked most of the few women members to work in the Administration of the centers and residences for men (and later for women), helped by his sister Carmen. He was aware that this momentarily reduced to one the career options of women members of Opus Dei, in clear contrast to the wide range of opportunities open to male members. He felt, however, that establishing a Christian family atmosphere in the houses of the Work was both essential and urgent. He did not think of giving priority to the Administration of the Work's centers as an obstacle to the development of the women's branch since taking care of the Administration is a vital part of the apostolate it is called to carry out.

The Founder emphasized that he understood Administration of the centers as an apostolic activity proper and specific to the women of the Work and, at the same time, an essential and permanent characteristic in the spirit of Opus Dei. On the other hand, the fact that practically all the women of the Work at that time dedicated their professional time to the Administration was a transitory phenonmon. Eventually, something like 10 percent of the women in Opus Dei would work in the Administration of centers. The rest would be dedicated to all different kinds of work, according to each one's personal interests, talents, and opportunities. To emphasize this fact, although in those years less than 15 percent of Spanish university students were women, he commented: "There will be daughters of mine who are professors, architects, journalists, doctors."[7] The Founder asked the first members of the women's branch to have faith in God "and a little in him, who was a poor sinner."[8] González Guzmán, Ortega, Botella, and the others believed him when he told them that their concentrating now on taking care of the men's centers (preparing menus, cleaning, and sewing vestments) would in large measure make possible the many varied activities that lay on the horizon.

When the Founder's family moved to Diego de León in 1940, Carmen Escrivá became the administrator of the new house and the women of the Work took over the Administration of the Jenner residence. She served as administrator of Diego de León for seven years.

The Founder encouraged his daughters to improve their professional and technical skills. He begged them to offer vocational and spiritual training classes to the employees working in the house, to adapt to their needs, and to lead the way in doing the hardest and most unpleasant tasks. He also thanked them for their work, because by putting their professionalism and their motherly heart into it, they created a welcoming family atmosphere.

In 1943, Narcisa González Guzmán, Encarnación Ortega, and Amparo Rodríguez Casado took on the Administration of the new Moncloa residence. The separate and independent part of the residence where they lived was the second center of the women's branch. The first center, Jorge Manrique, focused on apostolate with women in the academic or liberal professions, whereas the new center was dedicated to people connected with the Administration of the residence.

Thanks to the *Religiosas de María Inmaculada para el Servicio Domestico* (Sisters of Domestic Service), they were able to hire a few experienced young women mostly from rural areas. Even under the best of circumstances, taking care of a large center which would soon have a hundred residents would have been difficult. For the three young members of the Work, it was an enormous challenge. They lacked training and experience, were understaffed, faced frequent turnover among their staff, and found it hard to get enough food, which was rationed and very scarce in a country that had not recovered from the Civil War before suffering from the consequences of World War II.⁹

Two years later, in 1945, the Administration of the Abando residence in Bilbao began. It was the first center for women outside the Spanish capital. Halfway through the academic year, in March 1946, two employees, Dora del Hoyo and Concepción Andrés, joined the Work. They were the first numerary servants, women called to live apostolic celibacy and to work professionally in centers of Opus Dei helping to make them family homes. Over the following months they were joined by three other young women: Antonia Peñuela, Rosalía López, and Julia Bustillo. In 1947, the first center of studies for these numeraries began in the Administration area of Diego de León in Madrid.*

Notes

1. See Inmaculada Alva, "El apostolado del Opus Dei entre mujeres: un segundo comienzo (1937–1942)," *Studia et Documenta* 12 (2018), pp. 173–217.

2. Quoted in Recuerdo de Dolores Fisac Serna, Madrid, September 5, 1975, AGP A.5, 212-1-4.

3. Recollections of Encarnación Ortega Pardo, Valladolid, August 21, 1975, AGP A.5, 232-1-2. See also Maite del Riego Ganuza, *Encarnita Ortega Pardo: hablando de tú a Dios* (Madrid: Palabra, 2006); Francisca R. Quiroga, "Apuntes

---

* See *Diario de la Administración de Abando*, Bilbao, March 13, 1946. AGP U.2.2, D-243; Javier Medina Bayo, *Una luz encendida: Dora del Hoyo* (Madrid: Palabra, 2011). Women who worked taking care of other people's homes were normally called "servants" in Spain. It had positive connotations in the 1940s and 1950s. From 1946 to 1966 it was used in Opus Dei because it was the normal word in the society of the time. As we shall see, when this word acquired a pejorative connotation in the 1960s, Escrivá began to speak about "household employees" and, in the case of those who were members of the Work, "numerary assistants." What people mean today when they speak about servants is far removed from the rich personal and vocational qualities of the women who embraced celibacy in the Work and dedicated themselves to God through a life of prayer and work in caring for people. Nonetheless, to avoid anachronisms, we will use the words "servant" and "numerary servants" in parts 2 and 3 of this book and the words "household employees" and "numerary assistants" in the rest of the book.

para una reseña biográfica de Narcisa González Guzmán, una de las primeras mujeres del Opus Dei," *Studia et Documenta* 4 (2010), pp. 339–371; and Beatriz Torres Olivares, "Botella Raduán, Enrica," in *Diccionario de san Josemaría Escrivá de Balaguer*, pp. 163–164.

4. Recollections of Encarnación Ortega Pardo, Valladolid, August 21, 1975, AGP A.5, 232-1-2

5. *Intimate Notes*, 1101b (January 5, 1934); see also *Intimate Notes*, 137 (December 26, 1930).

6. See González Gullón, *Escondidos*, pp. 250–258 and 305–306.

7. Recollection of Narcisa González Guzmán, Madrid, September 5, 1975, AGP A.5, 216-3-1. The Founder wrote that "only some ten percent of the women members [of Opus Dei] will take care of the Administration." Handwritten note in "Plan del Curso para la Nuevas [Junio 1949]," AGP A.3, 179-1-11. See also Mercedes Montero, "Mujer y Universidad en España (1910–1936): Contexto histórico del punto 946 de *Camino*," *Studia et Documenta* 6 (2012), pp. 211–234.

8. Recollection of Encarnación Ortega Pardo, Valladolid, August 21, 1975, AGP A.5, 232-1-2. In a certain sense, the renunciation of other professional activities on the part of women working in the Administration can be compared with asking men to leave a promising professional future and be ordained priests.

9. See María Isabel Montero Casado de Amezúa, "Mujeres en el Opus Dei. Inicio del apostolado." in *Diccionario de san Josemaría Escrivá de Balaguer*, pp. 860–868.

CHAPTER 6

Priests of Opus Dei and Growth in Europe

In the first half of the 1940s, Opus Dei grew among college students and recent graduates in Madrid and several provincial capitals. As numbers increased, the Work needed more lay men and women to take on tasks of governance and spiritual direction, as well as priests to administer the sacraments, preach, and fill some leadership positions.

At the end of World War II, Opus Dei was finally able to begin its long-desired expansion outside of Spain, first in Western Europe and then in North America. Escrivá moved to Rome in 1946, because a Catholic institution that aspired to a worldwide presence needed to have its headquarters near the Vatican. He also hoped to avoid having the Work seen as a merely Spanish phenomenon or linked to that country's political regime.

Although Spain was isolated and closed-in on itself, academics and professionals could get government scholarships to go abroad. Some young men who had joined the Work just before the Civil War or in its immediate aftermath gladly accepted the challenge of being the pioneers in spreading its message of secular holiness to new places and cultures.

Section 1. Priests of Opus Dei

From the earliest days of Opus Dei, Escrivá had explained to secular priests the vocation to sanctity in the midst of the world as it applied to them. He understood that God calls diocesan priests to fulfill their ministry with perfection, through personal piety, the administration of the sacraments, and spiritual direction of the Christian community. Between 1932 and 1935, Escrivá worked with ten priests from various dioceses who lived in Madrid. They met every week for what he called "priestly conferences." He tried to help them to assimilate the spirit of Opus Dei so that they could transmit it to the laity, both men and women.

In February 1934, some of these priests joined Opus Dei and promised obedience to the Founder. Soon, however, the financial problems of the DYA residence led to tensions. Some of them thought Escrivá was moving too fast. He concluded that, despite their goodwill, these priests had little faith in his foundational mission. In February 1935 he put an end to the priestly conferences and stopped meeting with the priests on a regular basis. He decided that in the future, the priests of the Work would come from the laity.[1]

During the Civil War and, above all, in the immediate postwar period, several Spanish bishops invited the Founder to preach spiritual exercises to diocesan priests, religious communities, and lay people of Catholic Action. He soon became a famous preacher. In the 1939/40 school year, he gave five retreats to priests and seminarians in the dioceses of Ávila, León, and Madrid; and four retreats to university students, some for men and some for women. He also gave days of recollection in Madrid, Valencia, Valladolid, and Zaragoza. By end of the 1941/42 school year, he had preached nineteen retreats to priests and seminarians in a number of Spanish dioceses.

Escrivá avoided the flowery style of preaching common at the time. He spoke in a direct, almost colloquial way, relying on texts from the New Testament and a short outline. He also quoted the Fathers of the Church and texts of spiritual authors, including the Spiritual Exercises of Saint Ignatius, adapting them to the circumstances and character of his listeners. Frequently he drew on inspirations received in his own spiritual life and events that occurred in his pastoral ministry. Much of his preaching was what might technically be called *lectio divina*, a reading of the Scriptures accompanied by personal prayer to God.[2]

As the years went by, Opus Dei's need for clergy of its own became acute. The number of people attending activities in the centers of the Work was growing rapidly, as was the number of members. The Founder asked God to give him priests with his spirit, priests who could provide pastoral care to the members and to those who took part in Opus Dei's activities. Priests were also needed to govern the Work, since those who exercise the power of jurisdiction instituted by Christ in the Church must have received the sacrament of holy orders.

In mid-1940, the Founder asked Álvaro del Portillo and José María Hernández Garnica, who were about to finish their engineering degrees, if they wanted to be ordained priests. Both said yes. In January 1942, Bishop Eijo Garay arranged for them to be enrolled in the seminary of Madrid. Because of their training and age, they would take classes at the Diego de León center taught by José María Bueno Monreal, a professor at the seminary, rather than attend seminary classes. They passed their first exams in June 1942. At that time, two more men, José Luis Múzquiz and José Orlandis, began ecclesiastical studies. For a short time, the two groups had separate classes. In the fall of 1942, however, Orlandis moved to Rome and Múzquiz began to attend classes with Hernández Garnica and Del Portillo.[3]

Although these students were preparing to become priests, the Founder had not found a legal formula that would allow Opus Dei to have them ordained. According to the Code of Canon Law, there could be no unattached priests who were not subject to some ecclesiastical authority. Therefore, the code required priests to be incardinated in a diocese, a religious order, or a similar institution. Opus Dei's personal character precluded it from being considered similar to a diocese. Its secular character precluded its being treated as similar to a religious order.

On February 14, 1943, while celebrating Mass in the Jorge Manrique center, the Founder received an inspiration that solved the problem. As he later noted: "I began the Mass looking for the legal solution to be able to incardinate priests in the Work. I had been trying to find it for a long time, but to no avail. And that day, *intra missam*, after Communion, the Lord wanted to give it to me: the Priestly Society of the Holy Cross. He even gave me its seal: the sphere of the world with the cross inscribed [in it]."[4]

Escrivá understood that God was asking him to take a new foundational step that would permit Opus Dei to have its own priests. It consisted in creating a priestly association linked to Opus Dei, made up of priests who had previously been lay members. From the canon law point of view, this association would be a society of common life without vows. The clergy would be stably attached to the Priestly Society of the Holy Cross and would exercise their ministry primarily in favor of the mission of Opus Dei, taking pastoral care of its members and other people involved in its activities, and meeting their sacramental and liturgical needs.[5]

After receiving a favorable opinion from the nuncio in Spain and the bishop of Madrid, the Founder sent Álvaro del Portillo, secretary general of Opus Dei, to Rome to request the necessary *nihil obstat* from the Congregation for Religious, which oversaw societies of common life without vows. During the month he spent in the Eternal City—from May 25 to June 21, 1943—Del Portillo met with Pope Pius XII, the secretary of state, and other leaders of the Holy See.

In preparation for the imminent legal change, Opus Dei held what Escrivá called a "Work Week" from July 29 to August 7, 1943. Fourteen members met in Madrid to review the main aspects of the spirit of the Work, draw lessons from the apostolic activities carried out thus far, and propose further developments. They focused on the plan of life, the way of living the Christian virtues, the progress of the St. Raphael and St. Gabriel Work, the functioning of the college residences and the center of studies for the formation of the members of Opus Dei, and the financial management of the centers. They submitted their conclusions to the Founder and the central government of the Work.

Meanwhile, in Rome the message of Opus Dei and its request for canonical approval were well received. Considering the usual pace of the Vatican bureaucracy, things went quickly. On October 11, 1943, the Congregation for Religious granted its *nihil obstat* for the diocesan foundation. After receiving the news, Bishop Eijo Garay of Madrid canonically erected the Priestly Society of the Holy Cross on December 8. A month later, on January 25, 1944, he approved the constitutions of the society. News of this approval appeared in the official bulletins of twenty-nine Spanish dioceses.

The constitutions defined the Priestly Society of the Holy Cross as "a predominantly clerical male society of common life without vows," composed of priests of Opus Dei and lay members preparing for the priesthood. Following the legal practice of the time, the constitutions distinguished two ends: the "general end is the sanctification of its members through the practice of the evangelical counsels and the observance of the Society's own Constitutions; the specific end is to work especially so that intellectuals, who direct civil society, adhere fully to the precepts and the counsels of Christ our Lord."[6] To avoid anyone's thinking that canonical common life proper to religious orders and congregations applied to Opus Dei, the constitutions specified that "common life" should be understood in a broad sense. What was important in Opus Dei, they clarified, was not living under the same roof, but unity of spirit and of regulations.[7]

The priests of the Priestly Society were incardinated in the society, which was responsible for supporting them economically. The society's governmental structure was similar to the one approved in 1941 for Opus Dei, with a general president—who was called "Father"—at its head and with central, territorial, and local levels of government.

For the first time, Opus Dei appeared as a pastoral and apostolic phenomenon made up of lay people and priests, with an institutional presence of the priestly ministry. The Priestly Society was united to Opus Dei, the association which had been approved in 1941. The constitutions, like the 1941 statutes, said that Opus Dei had a section for men and a section for women, and that it had supernumerary, numerary, and inscribed members as those terms had been defined in 1941. They also added that there could be "auxiliary cooperators" who helped the Work with their prayers and donations.

The requirements of canon law forced Escrivá to incorporate in the statutes a distorted vision of the relationship between the Priestly Society and Opus Dei. The Priestly Society as a society of common life had a higher legal status than Opus Dei, which was only a pious union. In the Founder's words: "Opus Dei seemed something secondary, an association proper to and inseparable from the Priestly Society of the Holy Cross, when the reality is that neither of these two parts of our Work is secondary. Both are principal."[8] According to the constitutions, Opus Dei was the place where the Priestly Society carried out its activity. As Escrivá pointed out, this made Opus Dei seem to be "a part of the Priestly Society of the Holy Cross, whereas in reality the Priestly Society of the Holy Cross is only a small part of the Work."[9]

There was another drawback. Church law considered societies of common life similar to religious orders. Although their members did not publicly profess the evangelical counsels, they were required to live some form of life in common and to receive the *nihil obstat* of the Congregation for Religious. In contrast, the founding spirit of Opus Dei provided that both clergy and laity should be secular.

As he had accepted the inadequate legal status of pious union in 1941, the Founder accepted the new legal status despite its problems because it did not affect the Work's core or charismatic essence and was the only way at the time the Work could have the priests it needed. Escrivá would occasionally describe his acceptance of imperfect legal solutions as involving "giving in without giving up, with the intention of recovering."[10]

In December 1943, Escrivá, as president general of the newly erected Priestly Society, appointed its council. The bishop of Madrid confirmed the appointments: Álvaro del Portillo, secretary general; José Luis Múzquiz, vice secretary for the Work of St. Michael; José María Hernández Garnica, vice secretary for the Work of St. Gabriel; Pedro Casciaro, vice secretary for the Work of St. Raphael; and Ricardo Fernández Vallespín, general administrator. Until Opus Dei became a secular institute some five years later, these men helped the Founder direct the Work. When the Founder moved to Rome in 1946, Del Portillo became procurator general and Pedro Casciaro replaced him as secretary general while continuing to hold the post of vice secretary for the Work of St. Raphael.

In December 1943, Escrivá erected the center of ecclesiastical studies of the Priestly Society of the Holy Cross, which would coordinate the teaching staff and the formation of those preparing for the priesthood. Bishop Eijo Garay ordained the first three priests of Opus Dei on June 25, 1944: Álvaro del Portillo, José Luis Múzquiz, and José María Hernández Garnica. The Founder chose not to attend the ceremony because he wanted all the attention to be focused on the new priests. He stayed in Diego de León and celebrated Mass there.

After the ordination, the bishop of Madrid and the new priests had lunch in Diego de León with Escrivá and other members of the Work. In the late afternoon, once they had said goodbye to Bishop Eijo Garay, Escrivá led the meditation. One of the participants took some notes:

> He again insisted on the need for prayer and sacrifice, the foundation of our interior life. Humility (individual and collective), obedience, professional work. The loving fulfillment of the norms as a means of our sanctification. "I don't want to go into all the details of today's historic event," he said, "and so when the years go by and those who come to the Work later ask you questions about the day of the first ordination, you will have to tell them simply that the Father repeated to us in the prayer what he has always said: prayer, sacrifice and fulfill the norms well." And then he spoke to us of perseverance, and of love for the Cross, and said that dying is gain. He told us that soon a few of our brothers would be going to distant places.[11]

Section 2. Consolidation in Spain

By 1945, Opus Dei was reasonably well known in the Spanish Catholic world. The news of the approval of the Priestly Society of the Holy Cross and the ordination of three members of the Work had appeared in the national press and in confessional magazines like *Ecclesia, Signo, Illuminare,* and *Catolicismo*.[12] The Work had almost 250 members: 223 men and 20 women. The men had ten centers, located in six Spanish cities. The women had two centers in Madrid and two retreat houses nearby. The guidelines for the growth of both sections laid down by the Founder stressed the formation of people who took part in Opus Dei's activities, the opening of new centers, and the preparation of candidates for the priesthood.

Opus Dei continued to spread the message of holiness in ordinary life in the same way it had from the beginning. A member, or perhaps someone who came to the Work's activities but was not a member, would explain its spirit to a friend, and perhaps invite him or her to participate in an activity or to visit a residence promoted by members of the Work. Usually they were people met at university, although significant numbers of men came into contact with members of Opus Dei at the army's summer training camp in La Granja in the province of Segovia, which all male university students were required to attend. Some young women employed as maids came to know Opus Dei in the course of their work.

Escrivá described Opus Dei's apostolate with young people, the Work of St. Raphael, as the apple of his eye and the seedbed of the Work, because vocations to celibacy and to marriage sprang up there. He urged the members of the Work to dedicate special attention to this apostolate and to use the same means they had in the early days: study, academic events, spiritual direction, study circles (the name used to designate the classes on Christian life given in the St. Raphael Work from March 1946 on), visits to Our Lady's poor, teaching catechism to children in poor areas, meditations and monthly days of recollection, informal get-togethers, and sports.

Escrivá's book *The Way* was widely used to make Opus Dei's message known and to facilitate personal meditation. Isidoro Zorzano, who had died prematurely of a tumor in July 1943, served as a model of secular sanctity in professional work and an intercessor for spiritual and material favors. He was an excellent example because of his intense professional activity as an engineer, his deep piety and generous dedication to the apostolate, and his close union with the Founder. Escrivá himself promoted his cause of beatification and canonization, which was opened in 1948.

From the mid-1940s on, the Founder had to cut back severely on his personal pastoral activity. Most of his time was taken up with governing the Work, giving formation to his sons and daughters in Opus Dei, dealings with ecclesiastical authorities, and studying possible legal solutions which would respect the nature of the Work while locating it within the Church's legal structure.

In governing the Work, Escrivá counted on the immediate personal collaboration of its secretary general, Álvaro del Portillo, and on the advice of the members of the council. As the founder and president general, he dealt personally with critical issues such as the canonical situation of Opus Dei, its institutional relationship with the hierarchy and other Church entities, and arrangements for the formation of the members. He gradually delegated other matters. Before solving problems or answering questions that came up, whether they involved long- or short-term issues, the Founder prayed for light and consulted the General Council. Periodically, he reviewed with the members of the council the main matters of government such as the opening of new houses, the assignment of local directors and the staffing of the centers, and the economic situation of the houses and residences. In gradually developing general norms for the future development of the Work, the Founder considered not only its foundational spirit but also the practical solutions developed in the course of solving concrete problems.

The General Council gradually developed systems of communication with the local centers. They usually communicated in writing or, less frequently, in face-to-face meetings. Written communications covered issues such as the way of living the norms of Christian piety and the customs that constituted the plan of life for members of the Work, the progress of the activities of the St. Raphael Work, and proposals for people who could attend summer courses or move to other centers.

The office of the general administrator frequently reminded the local directors of the importance of all members' being personally detached from personal possessions and things they used at work or in the apostolate. It also tried to see to it that the local directors managed properly the collection of room and board, the prompt payment of the household staff, maintenance of the center, and similar matters.

Shortly after the opening of the Jorge Manrique center in 1943, the Founder urged his daughters to look for ways of spreading Christian doctrine through the media, including publishing houses, bookstores and lending libraries, newspapers, and magazines. Their first venture in this area was a small publishing house, Editorial Minerva, which had its headquarters in the Jorge Manrique center. It was probably the first Spanish publishing house run entirely by women. Its head was María Jiménez Salas, who did not belong to the Work. Minerva's initial plans were ambitious, including publication of works of literature, classic texts of spirituality, and collections of short stories by women writers. It also hoped to produce reading guides and annotated bibliographies. The business failed for lack of sales. It only published Escrivá's two books, *The Way* and *Holy Rosary*, and one classic book of spirituality, *Victoria del Amor*, by Francisco de Osuna, a sixteenth-century Franciscan.[13]

In January 1947, Editorial Minerva was reorganized under the name *Ediciones Rialp* and taken over by Florentino Pérez Embid and two other men of the Work, Rafael Calvo Serer and Raimundo Pániker. Rialp quickly prospered. In addition to Escrivá's works, its collections included the *Biblioteca del Pensamiento Actual* (Library of Current Thought), which by the 1950s included five dozen books on history, philosophy, and politics; "Adonais," dedicated to contemporary poetry; the "Neblí" series of classic books of spirituality; and the "Patmos" series of contemporary books of spirituality. One of the Patmos books, *El valor divino de lo humano*, by a priest of Opus Dei, Jesús Urteaga, which focused on following Christ in daily life, rapidly became a best seller.[14]

Members of the Work and friends with money and financial expertise established corporations and other legal entities to acquire, build, and renovate properties to be used as centers, residences, and retreat houses. For example, in 1945 three members of the Work, Pedro Casciaro, Miguel Fisac, and Ramón Guardans, created SAIDA (*Sociedad Anónima Inmobiliaria de Andalucía*), which acquired, remodeled, and managed the start-up of several centers that began at that time in the south of Spain. The Work referred to these corporations as "auxiliary societies." They were designed to ensure that their properties would continue to be available for the apostolic purposes for which they were acquired. The general administrator of the Work, with the help of a small group of legal and financial advisors, regularly reviewed the accounts of the auxiliary societies and the local centers. In addition to making suggestions for improvements, he sometimes asked an auxiliary society to make a grant to a center that was running at a deficit.*

Moncloa residence quickly became the showcase of Opus Dei's corporate apostolic activity for men. It was alive with activities and brought together many young people in a vibrant Christian atmosphere. In addition to the hundred or so residents, many of their friends came to study, receive spiritual formation, or attend cultural and sporting activities in a warm family environment. On September 16, 1944, Nuncio Cicognani and five Spanish bishops visited the house.

Outside Madrid, the members of Opus Dei focused on opening student residences. At the end of the 1944/45 school year, members of the Work began activities in Bilbao in a rented apartment which they named *Correo* (Post Office); and in Santiago de Compostela, in a house which they called *Rúa Nueva* (New Street). A year later, the Abando residence in Bilbao and the Albayzín residence in Granada opened. People of the Work had been living in Seville since 1943, in "Casa Seras," a residence run by the University of Seville's School of Hispanic-American Studies. In 1945, they opened a student residence

---

* For more information about the entities created by members of Opus Dei and their friends to handle the economic aspects of the Work's apostolates, see chapter 11 ("Institutional Apostolic Activities").

that they soon named Guadaira. In 1948, La Estila residence open in Santiago de Compostela.

The year 1945 saw significant growth of the women's branch. Its members began giving the circles to young women involved in the St. Raphael Work, as well as the classes of formation for members of the Work known as brief circles. They traveled more frequently to Valencia and Zaragoza, as well as to other Spanish cities, to talk about Opus Dei with friends and acquaintances. The Jorge Manrique center was replaced by a larger one, Zurbarán.

At a structural level, the naming in 1946 of Narcisa Gonzalez Guzman and Encarnación Ortega as Escrivá's advisors represented the beginning of a central governing body of the women's branch distinct from the organizational structure of the individual centers. Until then, there had been only the local councils of the various centers and a senior director who oversaw activities in Madrid. In March 1946, the two members of the incipient Central Advisory Board began to visit the various centers to strengthen their formation, organization, and economic management.

The first center of studies for the women's branch began in 1945 in Los Rosales. There were only twenty women in Opus Dei, and their work in the Administration of the centers and running Jorge Manrique center did not permit them to get away for long periods of time. The center of studies, therefore, began offering short summer training courses. Twelve women attended the first course, which took place in July and August. They came from middle-class families and had an intense life of Christian piety, great dedication to work, and the strength of character frequently found in those who had lived through the Civil War. Only one of them, Guadalupe Ortiz de Landázuri, was a college graduate.

The Founder and the priests of the Work contributed to the women's center of studies by preaching, giving lectures on the doctrine of the Church, teaching theoretical and practical classes on the spirit and customs of Opus Dei, and explaining how the members could give informal spiritual direction to their friends and acquaintances and explain to them the message of the Work. Escrivá invited his spiritual daughters to dream. In a few years, he told them, women of Opus Dei from all sorts of professional backgrounds would be working in many countries. Despite the stark contrast between this vision of the future and the small reality of the moment, they believed the Founder.

During the following years, similar training courses were held within the limits imposed by the need to continue providing Administration services in the centers. The older members gave spiritual direction to the younger ones. They explained Opus Dei and its spirit in detail, especially the sanctification of work and the interior life of prayer and sacrifice. They urged them to cultivate the virtue of simplicity, to eat enough and get enough rest. The more experienced members gave practical classes on how to handle cooking, cleaning, and sewing in the Administration of a center.

Los Rosales had a loom used for weaving oratory and table linens, a garden with vegetables and fruit trees, and a farm with chickens and rabbits. It covered part of its expenses by selling these products to other centers of the Work. In later years, the house was enlarged to include an area for retreats and the facilities were improved. To satisfy the growing demand for vestments for the oratories of the centers of the Work, the vestment and oratory linen workshop was renovated and expanded.

By summer 1949, there were more than eighty women members living in eleven Spanish cities. Thirty-two of them were able to attend a summer course in the Administration of La Estila residence in Santiago de Compostela.

Among the women who joined the Work, there were a growing number of domestic employees who worked in the Administration of Opus Dei's centers. Many of them came from farming villages where they had received little education. Given that 23 percent of Spanish women were illiterate, it is not surprising that some did not even know how to read or write. It was not common at the time for families to take an interest in their servants' cultural or technical improvement. With the Founder's encouragement, however, Opus Dei worked hard at providing them human, professional, and spiritual formation, starting with literacy when necessary. The women were grateful for the education they received, which made them aware that they were valued and appreciated. In order to give more continuity to the education of numerary servants and to improve the level of work done in the Administrations, a study center for them was opened in Diego de León in the spring of 1947. Afterwards, the directors drew up a spiritual, doctrinal, cultural, and professional curriculum, which included preparing menus, cleaning the house, and taking care of clothes.

Little by little, the women of Opus Dei began to carry out the full range of apostolic activities that the men had begun earlier. They opened their first university residence in 1947 when they converted Zurbarán into a residence with room for thirty-three occupants. The first steps were difficult since there was no tradition of higher education for women in Spain. Zurbarán's first director was Guadalupe Ortiz de Landázuri. The priest was José María Hernández Garnica.[15]

Opus Dei's message spread among women in different ways depending on people's circumstances. Aurora Nieto was a widowed woman with three children. She met Escrivá in Salamanca and asked to be allowed to join the Work in October 1945. She did not formally become a member until five years later, when it finally became possible to be a member without a commitment to celibacy. Ramona Sanjurjo, a nurse from Vigo, joined Opus Dei in April 1945, after attending a retreat a preached by Álvaro del Portillo. She immediately moved to the Jorge Manrique center in Madrid, but only a few weeks later developed tuberculosis, which forced her to return to her hometown, where she explained the message of the Work to many friends. In April 1948 she joined Opus Dei again as a supernumerary.[16]

The ordination of the first three priests of the Work proved a crucial step in its growth. Álvaro del Portillo helped the Founder in Madrid and took care of activities for men in the north of Spain, José María Hernández Garnica focused on the women of the Work and provided priestly services in Catalonia, Valencia, and the

Mediterranean coast. José Luis Múzquiz took responsibility for supporting the apostolate of the Work in Andalusia. Through their preaching and individual spiritual direction they helped many people become enthused with the idea of being saints in the midst of the world and passing on that ideal to their coworkers and relatives.

In 1946 six more priests were ordained. By 1950 there were twenty-one priests of Opus Dei. All of them held university degrees in addition to an ecclesiastical doctorate. They gave up promising professional futures to serve others as priests. This sacrifice was comparable in a certain sense to that of the women who dedicated themselves to the domestic administration of centers instead of pursuing other more prestigious careers. In the Founder's opinion, this personal gift greatly benefited many people.

Starting in 1944, people of Opus Dei began to use a country house called La Pililla, located in Piedravales in the province of Ávila, as a place where they could get out of the city for a few days of work or rest, as well as for retreats. In 1945 the Work opened Molinoviejo, a conference center referred to at the time as a House for Spiritual Exercises. It was near Madrid, in Ortigosa del Monte. During their early years, these houses were opened for short periods to accommodate specific activities. The Founder's sister, Carmen, ran the housekeeping staff until the women of the Work were able to relieve her.

The retreats preached by priests of the Work in Molinoviejo and La Pililla as well as in other locations were powerful instruments of evangelization. During days spent in silence and dialogue with God, many people came to understand Opus Dei's message, underwent profound conversions, and in some cases heard God's call to give themselves to him in Opus Dei or in other institutions of the Church.

Molinoviejo, La Pililla, and the Moncola and Albayzín student residences also hosted summer courses of formation and rest for men of the Work. These classes began in 1944, and from 1945 on were called Annual Courses. They involved three weeks of intensive classes on Christian doctrine and the spirit of Opus Dei, but they were also an opportunity for rest and recreation and gave members of the Work a chance to get to know each other better and enjoy each other's company. Starting in 1948, members from other countries began to attend. The first two summer courses for women were held in 1946 in Los Rosales. In 1949, a Portuguese woman and an Irish woman participated for the first time.

Section 3. The Founder Moves to Rome

In November 1942, Professor José Orlandis and doctoral candidate Salvador Canals moved to Rome on scholarships from the Ministry of Foreign Affairs. Escrivá told them they need not try to do anything about Opus Dei's legal situation. He would take care of that personally from Madrid. What he wanted them to do was to tell people about the Work. They suffered through the final three years of World War II in Rome, including bombings, the nine-month Nazi occupation of the city, and its liberation by the Allies. Despite the adverse circumstances, they were able to meet many people, including cardinals who were Vatican department heads and other Vatican officials, professors from pontifical and secular universities, diplomats and journalists from various countries, and members of the ancient Roman nobility. They were granted an audience by Pius XII in January 1943.[17]

After the end of the war in 1945, they returned to Spain for a few weeks. In January 1946, they were back in the Eternal City. There they met two Croatians who were studying at the Lateran Athenaeum and were trying to get the Holy See to establish diplomatic relations with their country. In April 1946 one of them, Vladimiro Vince, joined Opus Dei. He was the first person to join Opus Dei outside of Spain.

In February 1946, Álvaro del Portillo arrived in Rome. The Founder had asked him to try to obtain Vatican approval of the Priestly Society of the Holy Cross, which would let it operate all over the world. In technical terms, he wanted a *decretum laudis* (decree of praise) making the Priestly Society an institution of pontifical, not merely diocesan, right. Del Portillo requested that the legal structure with which the Priestly Society of the Holy Cross and the association of the faithful Opus Dei had been approved by the diocese of Madrid be approved by the Holy See for the whole Church. Specifically, he was thinking of an inter-diocesan society of common life without vows that would integrate in legal and pastoral unity the two realities of the Work—the Priestly Society and the Association—and that would be governed by the same directors. Vatican approval would open the doors to expansion throughout the world.

Del Portillo went to Rome with more than sixty letters of recommendation, written by Spanish cardinals and bishops who knew about the formative activities of Opus Dei. These letters showed the scope of the Work and the fact that the bishops of Spain approved of it. In addition, he took advantage of a consistory in the Vatican to solicit recommendations from Cardinals Frings of Cologne, Germany; Caggiano of Rosario, Argentina; Cerejeira of Lisbon, Portugal; Ruffini of Palermo, Italy; and Gouveia of Lourenço Marques in Portuguese East Africa (now Mozambique).

The secretary general of Opus Dei, however, was unable to complete the assignment the Founder had given him. On the one hand, the doctrine of sanctity in the midst of the world astonished many in the Vatican. On the other hand, the unity of the two entities—Opus Dei and the Priestly Society—implied a society of common life without vows composed of priests and lay people, men and women, celibate and married people—something completely new. A member of the Congregation for Religious told Del Portillo that Opus Dei had arrived in the Church "a century ahead of its time."[18]

Álvaro del Portillo understood that the only way to move things forward was for the Founder to come to Rome. Escrivá had been diagnosed with diabetes three years earlier and was in such poor health that travel was dangerous for him. Nonetheless, he arrived in the Eternal City on June 23, 1946. He stayed in an apartment rented by the members of the Work in Piazza Città Leonina, very close to the pontifical apartments. A few days later, Pope Pius XII granted him an audience and they discussed the approval. Despite the legal difficulties and the fact that it was still a small institution (239 men and 29 women, almost all of them living in Spain), the Founder thought that the Pope was interested in Opus Dei because of its impact.[19]

Escrivá thought that the imminent international expansion of Opus Dei required a group of men and women dedicated to governing the Work. On September 24, he gathered in Molinoviejo twenty men of the Work, including the members of the Council. In a small, free-standing chapel on the grounds, they made a special commitment to protect the material and spiritual unity of Opus Dei, to remain united to its superiors, exercising, when appropriate, fraternal correction, and to assure that the spirit of poverty lived from the beginning would never be lost.* A few weeks later, the Founder returned to Rome. On December 8, the Feast of the Immaculate Conception, the Pope received him again.

Although he made occasional trips to Spain, primarily to meet with members of the Council and the Advisory, from then on the Founder lived in Rome. Residing in Rome reflected the worldwide vocation of Opus Dei and facilitated regular contact with Vatican authorities. It also prevented the Franco regime from exploiting him or the Work.

Escrivá had been convinced for years that as a worldwide institution of the Church, Opus Dei should have its headquarters close to the Vatican. People he spoke with in Rome confirmed this conviction. While working on the legal approval process, he searched for a suitable site. Eventually he found in the Pinciano district a Florentine-style villa with a large garden where more buildings could be built. It had been the embassy of Hungary to the Holy See. Because of the instability of the political situation and the severe inflation Italy was undergoing, it cost only seventy-five thousand dollars. The owner was willing to accept a symbolic down payment.

---

* See AGP A.3, 87-7-7. Fraternal correction, which is deeply rooted in the gospel, is a "refined warning, full of supernatural sense, with which one tries to help a member of the Work overcome some habit that is foreign to our spirit": *Catechism*, 1947 (1st ed.), no. 145. AGP E.1.1, 181-1-1. As a manifestation of unity and reminder of the commitments made in 1946, the Founder gave a pocket cross—made from the wood of some beams from the chapel of Molinoviejo—to the first man and woman in each country who asked to be admitted to the Work and also to the councilors of each region.

In the summer of 1947, the members of the Work moved into the new house, which they called Villa Tevere. At first they had to live in the gatehouse, a small two-story building that they called the *Pensionato* (The Hostel). They could not take immediate possession of the main building because the former tenants, who claimed diplomatic immunity, refused to move out. As soon as they gained possession of the whole property in February 1949, they began extensive remodeling of the main building and construction of new buildings to adapt the property as Opus Dei's headquarters and the temporary location of its international center of formation.

In the fall of 1947, three Spanish members of the Work enrolled in the Pontifical Lateran University and one in the Sapienza University of Rome. These young men made friends with Italian students and invited them to meet the founder of Opus Dei and the other residents of the Pensionato. Most of these Italian students belonged to religious associations, especially Catholic Action and the *Federazione Universitaria Cattolica Italiana*. Very soon, in November 1947, the first Italian, Francesco Angelicchio, joined the Work. During the following three months Renato Mariani, Luigi Tirelli, and Mario Lantini also joined Opus Dei. They were struck by the cheerfulness of their Spanish fellow students and by the affection that Escrivá lavished on them. Angelicchio recalls that when he met the Founder for the first time, "he embraced me and called me 'my son,' adding with the emotion and joy of a true father: 'my first-born Italian.'"[20]

The Founder encouraged the development of Opus Dei in other Italian cities, in much the same way as he had done in Spain a decade earlier. In January 1949, he appointed Del Portillo the councilor of Italy, Opus Dei's leader in the country. Together with other members of the Work, Escrivá and del Portillo drew up an ambitious travel plan. During 1949, students of the Work made more than eighty trips to various destinations, including Milan and Pisa in the north and Palermo and Bari in the south, sometimes accompanied by a priest of the Work. They left on a Saturday morning and returned on Sunday night so as not to miss classes. Wherever they went, they would gather a handful of college students and explain to them the spirit of

Opus Dei. At the end of 1949 they rented an apartment in Palermo and another in Milan. These were the first centers of Opus Dei's Italian region. In November 1950 they opened a center in Rome and in September 1952, one in Naples.

Opus Dei's initial development among Italian women was the work of the members who took care of the Administration of the Pensionato. A number of the people they met in the beginning were mothers or sisters of the first Italian men of Opus Dei. In January 1952, the first Italian woman numerary, Gabriella Filippone, joined the Work. Soon after, she was joined by the first female supernumerary in the country, Gioconda Lantini. A year later, the women's branch opened its first center in Naples.

Section 4. Expansion in Western Europe

After World War II, Europe began a slow process of economic and social reconstruction. Some borders changed, but what changed above all was the mentality of many Europeans, who were convinced that such an atrocity should not be repeated. The geopolitical situation was very complex. Western democracies had to rebuild a state of law; Germany was occupied by the armies of several nations; and Eastern Europe remained within the Soviet communist orbit.

In contrast to the situation in Eastern Europe, freedom of worship permitted Opus Dei to expand in Western Europe. In addition to Italy, Escrivá focused on Portugal, France, Ireland, and Great Britain. Between 1946 and 1948, thirty members of the Work opened centers in these five European countries. This facilitated transmitting the message of the Work in English, French, Italian, and Portuguese and pointed the way toward establishing Opus Dei on other continents.

Traveling outside of Spain and residing in foreign countries was much easier for Spanish professors and graduate students than for most other Spaniards. The Ministry of Foreign Affairs, working with the CSIC, not only made it easy to obtain an exit visit for study and research abroad but also offered quite a few scholarships and research grants This made it possible for members of the Work in their mid-twenties to complete their studies outside Spain.

In each country, the men began first. They rented an apartment or small house near a prestigious university and gradually met college students and other academics in accordance with the Founder's idea of starting with intellectuals in order to reach all layers of society. Once the men established themselves, the women of the Work opened a center in the same city.

Just to maintain family ties, the members outside of Spain occasionally sent the Founder and members in Spain audio recordings or home movies with greetings. Most of their communication with Escrivá and the Council was by letter. They wrote to give personal news and to inform them about activities and needs that had arisen. The Founder, for his part, followed the expansion closely and wrote frequently to assure them of his prayer and support. From time to time he asked one of the central directors of the Work to visit them.

The first members to go to each country promptly met with the local bishop to introduce themselves and request permission to have an oratory. They worked in their respective professional areas, studied the language of the country, translated *The Way*, spread private devotion to Isidoro Zorzano, and organized lectures and other cultural activities that would let them get to know students. As soon as they could, they usually opened a small student residence. Naturally they drew inspiration from the Work's experience in Spain, but they showed considerable flexibility in adapting to local conditions.

Portugal

The first members of Opus Dei to visit Portugal were Laureano López Rodó and Ángel López Amo, who spent a few days at the University of Coimbra in 1944. Thanks to the efforts of Sr. Lúcia de Jesus, one of the children of Fatima, Escrivá obtained a visa to enter Portugal in 1945. That year he visited the country four times to lay the groundwork for Opus Dei's apostolate there, meeting with the patriarch of Lisbon and the bishop of Coimbra.

In February 1946 Francisco Martínez, a pharmacist, arrived in Coimbra to study there. A few weeks later he was joined by Gregorio Ortega, a lawyer, and Alvaro del Amo, a scientist. All three enrolled as postdoctoral students. They opened a center and began organizing cultural and religious activities. Thanks to their personal friendship with professors and students, they were soon able to open a small university residence named Montes Claros, and to publish a Portuguese translation of *The Way*. In June, Mário do Carmo Pacheco, a student of philosophy and literature, became the first Portuguese member of Opus Dei.

During the following two years they set up the larger Boavista residence in Porto and a center in Lisbon as well as publishing a Portuguese translation of Escrivá's book *Holy Rosary*. The first Indian member of Opus Dei, Emérico da Gama from the Portuguese colony of Goa in southwestern India, joined Opus Dei in Coimbra in 1949. Meanwhile, Francisco Xavier de Ayala, who had arrived in Portugal in October 1946, was ordained a priest and became Opus Dei's councilor in Portugal.

The women of the Work started making trips from Spain to Portugal in 1949. Two years later, Maria Sofia Pacheco (Mário's sister), Ester Teijeira, and Julia García opened the first women's center in Lisbon. In 1953, they started the Lar da Estrela student residence in the Portuguese capital. Soon after, the residence Da Carvalhosa opened its doors in Porto.[21]

England and Ireland

Beginning in England represented a serious challenge for Opus Dei, because the Protestant majority had long been hostile to Catholicism. In the 1940s, many members of the political and intellectual elite still did not consider a Catholic a true Englishman. On the other hand, the number of Catholic converts was increasing from year to year; the country had a global empire; its capital was a world crossroads; and its language was rapidly becoming the world's new lingua franca.

Eduardo Alastrué, Juan Antonio Galarraga, and Salvador Peris arrived in London on December 28, 1946, with study grants from the CSIC. They visited the archbishop of Westminster, Cardinal Bernard Griffin, who welcomed them warmly. Soon they were joined by Rafael Calvo Serer, who had come to work at the *Instituto de España* in London. When they arrived at the apartment they rented in Rutland Court, south of the City, the doorman was surprised that they had only their suitcases. It took some time to furnish the apartment with the help of donations from friends.

They concentrated first on trying to spread Opus Dei's message among college students. On Saturday afternoons they invited friends and acquaintances to the center to attend a talk or lecture or just to spend some time conversing. More than two years went by before Michael Richards, a student at University College London, became the first British member of Opus Dei in 1949. He was followed quickly by Richard Stork, who was temporarily living in Madrid. Stork returned to London in 1951 to study engineering.[22]

Opus Dei took its first steps in Ireland in October 1947, when an engineer, José Ramón Madurga, enrolled in the master's program of the Department of Engineering at the National University of Ireland (Dublin College). He roomed with a family until he managed to rent a small apartment. In order to meet more students, he joined several clubs and societies. At a meeting of the Spanish Club, he met Cormac Burke, who lived in University Hall, a residence run by the Jesuits.

Madurga spent Christmas with the members of the Work in London. Shortly after returning to Dublin, he explained Opus Dei in detail to Burke and suggested that God might be calling him. After consulting with a priest-friend who encouraged him, on January 9, 1947, Burke joined the Work. He and Madurga immediately set about translating *The Way* into English. Burke met the Founder during a summer course held at Molinovijeo in 1948. Escrivá told him that God would ask a lot of him, but that he would also give him extraordinary graces.

Salvio Carreiras, an industrial engineer, joined Madurga and Burke in Dublin during the 1948/49 school year. They rented a house which they called Northbrook. Many students began to come to formational activities at the center, and several of them joined Opus Dei, including Dick Mulcahy, Paul Cummings, and his brother Dan. Cormac Burke's sister, Honoria, and four of her friends also joined Opus Dei between March 1949 and June 1950: Máire Gibbons, Anna Barrett, Olive Mulcahy, and Eileen Maher. When he heard about this rapid initial development, which occurred before a priest or other women of Opus Dei came to Dublin, Escrivá referred to it as the "miracle of Ireland."

Five Spaniards joined the members of the Work living in London and Dublin for a summer course for members of Opus Dei in the Irish capital in 1949. José Orlandis preached a retreat in Dublin for members of the Work during the Christmas season. A year later, Madurga moved to Rome to receive priestly ordination. From Rome, Fr. Josemaría often wrote to his children in London and Dublin.

In 1951, Escrivá invited Juan Antonio Galarraga and Cormac Burke to join him in Rome for a few days. During their stay, he suggested that they establish a university residence in London. He knew they did not have nearly enough money, but he promised to support the project despite the fact that in Rome they were very short of money for building Villa Tevere. He also sent José López Navarro to be the first priest of the Work permanently assigned to supporting its apostolate in England and Ireland.[23]

France

The beginning of the men's branch of Opus Dei in France proved especially difficult. In fall 1947, Fernando Maycas went to the French capital for master's studies, and Álvaro Calleja and Julián Urbistondo enrolled in the Sorbonne. They stayed at the Colegio de España in the Ciudad Universitaria. The Founder was aware that they found adapting to life in Paris difficult and often wrote to encourage them: "May you be happy; ploughing is a hard thing."[24] Urbistondo was the first to return to Spain; Maycas and Calleja followed him in the summer of 1949. The activities of Opus Dei in France would not begin again until 1952, but then this time on a permanent basis.[25]

The first vocation of a French woman occurred in an unexpected fashion. A young Spanish woman who had herself just joined Opus Dei, Lourdes Bandeira, went to Bordeaux to learn French at the home of the Bardinets, who were family friends. One of the daughters, Catherine Bardinet, quickly became enthused with what Lourdes told her about Opus Dei and with what she learned about its spirit from *The Way*, which she read from cover to cover in a single night although her Spanish was not very good. She began to ask herself in prayer whether God was calling her to the Work, and on August 15, 1949, she joined Opus Dei. She lived at home with her parents for the next two years and traveled with them to Rome, where she met Escrivá. In 1951 she went to Los Rosales to study for six months.

Notes

1. See González Gullón, *DYA*, pp. 288–300.

2. See Nicolás Álvarez de las Asturias, "San Josemaría, predicador de ejercicios espirituales a sacerdotes diocesanos (1938–1942): Análisis de las fuentes conservadas," *Studia et Documenta* 9 (2015), pp. 277–321.

3. See José Luis González Gullón, "Los tres primeros sacerdotes del Opus Dei (mayo–junio 1944)," in Pablo Gefaell, ed., *Vir fidelis multum laudabitur* (Rome: EDUSC, 2014), pp. 93–106; and Federico M. Requena, "El claustro académico del Centro de Estudios Eclesiásticos de la Sociedad Sacerdotal de la Santa Cruz: los profesores de Teología del beato Álvaro del Portillo," *Studia et Documenta* 9 (2015), pp. 13–55.

4. Cited in John F. Coverdale, *Uncommon Faith. The Early Years of Opus Dei (1928–1943)* (Princeton NJ: Scepter 2002) p. 367.

5. See Handwritten note by Josemaría Escrivá de Balaguer, February 28, 1943, AGP L.1.1, 2-1-3.

6. *Constitutiones Societatis Sacerdotalis Sanctae Crucis* (1950), nos. 1 and 3. AGP L.1.1, 2-4-2.

7. See Letter 9, no. 12, AGP A.3, 92-2-2.

8. Letter 13, no. 160, AGP A.3, 92-6-2.

9. Letter 9, no. 17, AGP A.3, 92-2-2.

10. Letter 15, no. 18, AGP A.3, 93-1-4.

11. Notes on the days of the ordination of the first three priests of Opus Dei, May 23 to July 28, 1944, pp. 24–25, AGP A.1, 14-1-13; González Gullón, "Los tres primeros sacerdotes del Opus Dei," pp. 93–106. See also Fuenmayor, Gómez-Iglesias, and Illanes, pp. 119–127.

12. See clippings of these publications in AGP L.1.1, 18-1.

13. See Mercedes Montero, "La Editorial Minerva (1943–1946). Un ensayo de cultura popular y cristiana de las primeras mujeres del Opus Dei," *Studia et Documenta* 11 (2017), pp. 227–263.

14. See Mercedes Montero, *Historia de Ediciones Rialp: Orígenes y contexto, aciertos y errores*, (Madrid: Rialp, 2020). Urteaga's book was eventually translated into many languages. English versions were published under two different titles: *Man, the Saint*, and *Saints in the World*.

15. See Mercedes Montero, "Los comienzos de la labor del Opus Dei con universitarias: La Residencia Zurbarán de Madrid (1947–1950)," *Studia et Documenta* 4 (2010), pp. 15–44.

16. On May 31, 1953 Aurora Nieto became the first woman to join Opus Dei as a supernumerary. Ramona Sarjurjo made the oblation on May 26, 1955. See Francisca Colomer Pellicer, "Ramona Sanjurjo Aranaz y los inicios del Opus Dei en Vigo," *Studia et Documenta* 12 (2018), p. 311n32.

17. See Josep-Ignasi Sarayana, "Ante Pío XII y Mons. Montini: Audiencias a miembros del Opus Dei, en los diarios de José Orlandis (1942–1945)," *Studia et Documenta* 5 (2011), pp. 311–343; Luis Cano, "San Josemaría ante el Vaticano. Relaciones y trabajos durante el primer viaje a Roma: del 23 de junio al 31 de agosto de 1946," *Studia et Documenta* 6 (2012), pp. 165–209; Alfredo Méndiz, *Salvador Canals: Una biografía* (Madrid: Rialp, 2019); José Orlandis, *Memorias de Roma en guerra (1942–1945)*, 2nd ed. (Madrid: Rialp, 1998); and José Orlandis, *Mis recuerdos: Primeros tiempos del Opus Dei en Roma* (Madrid: Rialp, 1995).

18. Letter 17, no. 18, AGP A.3, 93-2-4; see also Letter 13, no. 166, AGP A.3, 92-6-2.

19. See "Relación sobre el estado actual de la Sociedad Sacerdotal de la Santa Cruz," 1946, AGP L.1.1, 5-1-1.

20. Recollections of Francesco Angelicchio, Rome, July 24, 1975, AGP A.5, 193-4-1. See also Cosimo di Fazio, "Italia," in *Diccionario de San Josemaría Escrivá de Balaguer*, pp. 658–662.

21. See Hugo de Azevedo, "Primeiras viagens de S. Josemaria a Portugal (1945)," *Studia et Documenta* 1 (2007), pp. 15–39.

22. See Maureen Mullins, "Great Britain," in *Diccionario de san Josemaría Escrivá de Balaguer*, pp. 585–589.

23. See Marie Heraughty, "Irlanda," in *Diccionario de san Josemaría Escrivá de Balaguer*, pp. 655–658.

24. Letter from Josemaría Escrivá to the members of the Work in Paris, Madrid, February 16, 1949, AGP A.3.4, 260-4, 490216-1.

25. See François Gondrand, "Francia," in *Diccionario de san Josemaría Escrivá de Balaguer*, pp. 543–547.

CHAPTER 7

Pontifical Approvals

Escrivá arrived in Rome in the early summer of 1946 to request the *decretum laudis* (decree of praise) which would approve Opus Dei for the entire Church. The Founder met with the *sostituto* of the secretary of state, Giovanni Battista Montini (the future Pope Paul VI), and with some consultants of the Congregation for Religious, including the Claretians Arcadio Maria Larraona and Siervo Goyeneche. They told him that for some time the Holy See had been studying an array of institutions that it grouped together under the heading of "new forms" of Christian life. The way their members gave themselves to God and carried out apostolate differed in important respects from the canonical states of perfection. For example, some did not profess public vows, wear a habit, or live canonical common life. They did not, therefore, fit within the framework established by canon law.

The Founder of the Work pointed out that these groups varied greatly among themselves. Some wanted to be religious orders or congregations or comparable to them, but without common life for apostolic reasons. Opus Dei and some other groups, however, belonged to the secular sphere. Faced with the fact that Vatican officials wanted to craft legislation that would cover the entire range, Escrivá moved prudently, trying to find acceptable compromises that would ensure that Opus Dei's foundational charism was fully respected. In his own words, "the law was of particular importance. A mistake, a concession in something substantial, could have irreparable effects. My soul was at stake, because I could not adulterate God's will. You will understand my stress and suffering."[1]

Fr. Arcadio Larraona, the undersecretary of the Congregation for Religious, was working on a legal structure for the "new forms." Escrivá, Del Portillo, and Canals collaborated actively with him on the project.[2] Their efforts came to fruition on February 2, 1947, with Pius XII's promulgation of the apostolic constitution *Provida Mater Ecclesia*. This document created the category of secular institutes, defined as "clerical or lay societies whose members, in order to acquire Christian perfection and fully exercise the apostolate, profess the evangelical counsels in the world."[3] The three fundamental characteristics of these institutes were: 1) full consecration to God through the profession of the evangelical counsels, which, in contrast to the religious orders and congregations, were not public and did not require canonical common life; 2) secularity of the members who remained in the world; and 3) the exercise of the Christian apostolate.

Section 1. An "Entirely" Secular Institute

On February 24, the Congregation for Religious approved Opus Dei as a secular institute of pontifical right with a *decretum laudis* (decree of praise) titled *Primum Institutum*. It also approved the constitutions, which were the same as those of 1944, with very minor changes. Following the usual practice of the Holy See, the approval was temporary, to allow for a period of experience before definitive approval.[4]

The Founder of the Work received the approval with joy. From the theological point of view, the Holy See confirmed that a vocation to Opus Dei involved the search for holiness in one's own state and in the exercise of one's profession or job. From the canonical point of view, a centralized, worldwide regime gave Opus Dei greater legal stability and opened the door its expansion throughout the world.

Nonetheless, Escrivá was troubled by some aspects of the underlying mentality reflected in *Provida Mater Ecclesia* and by some problematic points in its text. Although the first Christians had understood clearly that fully secular ordinary people could and should pursue authentic holiness in everyday life, the idea had largely been lost sight of in the Church. For centuries complete self-giving to God had been linked exclusively to public consecration and detachment from the world by embracing a vocation to a religious order or congregation. It was not going to be easy to change that.

In this sense, the fact that the text of the constitution put Opus Dei under the authority of the Congregation for Religious did not help. This situated the Work in the sphere of the institutes and canonical states of perfection, which traditionally involved a public consecration to God and detachment from the world to a greater or lesser degree. To try to avoid the implication that these practices applied to Opus Dei, the decree of praise indicated, at Escrivá's request, that the members of the Work "do not have a common religious life, nor do they take religious vows, nor do they use religious habits."[5]

In the minds of most Catholics, vows were associated with religious orders and congregations, but *Provida Mater Ecclesia* required the members of all secular institutes to take vows. Escrivá stressed that, unlike the public vows taken by members of religious orders and congregations, which publicly professed the three evangelical counsels, the vows the constitution required members of Opus Dei to take were private or social bonds. He also emphasized that the Work had no institutional interest in vows but only in its members' living the Christian virtues. Moreover, membership in Opus Dei (whether temporary through the Admission and Oblation or definitive through the Fidelity) depended not on taking vows but on expressing verbally one's personal commitment before God in a separate brief ceremony that did not include vows or other formulas of consecration.

Underlying these specific issues was a failure of many people to fully grasp the difference between the situation of the members of Opus Dei who dedicated themselves fully to God in ordinary life and without changing their state in life, and the situation of the members of religious orders and congregations designated by the theological and canonical concept of "state of perfection." The canonical state of perfection rested on public profession of the vows of poverty, obedience, and chastity,—a mode of consecration that implied a way of life

separated in various respects and to varying degrees from the world.*
A person who entered that state of perfection changed his state in the

---

* For centuries it had been held that the public profession of the evangelical counsels by the members of religious orders and congregations separated them in greater or lesser degree from secular realities and bore witness to the fact that the goal of human life is God, not created goods. It was thought this meant that they embraced a state or way of life (the "state of perfection") which facilitated sanctity. It was common doctrine that the public profession of the three evangelical counsels led to the fullness of communion with God because the members of religious orders and congregations took on an obligation to seek perfection which bound them legally and not only in conscience. Religious life was presented as the paradigm and fullness of Christian sanctity. It was not denied that a secular person could reach perfection through the fulfillment of the commands of the God's law, but frequently it was understood that it was more difficult for them to do so and that the perfection they could achieve was lesser because their living in the world was an obstacle.

During the twentieth century, both the Magisterium and theological thought gradually abandoned the ideas that a person's degree of perfection depended on his state in life and that living in the world was an obstacle to sanctity. Reflection on the Christian ideal came to center on the universal call to sanctity involved in Baptism. In 1939, Pope Pius XII affirmed: "God does not call all his children to the state of perfection; but he invites all of them to perfection in their state." (General Audience, December 6, 1939, in *Discorsi e radiomessaggi di Sua Santità Pio XII, vol I* (Città del Vaticano: Tip. Poliglotta Vaticana, 1940) p. 414.

The message Escrivá received in 1928 moves in this line and was solemnly proclaimed by the Second Vatican Council. He told lay men and women and secular priests immersed in secular realities that God calls them to "ordinary life carried out with perfection." Their "normal, ordinary life, which does not seem to be anything special, can," "he stressed," be a means of sanctity. There is no need to abandon one's own state in life." Carta 1, nn. 12 and 2, in Josemaría Escrivá de Balaguer, *Cartas* (edición crítico-histórica), Vol I (Madrid: Rialp, 2020), pp. 64 and 56. This was the aim of the institution he founded. "The Work was born to help Christians inserted in the fabric of civil society through their family, their friendships, their professional work, and their noble ambitions to understand that their life, just as it is, can be an occasion of an encounter with Christ, that is a way of sanctity and apostolate." Josemaría Escrivá de Balaguer, *Conversaciones con Mons. Escrivá de Balaguer* (edición crítico-histórica), (Madrid: Rialp 2012), n. 60. On the relationship between secular life and the consecrated life of the religious, cf. Ernst Burkhart and Javier López, *Vida cotidiana y santidad en la enseñanza de san Josemaría, vol. I*, (Madrid: Rialp, 2010), pp. 213-239; Sergio Lanza, "Secolarità" in *Dizionario di Ecclesiolgia* eds. Gianfranco Calabrse, Philip Goret, Orazio Francesco Piazza (Rome: Città Nova, 2010), pp. 1301-1305; Juan Fornés, "Fiel," in, *Diccionario General de Derecho Canónico* eds. Javier Otaduy, Antonio Viana, and Joaqauín Sedano (Pamplona: Aranzadi, 2012), pp. 984-988. On the concept of state in the Church, cf. Juan Fornés, *La noción de status en Derecho Canónico* (Pamplona: EUNSA, 1975).

Church and ceased to be an ordinary Christian. Joining Opus Dei did not change the member's canonical state. The Work was born to help these Christians, inserted in the fabric of civil society—with their family, their friendships, their professional work, their noble aspirations—to understand that their life, just as it is, can be an occasion for an encounter with Christ. In short, it is a path to holiness and apostolate. The legislation on secular institutes created a *secular state of perfection* that did not modify the canonical personality of its members. They were, at the same time, consecrated and secular persons, ordinary faithful (either secular priests or ordinary laypeople) who were in the midst of the world, immersed in a social and work situation in which they grew in sanctity and gave Christian witness. Their consecration to God, carried out privately through the evangelical counsels, was a means by which they manifested their full self-giving to God. On the other hand, each one sought holiness and exercised the apostolate in his social environment, among his peers.

In the preceding paragraphs we have talked about "consecration." Members of Opus Dei can be said to be consecrated, but not in the same sense as the religious. The Founder often reminded his spiritual sons and daughters of what he meant when he spoke about consecration in Opus Dei, which went hand in hand with full secularity: "I have said that the members are consecrated and have spoken about consecration in the Work, but only in the sense of absolute dedication. It has never occurred to me to give those words a technical canonical or religious interpretation."[6] It was also a constant in his preaching and writings that the members' self-gift to God left them in their own canonical state of life: "We are not like secularized religious, but authentically secular members of the Church who do not seek the life of evangelical perfection proper to religious, but Christian perfection in the world, each in his own state."[7]

As a way of underlining the secularity of the members of the Work, Alvaro del Portillo requested that the Founder be named an honorary prelate of His Holiness and granted the title of monsignor, an honor that the Holy See conferred only on secular priests. In April 1947, the Holy See granted the title to Escrivá.

The Founder worked to explain the new category of secular institutes both to the hierarchy and to members of other ecclesial institutions. On December 16, 1948, he gave an important lecture at the headquarters of the National Association of Propagandists in Madrid. He described secular institutes as "a new type of life of perfection." Across the centuries, the Church had witnessed the development of groups of hermits, monastic communities, mendicant orders and clerics regular, congregations with simple vows and societies of common life without vows. All these entities had in common the canonical state of perfection, which demanded separation from the world, although they differed from each in the degree to which they approached the world to carry out pastoral and apostolic tasks.

Secular institutes, Escrivá continued, were similar to these institutions in that they involved a radical search for sanctity. They were different, however, in that they opened up in the Church a path that affirmed the value of ordinary Christian life. They involved "a new form of life of perfection, in which the members are not religious, and do not, therefore, depart from the world. They come to fulfill in the world the evangelical counsels to acquire Christian perfection." "It is from the world itself," he added, "that these apostles arise, who dare to sanctify all the ordinary activities of men." Referring specifically to Opus Dei, he underlined that it seeks "the evangelical perfection of its members through the sanctification of ordinary work, in the most diverse fields of human activity." And, since they are secular, they act "in the world under their personal and exclusive responsibility. For this reason, they enjoy absolute professional freedom. Opus Dei does not interfere in these matters."[8]

Section 2. Government and Organization

After obtaining pontifical approval, Josemaría Escrivá appointed the members of the General Council of the new secular institute. Pedro Casciaro was secretary general; Álvaro del Portillo, procurator general; José Luis Múzquiz, vice secretary of the Work of St. Michael; Amadeo de Fuenmayor, vice secretary of the Work of St. Gabriel; Odón Moles, vice secretary of the Work of St. Raphael; Antonio Pérez, general administrator; and Antonio Fontán, prefect of studies. The Founder asked all of them to strive to live fully the spirit and the norms of piety foreseen in the Work, having as the foundation of their lives connecting with God and searching for holiness.

On September 24, 1947, the Founder met in Molinoviejo with a large group of members. In accordance with the constitutions of the newly approved secular institute, he appointed them as inscribed members; that is, numeraries specially dedicated to giving formation and governing the Work. They all made a spiritual commitment before God to exercise fraternal correction when necessary, not to seek positions in Opus Dei, and to consult the Father or the councilor on important matters.* The Founder appointed nineteen inscribed members as electors. They were to attend the general congresses of the Work, and when the time came they would choose his successor as head of the Work. In addition, he approved the assignment of the members to one or another of the twenty-three existing centers, the appointment of the directors of each center, and expansion in Rome, where an interregional center of studies was planned, in various European countries, and, when possible, in the Americas.⁹

Although Escrivá was living in Rome duirng these years, the General Council and Central Advisory as well as the centers of studies for men and women remained in Madrid because most of the people and activities of the Work were in Spain. The Founder and the members

---

* This triple spiritual commitment would also be made by all members before making the Fidelity and by the priests of Opus Dei. With the definitive approval of Opus Dei in 1950, the commitment took the form of an oath. See *Constitutiones Societatis Sacerdotalis Sanctae Crucis et Operis Dei* (1950), nos. 20 and 58. From 1969 onward, this commitment ceased being by oath and became a simple promise on one's honor as a Christian (Acts of the Special General Congress, September 9, 1969, AGP D.3).

In the 1941 statutes the term *inscribed members* had been used to designate people close to the Work but not officially members, who today would be called cooperators. Beginning in 1950, the term "inscribed members" has been used to designate certain numeraries who usually work full time in governing the Work and giving formation.

of the General Council and Central Advisory wrote letters each week to give directives and raise issues.

Over time, the directors of the General Council, with the help of some other numeraries who worked with them, gradually improved and expanded the service they provided to the rest of the Work. For example, the office of spiritual direction prepared outlines for the talks to be given in the circles for members and for the meditations preached by the priests. The General Council developed a system for numbering notes and other papers sent to the local centers and by the local centers to it. This permitted cross-referencing and improved coordination between the General Council and the centers.

The primary focus of the council's office of general administration was on helping the members of the Work to live personally the virtue of poverty, but it also oversaw the Work's finances. Management of the real estate holding companies that owned the centers and other not-for-profit corporations was in the hands of the people who had created them, but the office reviewed their balance sheets and other accounts.

The constitutions approved by the Holy See when it transformed Opus Dei into a secular institute determined its legal structure and set forth the principal features of its spirit and the way to live it. To know what God was asking of them in greater detail, the directors and other members also turned to the Work's oral tradition and practice as well as to written materials such as *The Way* and *Holy Rosary*, the Instructions on the *Supernatural Spirit of the Work of God*, *The Way of Proselytizing*, and *the Work of St. Raphael*, and two documents written by Escrivá in the mid-1940s: the *Catechism* and the *Guidelines for Directors*.

The catechism consisted of one hundred and fifty short questions and answers. It summarized the main characteristics of the spirit, the law, and the history of the Work. It explained, for example, that the members of the Work were ordinary faithful, that priests and laity formed a single class within Opus Dei, that the Christian spirit of the Work could be put into practice by people from all walks of life, and that the means employed by its members were "the sanctification of ordinary work and the perfect fulfillment of their professional and social duties."[10] Starting in 1945, a typewritten version was used in the centers of studies and summer courses. Three years later, a printed edition appeared that reflected the changes originated by the approval of the Work as a secular institute. All the members were asked to study it and even learn it by heart.

Guidelines was intended for central and local directors. It was a practical collection of criteria and experiences on how to govern and manage centers and apostolic activities. Escrivá had invited all the members to send him suggestions on ways of living the spirit of Opus Dei. After reviewing the suggestions, he published the first edition in 1948, with two versions, one for men and one for women. These documents were in effect during the 1950s.[11]

From August 24 to 29, 1948, twenty-eight numeraries, mostly central or local directors, met in Molinoviejo to review hundreds of suggestions received about the formation of the members, ways to improve the Work's apostolic activities, and plans for its growth. Escrivá commented with amusement that their main problem was that they were still young. He said the time had come to move faster and with a worldwide focus to bring the message of sanctification in ordinary life to many people. This meeting was Opus Dei's third Work Week.[12]

To prepare Opus Dei's expansion to America, Pedro Casciaro, who had been ordained a priest two years before; Ignacio de la Concha, a law professor; and José Vila, an historian; spent six months gathering information and meeting people in the United States, Canada, Mexico, Peru, Chile, and Argentina. They returned in September 1948 and prepared a detailed report for the Founder and the General Council.[13]

Until this time, the individual centers had reported directly to the General Council. On October 27, Escrivá instituted the regional level of government of Opus Dei. He set up seven districts and appointed their respective councilors: Spain (with Francisco Botella as councilor); Italy (Álvaro del Portillo), Portugal (Francisco Xavier de Ayala), Mexico (Pedro Casciaro), the United States (José Luis

Múzquiz), England (Juan Antonio Galarraga), and Ireland (José Ramón Madurga). These appointments produced some changes in the General Council. The most important was that Francisco Botella became secretary general, so he temporarily held both a central and a regional position.*

The women of the Work had their first Work Week in Los Rosales from November 26 to 29, 1948. The thirteen participants reviewed the activities the women's branch had carried out so far, particularly the Work of San Rafael and the Administration of the centers. They set ambitious goals for the future, encouraged by the fact that there was a large group of young women who were discerning their call to the Work.

Narcisa González Guzmán and Guadalupe Ortiz de Landázuri were appointed as the initial members of an incipient Central Advisory, which would play in the women's branch the role played by the General Council in the men's branch. In October 1949, the Advisory established its headquarters in Juan Bravo Street. It would be some time before it was fully staffed, but fairly soon Rosario Orbegozo, who was the senior director in Madrid, became the third member.[14] Gradually other women joined them.

The women who worked in the Administration gradually acquired experience. The Administrators, who were in charge of the Administration in each center, became more skilled at assigning tasks to the other members of the Administration, handling the accounting, preparing menus and budgets, and staying on top of what needed to be done in the house.

---

* Technically, only Spain was a "region." Italy, Portugal, Mexico, and the United States were "quasi-regions." England and Ireland were "delegations." To be a region, a district had to have a full regional commission and at least one center of studies for each branch. Quasi-regions were districts that were not yet sufficiently developed to meet these requirements. The term *delegation* applied to two different organizations: 1) Districts that were even less developed than a quasi-region and that depended on a region or directly on the president general, and 2) geographic subdivisions within a region that stood between the regional commission and the local centers. (See Rescript, October 25, 1948, AGP L.1.1, 10-1-22.) Generally, the boundaries of the districts coincided with those of a country.

The administrators developed training plans to help the servants become outstanding professional cooks and experts in cleaning, laundry, and home decoration.* They helped them see how their dedication contributed to creating real homes for the members of both branches and how they could give their work a supernatural meaning. Many of the maids came from impoverished rural social and educational backgrounds, so the administrators needed to help them mature and grow. They gradually gave them more responsibilities and helped them overcome their shyness and lack of confidence in dealing with people from higher social classes. This was a slow process, especially given how marked the differences between social classes were in Spain at the time. For the moment, it was necessary to respect their way of being and give them time and space in which to develop. For this reason, there were separate dining rooms for the numeraries and the numerary servants, so that during meals both could relax and feel at home.†

Escrivá stressed that the separation between the two sections was a foundational characteristic of the Work. It found expression even in the architecture of the centers. The first regulations for the Administration, published in 1947, specified that the women's branch would take care of the Administration of a men's residence only if the building allowed an absolute separation of the two houses, which *de jure* and *de facto* are totally independent.[15]

Section 3. Variety of Members

In the years immediately following the 1947 approval, the Congregation for Religious accepted a number of modifications to the

---

* We recall that the word *servant* is a paradigmatic case of semantic evolution of words, since it did not have in those years the pejorative connotations it now has. See chapter 5, section 2 ("The Administration").

† Women's empowerment increased in the following decades. These changes brought with them, as we will see, an end to the practice of having separate dining rooms and in general to differences in the way of life and living conditions of the various people working in the Administration.

constitutions proposed by the Founder, some of them of great importance. The most significant made it possible for married people and diocesan priests to join the Work, thereby expanding it well beyond the limits within which it had functioned until then.

Since the 1930s, the Founder had spiritually accompanied men who were attracted by what he was saying about the call to holiness in marriage and in ordinary life. He preached spiritual exercises for married professional men in Vitoria (1939) and Madrid (1942 and 1945). He also gave personal spiritual direction to a number of married professionals, employees, and workers. He encouraged them to seek holiness in ordinary life, in their work, and in family and social relationships. This idea was not only unusual, but shocking. For example, a married teacher, Víctor García Hoz, was surprised and overjoyed when Escrivá told him in 1941: "God is calling you to paths of contemplation."[16] He recommended that he and a married teacher, Tomás Alvira, live the norms and customs of Opus Dei, even though for the time being it was not possible for them to become members. In 1943, he suggested that José María Hernández Garnica, the recently appointed assistant secretary of the Work of St. Gabriel, take over the spiritual direction of Alvira and of García Hoz, who had recently become the first person to earn a doctorate in pedagogy from a Spanish university.

As soon as Opus Dei became a secular institute in February 1947, Tomás Alvira applied for admission. Two months later, Mariano Navarro Rubio and García Hoz did the same. For the moment, their commitment was of a purely spiritual nature, since there was still no possibility of married people being considered members from a legal point of view. But in February 1948, Escrivá got the Holy See to approve that people of any condition, whether single or married, could establish a stable legal bond with Opus Dei, although they would not be fully available for tasks of government and formation. They would be called *supernumeraries*.

Fifteen married professional men attended a week-long workshop in Molinoviejo in September 1948. Six were already supernumeraries, and the rest joined the Work at that time. In talks and meditations,

Escrivá explained how they could live the spirit of Opus Dei in their own family and professional circumstances. He stressed that the call to be saints in marriage was not a utopian aspiration but a divine vocation that for members of the Work involved complete dedication to God.[17]

Following the 1948 workshop, both branches of the Work greatly expanded their activities for married people, and the number of supernumeraries grew rapidly. By 1950, supernumeries made up almost 25 percent of the members.[18]

Being a numerary member of Opus Dei implied being available to take on tasks of government and formation within the Work. This required a college education and, in most cases, living in a center of the Work. By the late 1940s there were a number of people who felt God was calling them to live celibacy in Opus Dei but who had not gone to college or whose personal, family, or professional circumstances made it impossible for them to take on tasks of government or formation or live in a center of the Work. Escrivá raised with the Holy See the possibility of their joining the Work. He drew up a complement to the statute of the previous year on supernumeraries. On September 8, 1949, he received a rescript from the Congregation for Religious admitting the new category. These members came to be called *oblates*.*

The Founder also considered at this time how the message of the Work could reach the diocesan clergy. The foundational light was directed to the entire secular sphere of the Church, including both laity and priests. Before the Spanish Civil War, a dozen diocesan priests had joined Opus Dei. The experience had not, however, been satisfactory because those priests already had a different mindset and had not been able to make the spirit of Opus Dei their own. They had

---

* See Rescript, Rome, September 8, 1949, and note, June 2, 1950, AGP L.1.1, 10-1-30 and L.1.1, 12-1-5, respectively. In 1967 Escrivá changed the name from *oblate* to *associate*, since oblate could evoke consecrated religious, while associate was a term that came from the academic world. See General Note 50/67 (July 13, 1967), AGP E.1.3, 245-3. To avoid anachronisms, we will use *oblate* in parts 2 and 3 of this book and *associate* in the rest.

all ceased to belong to the Work, and Escrivá had put aside for the moment apostolate with diocesan priests. The approval of the Priestly Society of the Holy Cross in 1943 made it possible for Opus Dei to have some of its lay members ordained priests, but diocesan priests could not join the Priestly Society because they were already incardinated in their respective dioceses.

Escrivá was so firmly convinced that God wanted him to work with diocesan priests that he eventually concluded he should leave Opus Dei and found another secular institute or some other type of institution for diocesan priests to whom it would transmit the spirit of the Work. He communicated this informally to the Congregation for Religious, to the central directors of the Work, and to his brother and sister. Before he acted on this conviction, however, he found a way for diocesan priests to belong to Opus Dei.

In February 1950, he asked Pope Pius XII to grant definitive approval to Opus Dei as a secular institute. He presented a draft of new constitutions and the endorsement of one hundred and ten bishops and prelates from seventeen countries. Two months later, the Congregation for Religious decided to delay the approval for a while in order to study the future constitutions better.

The delay proved providential. While Escrivá waited for the Holy See to act, God showed him a way in which diocesan priests could become associate or supernumerary members of the Priestly Society of the Holy Cross without changing or diminishing their diocesan character. The local bishop would continue to be their only superior. The Priestly Society would offer them spiritual help to seek holiness in the midst of the world, precisely in their priestly work, and they would benefit from Opus Dei's family atmosphere. In Escrivá's words, "If it is possible to speak in this way, for priests their professional work, in which they must sanctify themselves and with which they must sanctify others, is the ministerial priesthood of the Bread and the Word."[19] The spiritual character of the call to Opus Dei would strengthen their union with their respective bishops in accordance with the maxim *Nihil sine Episcopo* ("Nothing without the Bishop"). It would also reinforce their unity with the other priests of their diocese. Escrivá wrote a statute for diocesan priests and presented it to the congregation on June 2, 1950, to be added to the material that was being studied.[20]

Section 4. Developments and Difficulties

Just two weeks later, on June 16, the Holy See issued the decree *Primum inter Instituta*, which granted the definitive approval of the Priestly Society of the Holy Cross and Opus Dei as a secular institute, as well as its new constitutions. It began with a summary of the spirit of Opus Dei in the light of which the rest of the legal text was to be interpreted. It underlined the secularity of the members, the sense of divine filiation as the foundation of their spiritual life, and the search for perfection through the "exercise of the moral and Christian virtues and especially through the sanctification of everyday professional work."[21]

The constitutions set out the nature of the institute and its worldwide, centralized legal regime. In accordance with the provisions of the law for institutes of perfection, a distinction was made between the general aim of Opus Dei—holiness through any professional work—and the specific aim, which was to bring the light of the gospel to intellectuals in order to reach all classes of civil society through them. Among the corporate tasks of an apostolic nature the institute could undertake, the constitutions specifically mentioned student residences and retreat houses.[22] They also underlined the unity of the pastoral function, including the fact that the Priestly Society of the Holy Cross, "being *aliquid intrinsecum* to Opus Dei, has the same superiors who exercise in the Priestly Society the same faculties as in Opus Dei."[23]

The decree approving Opus Dei noted that it was composed of two sections: one for men and one for women, each with great legal and administrative autonomy at all three levels of government—central, regional, and local. The president general and in each region the regional councilor give unity to the government of what is a single pastoral and apostolic enterprise.

All the members, whether men or women, priests or laity, single or married, would have the same spiritual call and, therefore, would form a single class. The president general, the councilors in each region, and certain other directors had to be priests, but the statutes foresaw that lay men and women would play central roles in the apostolate of the Work, its formational activities, and its government.

To accommodate their diverse personal conditions, the statutes foresaw three groups of members. *Numeraries* are celibate. They must be college graduates—or on their way to being college graduates—and also complete higher ecclesiastical studies. They usually live in Opus Dei centers, and are available to take on tasks of formation and government in the Work. *Oblates* also commit themselves to celibacy. They do not usually live in centers of Opus Dei, but rather with their relatives or wherever else is considered appropriate. They need not be college graduates nor undertake higher ecclesiastical studies. Their degree of availability for tasks of formation and for working in corporate or personal work apostolates varies with their personal circumstances and work. *Supernumeraries* do not make a commitment to celibacy. Whether single, married, or widowed, they use "their own family occupations and their professions as means of sanctification and apostolate."[24]

In addition to members, the statutes provide for cooperators of Opus Dei. They can be Catholics, other Christians, members of other religions, or nonbelievers. They support the activities of the Work spiritually and economically and benefit from the prayers of the members, the indulgences granted by the Holy See to cooperators, and the formational activities the Work offers them. Diocesan priests can also be cooperators. Some of them, called ecclesiastical assistants, may be asked to provide spiritual direction to members in places where there are no priests of the Work. Other secular and religious priests who collaborate in various ways receive a "letter of brotherhood." Finally, communities of contemplative religious men and women who pray for Opus Dei can be named cooperators.[25]

The decree of approval explicitly indicated that the members of the Work were not consecrated religious. But, in a way, it assimilated them to the religious by requiring both married and unmarried members to take private vows of poverty, chastity, and obedience, each according to his or her state. The Founder explained to his spiritual children that they would take these vows as they had done up to now, independent of the ceremonies that incorporated them into Opus Dei, whether for a period of time or for life.

Escrivá was confident that definitive approval would end the misunderstandings Opus Dei had endured. Instead, he encountered new problems. It all began when several Italians students, who had met members of the Work living in the *Pensionato*, joined the Work. The father of one of them, Umberto Farri, was upset by his son's decision and consulted a Jesuit who warned him against the Work Mr. Farri, together with three other parents with children in Opus Dei, sent a letter to Pope Pius XII on April 25, 1951. They complained that their children had grown distant from their families and had not discussed with their spiritual directors their decision to join the Work. They asked the Holy Father to intervene so that their children would return to their former ways and make a final decision only after consulting learned and experienced priests.[26]

It was a difficult moment because the Work had only recently received the Holy See's definitive approval. In addition, the Founder was away from Rome, presiding over the first General Congress of Opus Dei's men's branch, which took place in Spain from May 1 to 5. His reaction upon returning to the Eternal City was above all to pray. On May 14, he consecrated Opus Dei and the families of its members to the Holy Family, praying that the discord would end. Within a few months, the families withdrew their complaint.

In the summer, a more serious problem arose. Escrivá had begun to notice a "change in some people in the Curia. One day a slightly critical comment reached his ear. Then a cardinal whom he had known well for a long time denied in public that he had ever had any dealings with him."[27] The Founder decided to seek the intercession of the Blessed Virgin. On August 15, he celebrated Mass in the Holy House at the Shrine of Loreto. At the end of Mass, he consecrated Opus Dei to the Most Sweet Heart of Mary. Over the course of the next two months, he renewed the consecration at the Marian shrines of Pompeii, Divino Amore, Lourdes, Zaragoza, and Fatima. He prayed to Our Lady, repeating frequently the aspiration *Cor Mariae dulcissimum, iter para tutum!* (Sweetest heart of Mary, prepare us a safe way!).

In September, Cardinal Schuster, Archbishop of Milan, warned members of the Work living in his diocese that the Work faced a serious difficulty. He had heard accusations of promiscuity among the members and of being too quick to recruit people.[28] A few days later, at Escrivá's direction, the members in Milan told the cardinal about the gossip and accusations they had suffered in Spain a decade earlier.

Four months later, in January 1952, the Congregation for Religious asked for "a copy of the Constitutions of Opus Dei and the internal regulations of the Administration, with a doctrinal and practical written report on the governance of the Institute's two Sections and the concrete ways in which the unprecedented collaboration between them is carried out." The request showed that the congregation had doubts about the relationship between the two sections of the Work and, specifically, about the Administration of the men's houses. Within twenty-four hours, Del Portillo sent a report detailing the strict separation that existed in the governance and in the activities of the two sections of the Work. In the report, he expressed his surprise that the congregation should request texts which it undoubtedly already had, since it had approved them only a year and a half earlier.

Later that month, the Cardinal-Archbishop of Milan told the members who were starting Opus Dei in his diocese that "reading the history of God's works and the lives of their founders, he had been struck by how the Lord always allowed opposition and persecutions. He pointed out that some new institutions had be subjected to official inspections by the Holy See and some founders had been removed as the superiors of the institutions they had founded."[29] He diplomatically suggested that the underlying motive for the crude accusation of promiscuity was rejection of the unity of men and women under one head and the desire to remove the Founder and then dismember the two sections of Opus Dei.

In February, Cardinal Schuster spoke for the third time with the members of the Work. He asked them to tell Monsignor Escrivá to remember "his countryman St. Joseph of Calasanz,"[30] who had been deposed as superior general of the Piarists, which he had founded. Escrivá immediately spoke with the secretary of the Congregation for Religious, who confirmed, without giving names, that some people in the Curia were attacking the statutes of Opus Dei. Then he went to Msgr. Federico Tedeschini, who was the cardinal protector of Opus Dei.[31]

On March 18, 1952, Pope Pius XII received Cardinal Tedeschini in audience. The prelate read him a letter from Escrivá in which he expressed his sorrow at the attacks on Opus Dei and asked that "these denunciations be made known to us openly, with concrete evidence."[32] He added that if at any point the separation between the two sections was not clear, he would be happy to modify the Internal Regulations for Administrations. As he read the letter, the cardinal stressed that a modification of its legal structure would discredit Opus Dei. Pius XII responded, *Chi pensa a quello?* (Who is thinking about that?)[33] Since he did not wish to take any action, the Pope limited himself to approving that the Founder revise the Regulations for the Administration of the centers.[34]

A few months later, on October 26, 1952, the Founder consecrated Opus Dei to the Sacred Heart of Jesus. Under the invocation *Cor Iesu sacratissimum, dona nobis pacem!* (Most Sacred Heart of Jesus, give us peace!), he asked for peace: inner peace for each member, peace so that Opus Dei could spread everywhere without further opposition, and peace for the world.

About this time, Archbishop Luigi Traglia, the viceregent of Rome (the principal assistant to the Cardinal Vicar of Rome), reminded Escrivá of the Italian maxim *Bisogna fare il morto per non essere ammazzato* (You need to play dead to avoid being killed). The Founder thanked him and took the suggestion to heart. He continued to maintain appropriate relations with the Holy See and with the Italian authorities, but avoided public appearances. Concretely, he did not attend official events or receptions at the Spanish Embassy

Escrivá with Juan Jiménez Vargas at the sanctuary of Cerro de los Angeles outside Madrid in 1933. Vargas, one of the first members of Opus Dei, played a crucial role in supporting and protecting the Founder during the Spanish Civil War. He would eventually become a professor of physiology and the founding dean of the School of Medicine of the University of Navarra.

Residents on the terrace of the DYA academy-student residence in Madrid in May 1936. DYA was the first collective activity of Opus Dei.

The first members of Opus Dei were university students or graduates who embraced celibacy and tried to spread the Christian message to friends, fellow students, and colleagues. Early members at the Jenner Residence in Madrid in 1940: Isidoro Zorzano, the oldest member of Opus Dei and the first to have a cause of canonization opened; Fernando Valenciano, a future member of Opus Dei's General Council; and Teodoro Ruiz Jusué who began Opus Dei's apostolic activities in Colombia.

Guadalupe Ortiz de Landázuri leading a seminar in Bilbao in 1947. In the mid-1940s, the first women members began taking responsibility for governmental and formational activities of the Work. They were pioneers in the adventure of transmitting its spirit.

An artisanal workshop for the fabrication of liturgical vestments, tapestries, and other decorative items established by women of Opus Dei on the grounds of Los Rosales Retreat House. Over time the weavers, embroiderers, and other artisans who worked there became highly skilled and began to contribute to the development of sacred art. Today the Rosales Artisanal Workshop forms part of Granda Liturgical Arts and is known worldwide for the quality of its products.

The participants in a course in Los Rosales, the first center of studies of the women's branch, celebrate the Holy See's 1947 approval of Opus Dei. Numerary and associate members attend each year a multi-week course which combines classes in philosophy and theology with a review of some aspects of the spirit of the Work and an opportunity to relax.

Juan Larrea, future Archbishop of Guayaquil, Ecuador, and Fernando Ocaso, who helped start Opus Dei in Japan, with St. Josemaria on the terrace of the Pensionato in Rome in 1951. The founder's move to Rome facilitated Opus Dei's international expansion as well as regular contact with the Holy See.

A 1952 class at Gaztalueta school in the outskirts of Bilbao (Spain). Gaztalueta, founded in 1951, was the first school started by members of Opus Dei. It laid stress on character development and adopted as its motto "Let your 'yes' be 'yes,' and your 'no' be 'no'." Gaztalueta adopted a system of individual mentoring which has come to characterize all schools connected with Opus Dei.

Five young women joined Opus Dei in Ireland before the first members of the Women's Branch came from Spain to the country. Four of them on a pilgrimage to the shrine of Knock in 1953: Eileen Maher, Olive Mulcahy, Máire Gibbons, and Teddy (Honoria) Burke.

The participants in a 1954 workshop outside a small chapel on the grounds of the Molinoviejo retreat house near Madrid. The Work offers supernumerary members a week-long residential course with classes on the spirit of Opus Dei, philosophy and theology. These courses are an opportunity to get to know other members better and to experience more deeply the family atmosphere of the Work.

Members of the Central Advisory in 1956 with the Founder's sister Carmen Escrivá de Balaguer y Albas (front row, right), who was living at the time in Rome. In the front row on the left, Blessed Guadalupe Ortiz de Landázuri who had recently been appointed to the Central Advisory. The Central Advisory helps the head of Opus Dei to direct the women's branch and its activities.

Associates during a formational course in the Estila Retreat House in Santiago de Compostela, Spain in 1957. Men and women associates live celibacy and carry out the entire gamut of professional activities.

A meeting of the editors of the Spanish family graphic magazine *La Actualidad Española* in January, 1958. The magazine began publication in 1952. It offered readers news and feature articles inspired by a Catholic outlook but without focusing on religious topics. It was quite successful in the 1960s, but in the 1970s it suffered the decline experienced by almost all graphic magazines.

Catherine Bardinet and Thérèse Truel in 1958 on a train bound for the French capital to begin the activities of the women's branch there. Paris's influence on world culture made the founder especially interested in spreading from there Opus Dei's message of sanctification in the midst of the world.

Olga Marlin (right), with a group of young African and Indian women in Nairobi, Kenya. Marlin was the first Regional Secretary of Opus Dei in Kenya. Opus Dei's establishment in Kenya, Japan, and Australia at the beginning of the 1960s gave it a presence on six continents.

A 1959 painting class at Montelar School of Homemaking and Art in Madrid. In the 1950s and 1960s, middle and upper class Spanish women were beginning to play a more active role in running their homes and felt the need for training. Schools of Homemaking and Art started by members of the women's branch offered them classes in home economics, cooking, child rearing, and art as well Christian formation and opportunities for volunteer social service.

Ernesto Cofiño (center with a sport coat) with a group of supernumeraries and cooperators at the end of a retreat in Altavista Retreat Center in Guatemala City in 1962. Cofiño was the first doctor to specialize in pediatrics in Guatemala. His cause of canonization has been opened.

in Rome. This seems to have reduced negative or scornful comments against Opus Dei and to have made it more difficult to associate it with Spain or its government. It also permitted Escrivá to devote more time to the formation of his sons and daughters and to the spread of the message he had received two decades earlier.

Another issue that could have affected the development of Opus Dei in unpredictable ways was a number of attempts to appoint Escrivá a bishop in the 1940s and first half of the 1950s. This possibility first arose in 1941, when the Founder became well-known in the ecclesiastical world, largely because of the spiritual exercises he preached and his dealings with many clergymen. People talked about him as a good candidate to cover a vacant diocese or to occupy some other important position in the Church. Escrivá was so opposed that he asked Bishop Eijo Garay for permission to take a vow not to accept being made a bishop, but the prelate refused his request.

The question appeared again in more concrete form in 1944. The Franco regime had the privilege of presenting to the Holy See a list of candidates for bishop. Both the minister of education and the nuncio in Spain raised the possibility of Escrivá's becoming the military vicar general. This might have had some advantages and would have been compatible with his continuing to direct Opus Dei. Álvaro del Portillo spoke about this possibility in Rome with Cardinal Lavitrano, the prefect of the Congregation for Religious, who in turn mentioned it to Pope Pius XII. Bishop Eijo Garay also supported the idea, but in the end nothing came of it.

In 1950, Escrivá again appeared on lists of names presented to the Holy See by the Spanish government to become the bishop of a dioceses or military vicar general. At the request of Cardinal Tedeschini, who wanted the Founder to become a bishop, Álvaro del Portillo discussed this possibility in the Madrid nunciature. Neither the nuncio nor the Spanish minister of foreign affairs favored the idea. Although again nothing came of them, these events gave a false impression of closeness between the Franco regime and the Founder which did not help his reputation in the Vatican.

Five years later, Tedeschini told Escrivá about the attempts to elevate him to the episcopacy that had been made up to that time. The Founder vigorously rejected the idea of being ordained bishop. He went to the Secretariat of State and told Bishop Antonio Samorè and Monsignor Domenico Tardini, soon to be cardinal secretary of state, that he would not accept appointment even as archbishop of Toledo, the primate of Spain.[35] This definitively put an end to any thought of making him a bishop.

Notes

1. Letter 31, no. 6, AGP A.3, 94-2-2.
2. See Méndiz, pp. 166–176.
3. Pius XII, apostolic constitution *Provida Mater Ecclesia. De statibus canonicis institutisque saecularibus christianae perfectionis adquirendae*, February 2, 1947, in AAS 39 (1947), p. 114. Shortly thereafter, two other papal documents were promulgated—the Motu proprio *Primo feliciter* (March 12, 1948) and the Instruction *Cum Sanctissimus* (March 19, 1948)—which insisted on secularity as the distinctive mark of secular institutes.
4. See AGP L.1.1, 7-2-2, which contains a bound copy of the *Laudis Decretum* and the *Constitutiones Societatis Sacerdotalis Sanctae Crucis et Operis Dei*.
5. Decree *Primum institutum*, February 24, 1947, AGP L.1.1, 7-2-2.
6. Handwritten report, January 9, 1943, AGP L.1.1, 1-3-8.
7. Letter 23, no. 36, AGP A.3, 93-3-3.
8. Josemaría Escrivá de Balaguer, *Escritos varios (1927–1974)*, edición crítico-histórica (Madrid:Rialp, 2018), pp. 182–184, 189. The text of the lecture was original published in the *Boletín de la Asociación Católica Nacional de Propagandistas*, 25, no. 427 (January 15, 1949), pp. 1–5.
9. See AGP A.3, 87-7-7; Minute book of the General Council (September 24, 1947), pp. 23–27, AGP E.1.2.
10. *Catechism*, 1st ed. (1947), no. 7. AGP E.1.1, 181-1-3.
11. See AGP Q.1.7, 9-50.
12. See AGP E.2.2, 171-3 and 171-4. The first Work Week was the Study Week of 1940, which was held in three sessions. The second Work Week had been held during the summer of 1943. See AGP E.2.2, 171-2-1; and

interview of the authors with Fernando Valenciano Polack, Rome, December 14, 2017.

13. See Diario del viaje exploratorio por América, AGP M.2.1, 23-1-1.

14. See Diario de Juan Bravo, October 25, 1949, AGP U.2.2, D-1012.

15. "Opus Dei: Reglamento interno de la Administración," Rome, March 19,1947, AGP Q.1.7, 1-5. The first printed edition of these regulations is dated February 14, 1950.

16. Víctor García Hoz, *Tras las huellas del beato Josemaría Escrivá de Balaguer* (Madrid: Rialp, 1997), p. 35.

17. See Luis Cano, "Los primeros supernumerarios del Opus Dei: La convivencia de 1948," *Studia et Documenta* 12 (2018), pp. 251–302.

18. See "Report on the Current State of the Opus Dei Secular Institute." AGP L.1.1, 11-3-5.

19. Letter 20, no. 148, AGP A.3, 95-3-1.

20. See "Statuto riguardante i Sodali Sacerdoti diocesani della Società Sacerdotale della Santa Croce," June 2, 1950, AGP L.1.1, 12-1-6; and Lucas F. Mateo-Seco and Rafael Rodríguez-Ocaña, *Sacerdotes en el Opus Dei: secularidad, vocación y ministerio* (Pamplona: EUNSA, 1994).

21. Decree *Primun inter*, no. 7. See also Letter of Álvaro del Portillo to the members of the General Council, January 31, 1947, AGP L 1.1, 8-1-5; and Fuenmayor, Gómez-Iglesias, and Illanes, *Itinerario Jurídico*.

22. *Constitutiones Societatis Sacerdotalis Sanctae Crucis et Operis Dei* (1950), no. 4, §2. AGP L1.1, 12-3-2.

23. *Constitutiones Societatis Sacerdotalis Sanctae Crucis et Operis Dei* (1950), no. 64. AGP L1.1, 12-3-2.

24. *Constitutiones Societatis Sacerdotalis Sanctae Crucis et Operis Dei* (1950), no. 27, §1. AGP L1.1, 12-3-2. The constitutions stated that numeraries were members of the secular institute in the strict sense. Escrivá said that he had to accept this legal classification but that the vocation was the same for everyone.

25. *Constitutiones Societatis Sacerdotalis Sanctae Crucis et Operis Dei* (1950), nos. 13–29. AGP L1.1, 12-3-2.

26. See AGP A.1, 53-1-2.

27. Andrés Vázquez de Prada, *The Founder of Opus Dei*, vol. 3, *The Divine Ways on Earth* (New York: Scepter, 2005), p. 140.

28. Among other things, the prelate commented to them bluntly: "Mi hanno detto della vita che non era tanto limpida" (I've been told your life isn't as clean as it should be). Report by Juan Udaondo on the visit to Cardinal Schuster, Milan, September 22, 1951, AGP A.1, 52-2-1.

29. Report by Juan Udaondo on the visit to Cardinal Schuster, Milan, August 15, 1951, AGP A.1, 52-2-3. That Opus Dei had two sections united institutionally was a privilege, since only by exception were secular institutes with men and women approved. See Fuenmayor, Gómez-Iglesias, and Illanes, pp. 317–318).

30. Letter 31, no. 44, AGP A.3, 94-2-2.

31. For centuries "cardinal protectors" had been appointed to defend within the Curia the interests of institutions or countries. Opus Dei had four cardinal protectors: Luigi Lavitrano, from May 1947 to August 1950; Federico Tedeschini, from January 1951 to November 1959; Domenico Tardini, from December 1959 to July 1961; and Pietro Ciriaci, from October 1961 to December 1966. This ecclesiastical position was suppressed by the Holy See in April 1964, although some cardinals kept the title for a while longer. See AGP L.1.1, 17-2-2; AGP L.1.1, 17-2-3; AGP L.1.1, 17-2-4.

32. Letter from Josemaría Escrivá de Balaguer to Federico Tedeschini, Rome, March 12, 1952, AGP A.1, 52-2-7 The letter is also signed by the secretary general of Opus Dei, Álvaro del Portillo.

33. Handwritten report by Álvaro del Portillo, Rome, March 26, 1952, AGP 52-2-10.

34. The revised version of the Internal Regulations for the Administration, written in Spanish and Latin, is dated April 27, 1954 (see AGP Q.1.7, 1-7).

35. Handwritten report by Álvaro del Portillo, Rome, December 29, 1961, AGP 17-4-8.

PART III

Spreading throughout the World
(1950–1962)

As the second half of the twentieth century began, the international scene was dominated by the Cold War, a struggle for political, military, and economic supremacy between the two great powers that won had the Second World War. The United States and the Soviet Union clashed indirectly on the terrain of allied countries—for example, in the Korean War (1950–1953)—and in a relentless arms race, which involved the manufacture of thousands of nuclear warheads.

Thanks to the economic power of the United States, Western countries recovered from the devastation of the global conflict and experienced rapid economic development. The Treaty of Rome (1957) created the European Economic Community, composed initially of Belgium, France, Germany, Italy, Luxembourg, and the Netherlands.

The United States also set the tone for popular culture in the West. Television became widespread. In addition to jazz, rock and roll dominated the music scene, with figures like Chuck Berry and Elvis Presley. Teenagers began to play an important role in the economy as consumers.

For its part, the bloc of dictatorial communist regimes—led by Soviet Russia and united militarily since 1955 by the Warsaw Pact—did not establish the egalitarian society it promised, despite its tight control over the population. Nevertheless, the intellectual and social influence of communism spread. In 1959, Fidel Castro's Cuban revolution triumphed.

During these years, the papacy of Pius XII enjoyed great prestige. The world saw in the Church a solid institution. Evangelization proceeded at an unprecedented pace, thanks in part to the many people who embraced the priestly and religious state in Western Europe and North and South America. Pius XII was the first pontiff with a major presence in the audiovisual media.

In the academic sphere, Catholic intellectuals lamented the growing separation between science and religion, manifested in the more aggressive forces of secularization, which sought to banish faith and religious practices from the public sphere. In the Soviet Union, its European satellites, China, and other countries with totalitarian communist systems, thousands of Christians martyrs bore witness to their faith. Often this repression was hidden from the eyes of those who formed and influenced international public opinion.

CHAPTER 8

Organization of Opus Dei

Opus Dei had received the definitive approval of the Holy See, but now the Founder and his spiritual sons and daughters faced new challenges, both in developing the structure of the institution and in spreading its message of holiness in ordinary working life to new countries and new environments.

It is not clear how many members Opus Dei had at the beginning of the 1950s perhaps somewhere between 500 and 1,000.[1] It had 23 priests and another 46 numeraries studying philosophy and theology. It had seven districts. The region of Spain was by far the most developed. It had centers in Madrid, Valencia, Barcelona, Valladolid, Bilbao, Seville, Córdoba, and Santiago de Compostela, and had two study centers, one for women and another for men, and two retreat houses.

Section 1. The Work as a Family

As part of the Church, the members of Opus Dei formed and felt part of the great Christian family. Moreover, they were deeply united among themselves by their awareness of having received the same divine call to be and to do Opus Dei. In Escrivá's words, the members of the Work were united by "supernatural bonds," by "bonds stronger than those of blood."[2] He wanted life in Opus Dei to reflect the life of the Holy Family of Nazareth. He envisioned the Work as a close-knit Christian family with relationships of parenthood, sonship, and brotherhood, marked by a love he liked to describe as "the warmth of a home."[3]

The Founder embodied spiritual fatherhood. He radiated great faith in God, love for his children, and charm, united to determination to carry out the Work. He did not hesitate to show them his love and his concern that they be happy and healthy:

> I love you because you are God's children, because you have freely decided to be my children, because you try to be holy, because you are very faithful and *muy majos* [great guys]: All my children are great guys. I love you with the same affection that your mothers feel for you. I love you with your bodies and your souls, with your virtues and your defects.[4]

The members responded to the Founder's fatherhood with a strong sense of being his sons and daughters. The people of Opus Dei combined closeness to the Father with the respect due him as founder and priest. After he moved to Rome, it was no longer possible for most people in the Work to see him often, so they sent him personal letters. Escrivá encouraged all the members of the Work to write to him directly whenever they wanted.

The central directors of the Work dealt with him personally every day, both in the office and in family life. The other people who lived in Villa Tevere had less contact with him, but saw him quite frequently in meditations and circles and in informal family gatherings they called *tertulias* (get-togethers). There they spoke about everything. He went seamlessly and with complete naturalness from talking about some recent event or something that had happened to him that morning to talking about the Blessed Virgin or the Trinity. In these informal get-togethers, members of the Work learned its spirit while relaxing and having a good time. The person who kept the diary of Villa Tevere in 1950 describes them as "gatherings in which we are filled with enthusiasm and in which we also have a lot of fun and laughter."[5]

Those who lived with Escrivá in Villa Tevere witnessed his energy in promoting Opus Dei and undertaking new projects. They often heard him speak passionately about God and the Work. They understood why he defined himself as "a man in love with God, with Christ's most holy humanity," and what he meant when he spoke about "courting" and "serenading" God, about singing to God songs of human love, about God's "pampering" and "caressing" us.[6] Escrivá warmly loved his sons and daughters in Opus Dei and, at the same time, demanded the best of them. He reprimanded them when necessary, but he tried hard to avoid their being hurt.

He often reminded them that the important thing in Opus Dei was doing well many small things that no one would notice: fulfilling their everyday duties and keeping to their schedule, working well, being joyful and kind to others, and taking care of the house. One day in a get-together in December 1950, he said that "although there had been many extraordinary events in the history the Work, the main thing is not that, but that each of us fulfill lovingly our small tasks and obligations."[7]

Few knew that he needed daily insulin injections to control acute diabetes that caused frequent headaches, vision problems, and circulatory issues. On April 27, 1954, the Feast of Our Lady of Montserrat, Álvaro del Portillo administered his dose of insulin. Shortly thereafter, Escrivá went into anaphylactic shock. He felt he was dying, asked Del Portillo to give him sacramental absolution, and immediately lost consciousness. He recovered from the attack, and his doctor found that he had been inexplicably cured of diabetes. Although he would suffer for the rest of his life from some consequences of diabetes, especially kidney insufficiency, he did not need insulin anymore.

Although Escrivá's sister Carmen never became a member of the Work, since 1939 she had helped her brother create a family in Opus Dei, dedicating her life to working in the Administration of various centers. She moved to Rome in 1952. There she met "nephews" and "nieces" from many countries. She was concerned about their health, sent them pastries and candy especially on feast days, and went for walks or day trips with them to give them a chance to rest. She also frequently accompanied the women when they did the shopping. Her "nieces and nephews" responded to her affection, treating her with love, respect, and gratitude for her generous dedication to Opus Dei.[8] In March 1957, she was diagnosed with liver cancer. She faced her illness with serenity and a Christian spirit, closely accompanied by her brother, Álvaro del Portillo, and Encarnación Ortega. She died on June 20 and was buried in the crypt of Villa Tevere. Although deeply moved, the Founder offered this loss to God. He attributed to God the conviction he had from the first moment that his sister was in heaven.

The Founder urged all the members of the Work, whether single or married, to cultivate a deep and practical sense of being brothers and sisters, a sense that would color their entire lives. He was not content with general exhortations but insisted on the importance of specific manifestations of fraternity such as spending time together in informal get-togethers, celebrating birthdays, making sure that others got enough rest, and taking care of the sick. This, he underlined, was an essential element of the spirit of Opus Dei: "The day you live like strangers or are unconcerned about the others, you will have killed Opus Dei!"[9]

Escrivá wanted the members of the Work to take seriously Jesus' exhortation to correct one another, and he fashioned a specific, practical way for them to put fraternal correction into practice. When a member thought that some habit of another member was contrary to the spirit of the Work, he should ask the local director if the habit was worth correcting and if this was a good time to do so. He should then take the other member aside and tell him face-to-face, with charity but clearly, that he needed to try to improve in that area. Escrivá didn't want to be deprived himself of this sort of help, so he established that the president general of the Work should have two *custodes* (guardians), who would live with him. One would help him in his spiritual life and the other would focus on his health and other external aspects of his life. In 1952 he named Álvaro del Portillo and Francisco Vives as his *custodies*. In 1956, Javier Echevarría replaced Vives.

From the earliest days of the Work, Escrivá was concerned about fostering unity by keeping the members informed about what the others were doing and what was happening in various places. During the summer vacations of 1934 and 1935, when the students who came to DYA were scattered all over the country, he put together a typewritten newsletter called *Noticias* (News Items) with information about the comings and goings and activities of the students as well as brief spiritual comments. This not only kept them informed about each other's doings but helped them feel like active participants in a joint project. He did something similar during the final months of the

Spanish Civil War and the immediate postwar period (March 1938–September 1939).

The idea was taken up again in 1948, when the General Council began publishing a monthly *Hoja informativa* (Information Sheet) for the men's branch. The Central Advisory Board followed suit for the women's branch in 1950. These publications were still typewritten, amateur affairs, but they were more developed than the earlier efforts. Each month's issue opened with a few words from Escrivá. The letters and articles with information about the development of the Work in the countries of Europe and America were generally longer than the very brief news items of *Noticias*. Some issues offered ascetical commentaries about how to live the customs of Opus Dei.

A major step forward in quality took place in 1954 with the first issue of *Crónica* (Chronicle) for the men's branch and *Noticias* (News) for the women's branch. These monthly publications were typeset, printed, and bound in the small print shop that the women's branch had established in Villa Tevere for internal documents and writings of the Founder. The men's branch also began a bimonthly publication for cooperators and other friends called *Obras* (Undertakings).

The magazines opened with some words of the Founder, followed by an essay on a topic connected with the spiritual life or the apostolate. The bulk of the magazines was made up of articles about people and apostolic activities of Opus Dei. Three more or less fixed sections were built around photographs. *Album antiguo* offered photos from the early days of the Work. *De Villa Tevere* had photos of the Work's headquarters. *Nos han enviado una foto* (They sent us a photo) featured members of the Work working in diverse professions and environments.

Singing in the get-togethers was another element of unity. Sometimes they sang traditional tunes like "*Madre en la puerta hay un niño*," a Christmas carol the Founder's mother had sung to her children when they were young. *Tan buen ganadico* by the fifteenth-century poet and composer Juan de la Encina reminded them of the role of the Father as shepherd of Opus Dei. Other times they sang songs the Founder had encouraged Luis Borobio, Jesús Urteaga, and Alfredo García to write at the end of the nineteen-forties. Most had lively lyrics and melodies, and referred to the development of the Work or aspects of its spirit. They referred to these songs as "Songs of the Work." Escrivá sometimes described them as songs of "human love with a divine meaning" because they moved him to pray.

Section 2. The Administration of the Centers

The Founder wanted the women of the Work to carry out all kinds of work in society, just as the men did. By the 1950s, female oblates and supernumeraries could be found working in a wide range of jobs and professions. Women numeraries, however, because of the needs of the growth of Opus Dei, worked mostly in government and formation tasks, in the care of Administrations, and in the direction of corporate apostolates such as student residences, retreat houses, home schools, and farms for women farmers.[10] In this section, we will focus on women who worked in the Administration of centers and particularly on those who became numerary assistants, or as they were called at the time, numerary servants.

In Spain and many other countries at similar levels of economic and social development, young women from small towns and rural areas often sought work in the cities in domestic service. The message of Opus Dei about the search for sanctity through daily work reached them through residential internships in the Administrations of the residences promoted by the Work. There they receive practical training in the activities of the home as well as general education, where necessary including literacy and other basic skills. They covered their tuition and expenses with their part-time work. As was common at the time, many were minors who attended the boarding school with their parents' permission. Recruiting for these programs was carried out through families in each town who already knew about the programs and through parish priests, some of whom belonged to the Priestly Society of the Holy Cross.[11]

Another forum for the professional, human, and religious development of domestic workers was the so-called "Sunday schools." Oblate and supernumerary young women gave classes in reading, writing, arithmetic, cooking, cleaning, laundry, sewing, and dressmaking for a couple of hours, twice a week—generally on Sundays and one working day—at times compatible with the employee's work in hotels and private homes. The students paid a small fee. Those who were interested also received a class of religion given by a priest of the Work and were offered the possibility of having spiritual direction. The first Sunday Schools were held in Los Rosales and Molinoviejo conference centers, but soon they began to function in large cities, generally in the area of the Administration of residences and in premises lent by cooperators of Opus Dei. They were especially successful in Spain. By 1961 there were two schools each in Barcelona, Bilbao, and Madrid, and one in Córdoba, Granada, Seville, and Valencia.[12]

Many young women valued the opportunity to work (whether as interns or full-time employees) in the Administration of a center rather than in a private family home, a hotel, or a restaurant, since it gave them more opportunity to grow professionally, educationally, and socially. They also came to understand that although their work was not socially prestigious, it had great value and should be considered a very worthwhile profession. They were impressed by the fact that the administrators, "ladies," as they were called at the time, who came from well-to-do families and had high school diplomas, made an effort to adapt to their intellectual and social level and treated them with great respect and courtesy.*

Some of these women who worked as cooks, cleaners, laundresses, and the like joined Opus Dei because they came to understand that working to create a home for the members who lived in the center would allow them to unite a specific call to holiness with service to people.

---

* Marta Cojolón, the first assistant numerary in Guatemala, remembered the impression she got from the treatment she and her friends received from one of the numeraries who went to start Opus Dei in her country: "I don't know how to explain it, but I saw that that Spanish lady didn't make distinctions, nor did she treat us differently because we were indigenous." Quoted in Antonio Rodríguez Pedrazuela, *Un mar sin orillas: El trabajo del Opus Dei en Centroamérica*, 5th ed. (Madrid: Rialp, 2002), p. 144.

Like other colleagues from similar social backgrounds, many of them had become familiar with these tasks in their parents' home, or in private homes. The discovery of a vocation to Opus Dei added a transcendent dimension to their lives and a concrete way of manifesting their motherly heart. Their donation to God in celibacy, sustained by a life of personal piety and the care of the people of the Work and of those who participated in the center's activities, illuminated their lives with meaning. They believed Escrivá when he told them that their dedication shaped the Work as a family and that their profession was a model of dedication to God in daily tasks.*

The first summer course, or annual course for numerary servants, was held in Los Rosales in 1951. Also at that time, a center of studies for them began in Molinoviejo. The course lasted six months and covered three areas. First, professional training, with classes on cooking, house cleaning, and laundry. Second, spiritual formation, both in the faith and practice of Christian virtues and in the spirit of Opus Dei. Finally, cultural formation, so that all would learn to read and write well, and would have a foundation in geography and arithmetic. Once they completed the center of studies, the students usually went to work in the Administration of large centers like student residents and retreat houses, where they could easily develop their skills.[13]

Regions other than Spain gradually established centers of studies for numerary assistants. This was facilitated by being able to use the facilities of conference centers, called retreat houses at the time, which necessarily had a large area for the Administration. The number of retreat houses had grown rapidly since 1955, when the central government of the Work had asked all the regions to build one as soon as possible. Experience had demonstrated that having appropriate

---

* As we will see, decades later there were women in the Administration with middle and higher studies, since the social origin or the type of studies carried out do not configure the vocation of the numerary servants, called assistant numeraries from 1966. In this sense, the circumstances of the 1940s and 1950s were happily modified in society and the Church, and therefore also in Opus Dei.

premises would help people of Opus Dei and those who participated in formative activities like retreats and workshops to feel immersed in the family atmosphere of the Work.

In the 1950s, in most countries, little professional training was available for people who wanted to pursue careers in home economics or areas such as running catering or other hospitality services. Not surprisingly, therefore, the administrators of Opus Dei centers mostly learned on the job. Over time, however, they began to have more opportunities to learn accounting, direction of work teams, and personnel management.

The services the Administrations were able to provide were much improved when they began to centralize purchasing, which permitted obtaining wholesale prices. In 1954, the women of the Work in the Madrid area began an incipient centralized purchasing service in the area of the Lagasca Administration. The Gestoría, as they called it, purchased food and later laundry and cleaning products in bulk and then distributed them among the men's and women's centers.[14]

Later, the idea of wholesale purchases was followed in Barcelona, Seville, Valencia, and Valladolid, cities that were home to delegations of Opus Dei. In Pamplona it began in 1962 under the name of DECEPAL, serving the University of Navarra and the University Clinic. Years later, the model was copied in regions where the Work was more developed. For example, in Mexico City, a centralized service attended to the purchase of groceries and laundry for all the Administrations.

Section 3. The "Battle of Formation"

At the beginning of the 1950s, the Work was growing by leaps and bounds. The few hundred members of the previous decade had become something like a thousand. They were present in a dozen countries and were carrying out a wide range of activities. It was essential to insure that all these people spread over such a large area come to know well the Church's doctrine and the spirit of Opus Dei. Escrivá stressed that, "without adequate formation, we can do nothing.

Holiness and apostolate: these are the aims we set ourselves corporately. And to achieve these ends, we need formation. For our holiness, doctrine. For the apostolate, doctrine. And for doctrine, time, in the right place, with the right means."*

The Founder sometimes used a military metaphor when talking about formation. He said that Opus Dei had won the ascetical and theological battle in 1943, when the Church had confirmed its spirituality, the call to holiness in the secular sphere, by granting its *nihil obstat* for the erection of the Priestly Society of the Holy Cross within the lay body of Opus Dei. In 1950, it had won the legal battle with the approval of the entire social phenomenon: Opus Dei and the Priestly Society of the Holy Cross as an institute of pontifical right, with a centralized regime and the ability to have priests of its own. Now, however, it was engaged in a battle of formation; that is, the institutional effort to teach its members the Christian faith and the spirit of the Work in depth, so that they could "put into practice the specific aim of Opus Dei by example, by doctrine and by work."[15] Their incarnating the charism in its fullness would make it possible for it to be spread in its entirety.

As the Founder saw it, the formation Opus Dei offered had multiple aspects: human (primarily the natural virtues), professional, doctrinal-religious, spiritual, and apostolic. It was also given in many different ways: personally through spiritual direction, confession, and fraternal correction, and collectively through meditation, talks, classes, circles, days of recollection, retreats, and workshops. Formation in Opus Dei took place throughout the entire lifetime of the members because they had to assimilate it and incorporate it into the ever-changing circumstances of their lives. For that reason, he said, "it never ends."[16]

---

* Josemaría Escrivá, Meditation, November 21, 1954, quoted in *Meditations*, vol. 3, p. 449. AGP Library, P06. According to the founder of the Work, the three "dominant passions" of the members of Opus Dei are "to give doctrine, to direct in one way or another the souls that come to the warmth of our apostolates, and to love the unity of the Work." Recollections of Cipriano Rodríguez Santa María, Manizales, August, 1975, AGP A.5, 344-1-2. Rodríguez heard Escrivá say this in April or May 1958.

In 1951, Escrivá established the *Studium generale*, Opus Dei's instructional arm that offered university level theological studies in the Work's centers of studies and during annual courses.* He also approved a Plan of Studies, which laid out the curriculum for the undergraduate level philosophy and theology courses that all the numeraries of the men's branch would take (two years of philosophy and four years of theology.) The curriculum was patterned on that of the pontifical athenaeums and universities in Rome. In addition, the numerary priests would have periodic review exams in ecclesiastical subjects, would have to pass a series of exams to renew their licenses to celebrate the sacraments, and would attend monthly sessions on moral and liturgical subjects.

In 1955 he approved a similar plan of studies for the numeraries of the women's branch, with one year of philosophy and four of theology. The numerary servants would receive systematic instruction in Catholic teaching and doctrine appropriate to their background and education as well as classes of general culture.[17]

Classes were given in regional and interregional centers of studies. The regional centers of studies were organized and supervised by the regional commissions and advisories.[18] Interregional centers of studies welcomed students from various regions and were overseen by the General Council or the Central Advisory. They were intended for the training of future professors in the regional centers of studies, people who would work in government positions within the Work, and future priests.

---

*The *Studium generale* is the organism within Opus Dei responsible for the philosophical and theological training of the faithful of the Work. It is a specialized university-level institution which has faculty members and students but no campus of its own. It provides instruction in the interregional and regional centers of studies. Each region that is sufficiently developed creates its own *Studium generale*. The regional vicar with his respective councils appoints the professors from among the members of the Work who have the appropriate academic degree. The *Studium generale* does not itself grant degrees, but its classes are usually recognized by degree-granting ecclesiastical educational entities. See *Constitutiones Societatis Sacerdotalis Sanctae Crucis et Operis Dei*, 1950, nos. 127–142; and *Codex iuris particularis Operis Dei*, 1982, nos. 96–107.

The first interregional center of studies, Diego de León in Madrid, was followed by two interregional centers of studies in Rome, one for men and one for women. On June 29, 1948, Escrivá erected the Roman College of the Holy Cross for men, and named del Portillo its rector. Over the years, many people from all over the world have come to the Roman College to complete their four-year theological studies and to obtain their master's degree and doctorate in theology, canon law or ecclesiastical philosophy at a pontifical university. Studying in Rome helped the members of the Work grow in love for the Church and the Pope, and, until Escrivá's death in 1975, to learn the spirit of Opus Dei from the lips of the Founder. Escrivá invited some of the students to become priests and serve the Church with their ministry, particularly in the pastoral activities of Opus Dei. He saw the Roman College as "the *instrument of instruments*, to *romanize the Work* and keep it united"[19] and sometimes referred to it as "the apple of my eye."[20]

The Roman College of the Holy Cross began classes in October 1948 with ten students, four of whom enrolled in the Pontifical Athenaeum Angelicum. By 1950 there were twenty students, and two years later, forty. In 1953, the number of students jumped to 120. They came from Spain, Ireland, Italy, Mexico, and Portugal. In addition to studying, they helped supervise the construction of new buildings in what had been the garden of Villa Tevere. Space was so short that they slept in three-level bunk beds. To add to the crowding, many Italian and foreign friends of the students visited Villa Tevere.[21]

Despite all these limitations, in 1956, sixty students earned doctorates in one or another of the pontifical universities. The Roman College assured Opus Dei a steady flow of newly ordained priests as well as trained regional and local directors and professors for the regional centers of studies. Whatever role they played, the alumni contributed decisively to the unity and universal vision of the members of the Work.

A system of scholarships was established by the general administration office to subsidize the students of the Roman College of the Holy Cross. The general principle was that each region should pay for the students it sent to Rome, but Spain, which had more resources, was asked to help support those whose region could not pay their expenses.

To alleviate the effects of serious overcrowding during the school year, Álvaro del Portillo sought a summer home for the young people of the Roman College. In 1952, he bought, with financing from the seller, Marquis Giovanni Bisleti, a two-thousand-acre (eight hundred hectare) farm located on the Mediterranean shore about sixty miles (ninety-six kilometers) south of Rome, near the town of Terracina. They called the property Salto di Fondi, taking the name from a nearby village. A small part of the land was reserved for the summer home of the Roman College. The rest was divided into parcels and offered for sale on favorable terms to the three hundred peasant families that had worked the land. This made it possible for the former landless laborers to become small landowners. Their payments, although small, provided a bit of income to the Work, and some of the produce of the land was used to feed the people living in Villa Tevere.

Carmen and Santiago Escrivá moved to Italy in the summer of 1952. Carmen oversaw domestic services at Salto di Fondi during the first academic year. During the following summer the students of the Roman College and the women of the Work took turns using Salto di Fondi for a few weeks of rest and classes.

The Roman College of Holy Mary for women was erected by Escrivá on December 12, 1953. This center, like the Roman College of the Holy Cross, aimed to strengthen the students' personal union with God, increase their love for the Church and the Pope, strengthen the unity in Opus Dei, and contribute to the transmission of its message throughout the world. Specifically, it would prepare women to become professors in the centers of study and directors of the Work and its corporate activities. Offering women advanced theological instruction was a pioneering move on Escrivá's part. The pontifical universities would not allow women access to their ecclesiastical schools until 1965.

In 1954 seven students enrolled in the Roman College of Santa Maria. They came from Spain, Ireland, Italy, and Mexico. Space was so limited that there could only be one small group at a time. It was urgent to have trained women in the regions. During the first five years, therefore, students stayed for a maximum of one eight-month course. They then returned to their region or went to help start Opus Dei somewhere else, thereby making room for a new group.

In July 1959, the Roman College of Holy Mary ceased operations at the Villa Tevere headquarters. A few months later, a $170,000 construction project began to adapt Villa delle Rose, a retreat house in Castel Gandolfo that Opus Dei had used since 1949, to be the home of the Roman College of Holy Mary. On February 14, 1963, Escrivá celebrated Mass in the new location. A few days later an inaugural class given by Amadeo de Fuenmayor, professor of civil law, marked the resumption of classes.[22]

In accordance with the directives of the Holy See, the Founder indicated that in classes in the interregional and regional centers of studies professors should follow the principles and doctrine of St. Thomas Aquinas. At the same time, he defended each individual's freedom to form his own opinions as long as they did not contradict the teachings of the Church. To protect this freedom, he forbade defending or promoting collectively a particular philosophical, theological, or canonical school of thought.

The "battle of the formation" was fought not only in Rome but also in the regions. The regional commissions and advisories progressively implemented the curriculum and appointed the corresponding professors and spiritual directors of the *Studium generale*. The first centers of studies were created in Spain (Diego de León for men, and Los Rosales and Molinoviejo for women), but they were followed by others in Argentina, Mexico, Colombia, the United States, Ireland, and Italy. For example, the women's branch opened a center of studies in Mexico City in 1955. A year later it inaugurated in Montefalco a year-long training course for numeraries who worked in the Administration.

Section 4. Moving the Central Government of Opus Dei to Rome

As Opus Dei grew numerically and spread geographically, it became increasingly important to create management teams, people who understood and practiced what Escrivá called the art "of governing by serving."[23] In a document he called *Instruction for Directors*, he set forth some of the principles and attitudes he wanted reflected in the governance of Opus Dei: "always having supernatural outlook, a sense of responsibility, love of other people's freedom (which requires listening to them!), love of one's own freedom, the conviction that government must be collegial, that the Directors can make mistakes, and that when they do, they are obliged to remedy the situation."[24]

The *Instruction for Directors* stressed that the directors should be aware that they needed to count on God's grace in carrying out the tasks entrusted to them. Therefore, government in the Work should be rooted in sincere piety and a desire to put into practice in one's own life the message of holiness and apostolate in the midst of the world.

Escrivá stressed that governing should be seen as a way of serving, not as an honor or a privilege. Directors need to help others become fully rounded persons. They are called to transmit the spirit of Opus Dei by word and example, and to be concerned about the physical health and spiritual well-being of each person entrusted to their care. Their work is usually hidden, involving decisions made by a group rather than individually. They should be detached from positions of government, not wanting to be appointed to them or to hold onto them, and not making themselves indispensable.

Government in Opus Dei should be approached as a professional job. Issues should be studied calmly in light of the spirit and law of the Work, keeping in mind the people affected. Directors should avoid both unnecessary delays and precipitate action. Escrivá reminded them that "urgent matters can wait, and very urgent matters must wait."[25]

Decisions in Opus Dei should be made by several people, not by an individual. Escrivá stressed that collegiality in this sense was an essential characteristic of governance in Opus Dei. He expressed abhorrence for what he called the "proprietary director" or "tyrannical director," who decided matters solely on the basis of his personal views. He urged those who were taking up a new position to avoid thinking that everything that had been done before needed to be changed immediately, and he warned against the danger of judging the effectiveness of undertakings solely on the basis of their immediate results.

As a way of implementing collegial government without wasting time in lengthy meetings, the *Instruction for Directors* established a practice that relied more on exchanging views in writing than in holding meetings. Each director involved in a particular matter should give his opinion in writing after gathering the necessary data and studying the issue. In many cases a decision could be reached without any meeting. If a meeting was needed, the participants would have information at hand and would know in advance how each director saw things.

For Opus Dei to function smoothly, it was essential that there be unity and trust among the directors that served at the central, regional, and local levels, and that each level take full responsibility for its own area of competence while recognizing its limits and respecting the freedom of those beneath it. Local and regional directors were urged to refer to the next higher level of government not only those questions that exceeded their competence but also decisions they had authority to take but on which they could not agree among themselves. When it was necessary to consult higher authorities, Escrivá warned against the temptation to leave out disagreeable facts or to sugarcoat things for fear of upsetting people or simply looking bad. He assured them that if issues were raised with transparency and simplicity, there was always time to change a poor decision or to improve a good one.

As we have seen, in 1949, in response to Opus Dei's growth and spread to new countries, the Founder established three levels of government: central, regional, and local. The central government was headed by the general president, who, according to the constitutions, had to be a priest. He was referred to as the Father. He governed with the General Council for men and the Central Advisory for women. On the most important matters, the approval of these bodies was required for a decision to be valid. At the regional level, there was a Regional Commission for men, presided over by a priest called the regional councilor, and a Regional Advisory, presided over by the woman who was the regional secretary. Finally, at the local level, the centers of Opus Dei were governed by a local council made up of a director, an assistant director, and a secretary.

To reinforce the unity of the Work, Escrivá created the position of regional delegate (designated in those years with the Latin term *missus*), who formed part of both the central and regional governing bodies. They spent most of their time in the region and tried to keep intimately informed about its situation and activities, but they traveled regularly to Rome and reported directly to the Father. If they felt a decision taken by the councilor with the Regional Council or the Regional Advisory was badly mistaken, they could suspend it and consult the General Council or the Central Advisory.

Because Escrivá wanted the women of Opus Dei to take full responsibility for leading the women's branch without being subordinated to men, he established that the regional secretary would preside over the meetings of the Regional Advisory. The councilor, as representative of the Father, and the priest secretary attended the meetings to facilitate the practical unity between the approaches and activities of the two sections.

For a number of years the General Council and the Central Advisory continued to be based in Madrid, because the majority of the members lived in Spain and a large part of the Work's international expansion was based there. Nonetheless, the president general (Escrivá) and the procurator general (Del Portillo) resided in Rome to facilitate communication with the Holy See and because Escrivá hoped that his living outside Spain would help quiet criticism of Opus Dei within the Church. This arrangement was awkward because it slowed decision-making and forced the Founder to travel frequently to Spain and spend much time corresponding with the directors there. It was not, however, a serious problem, since he knew he could trust the decisions made in his absence by the central directors.

In 1951, Escrivá proposed that the central governing bodies move to Rome. After consulting the electors, he decided to wait a little and, in the meantime, to live between the two cities, alternating two months in each place. It soon became apparent, however, that the need to be in touch with the Vatican made it impractical for Escrivá to spend much time in Madrid, so the secretary general, who was based in Madrid, and the procurator general, who was based in Rome, began to travel frequently between the two cities.

The Central Advisory moved to the Eternal City in the summer of 1953. The Founder and the outgoing Advisory appointed Encarnación Ortega as central secretary, Marisa Sánchez de Movellán as secretary of the Central Advisory, María del Carmen Tapia as vice-secretary of the Work of St. Michael, María José Monterde as vice secretary of the Work of St. Gabriel, Lourdes Toranzo as vice secretary of the Work of St. Raphael, Pilar Salcedo as prefect of studies, Gabriela Duclaud as prefect of servants, and Catherine Bardinet as procurator.[26]

At the end of August 1956, shortly after the second General Congress of Opus Dei, the General Council moved to Rome. Escrivá ratified the appointments of Álvaro del Portillo as secretary general; Giorgio De Filippi as procurator general; Severino Monzó as priest central secretary; Richard Rieman as vice secretary of St. Michael, Nuno Girão Ferreira as vice secretary of St. Gabriel; Bernardo Fernández Ardavín as vice secretary of St. Raphael; Julián Herranz Casado as prefect of studies; and Joaquín Alonso Pacheco as general administrator.[27]

Most of the members of the newly named General Council and Central Advisory were quite young—on average a little over thirty-five—and they had had little experience of government. The women came from Spain, France, and Mexico; the men from Spain,

Italy, Mexico, the United States, and Portugal. The Founder decided to appoint so many young, inexperienced people because he thought that serving in the central organs of government of the Work would prepare them to work later on regional commissions and advisories. Furthermore, he did not want to deprive Spain, which was so important for Opus Dei, of experienced directors.

At both the central and regional levels the various offices divided up work in the following fashion. The offices of the vice secretaries of St. Michael and St. Gabriel oversaw the incorporation of members and life in the centers. The prefecture of servants in the women's branch was in charge of the formation and training of the members who worked in the Administration. The office of St. Raphael was responsible for activities with young people. The prefecture of studies oversaw the doctrinal formation of the members of the Work and schools. The general administrator's office, called in the Advisory the Consultancy, reviewed the accounts and budgets of the regions, with particular attention to the construction of Villa Tevere and corporate activities. The office of spiritual direction took care of the formation of the laity and the priests of the Priestly Society of the Holy Cross. The procurator managed relations with ecclesiastical authorities. The general secretariat kept track of correspondence with the regions; created indices, record books, and file systems; and handled the flow of work to and from the various offices.

Staffing of the offices of the Central Advisory was minimal because the total number of members of the women's branch was still small. In addition, the demands of the Administration of Villa Tevere were growing so rapidly because of the increasing numbers of buildings and students that all the women working in the offices needed for the moment to spend part of their time working in the Administration.

The constitutions provided for a general congress every five years, with a session for the men's branch and another for the women's branch. The electors would gather to review the projects undertaken since the previous congress, assess the progress of corporate and institutional activities, appoint the members of the General Council and the Central Advisory Board, and make plans for the apostolate during the next five years.

The First General Congress of the men's branch was held in Molinoviejo from May 1 to 5, 1951. The women met in Los Rosales from October 11 to 13, 1951. Twenty men and twelve women from various regions attended. They proposed a five-year plan for the formation of members and the development of the St. Michael, St. Gabriel, and St. Raphael Works. In addition, they studied ways to consolidate the Work in countries where it was already present and made plans for expanding to new countries. Finally they considered the implementation of corporate apostolic activates, many of which were just getting started.[28]

The Second General Congress of Opus Dei took place in 1956. The session for the men's branch was held in Einsiedeln, Switzerland, from August 23 to 25. The women met in Rome from October 23 to 25. In addition to appointing the central directors, the congress approved moving the General Council from Madrid to Rome, and creating delegations dependent on the Regional Commission and the Regional Advisory of Spain. Because it was the Founder's native language and the language in which he wrote, the General Congress adopted Spanish as the official language to be used at Opus Dei's meetings and in its internal documents. To facilitate its use, the General Congress provided that Spanish would be taught in the Work's centers of studies. The congress entrusted to the general secretary, Álvaro del Portillo, the completion of the central house, the headquarters of the two Roman Colleges (of the Holy Cross for men and of Holy Mary for women), and the project in Salto di Fondi. Similarly the congress entrusted to the councilor of Spain, Antonio Pérez, the development of what would eventually become the University of Navarre and was called at the time the *Estudio General de Navarra*.

At the proposal of the Founder, the Second General Congress approved four other resolutions. The first called for trying to develop as a priority task for the next five years "the apostolate of public opinion," which consisted in promoting undertakings in the field of communications: "(press, radio, television, news agencies, etc.) in order to spread among all classes of civil society the Church's views on current religious, scientific, educational, and social issues."[29] The second urged that as soon as possible, experienced men and women who had been responsible for the tasks of government and formation in the Work be named delegates in both branches. The third called for creating two additional interregional centers of studies, one in Washington and the other in Pamplona. The last encouraged the apostolic emigration of families of supernumeraries and cooperators who wanted to spread the message of Opus Dei to other places.

During the 1950s Escrivá dedicated a great deal of time and energy to the construction of Villa Tevere, because he was convinced that completion of the central headquarters would facilitate the development of the Work, its expansion, and most directly its governance. Conversely, he thought interrupting the project would be a serious setback for the Work as a whole. The remodeling of existing buildings and the construction of new ones, which began in 1949, absorbed most of the Work's economic resources.

During the first six years, the contractor was a small company which could not provide significant interim financing. Del Portillo, who had primary responsibility for financing the project, had to pay for material immediately, and, even more stressful, the workers had to be paid in cash every week. Failure to pay them would not only bring the project to a halt but leave their families without money for food, heat, and rent. Money was almost always short. At the beginning of many weeks, it was unclear where Del Portillo could find the money needed by the end of the week. On several occasions he traveled to Madrid to study with the general administrator how more money could be raised through individual donations, bank loans, and finance companies. He also organized a collection in the other regions, even in those that were just beginning, asking them to send what they could, even small amounts. The stress undermined his health, but he kept going and managed to keep the project moving forward. The situation improved in 1955 when he was able to hire a larger construction company that offered credit and delays in payment.

Little by little, the various buildings that made up Villa Tevere were finished, including the Villa Vecchia, for the president and members of the General Council, and the Montagnola, for the women of the Central Advisory. Three architects—Fernando Delapuente, Jesús Alberto Cagigal, and above all Jesús Álvarez Gazapo—directed the construction. Two artists, Manuel Cabellero and Salvador Pérez, worked full-time on decoration. Escrivá followed the construction and decoration closely and made numerous suggestions. In January 1960 he had the joy of blessing the last stone of the buildings of the Villa Tevere complex.

In the 1940s, much of the government of the Work was informal. Many times the Founder told the directors orally or with a handwritten note what he wanted done. After he moved to Rome, day-to-day relations between the central and regional governments were carried on by mail with numbered written communications. This formalized system improved follow-up at the cost of increased bureaucracy.

As we have seen, close coordination between the central and regional authorities, was facilitated by the delegates. When particularly difficult or important issues arose, the councilor or some other regional director would travel to Rome to talk with the Father and the central directors. Every five years the Father sent several representatives to each region to study the situation there and report back. In addition to these periodic visits, extraordinary visits took place when needed.

Occasionally the councilors of neighboring regions met to consider common issues. In addition, there were Work Weeks for the electors and regional directors, and workshops in Rome for local or regional directors, where they could receive suggestions and ideas, exchange experiences, and propose new projects. The first meeting of regional councilors was held in Rome in October 1957.

The number of Regional Commissions and Advisories increased steadily during the 1950s. At the beginning of the decade, Opus Dei was divided into seven regions. A decade later there were fifteen. In a number of countries, the regional governments were gradually able to fill positions that had been vacant for lack of sufficient personnel.

For example, in 1956, in several regions where activities with diocesan priests and with women had grown, priests were appointed as priest secretaries and spiritual directors.

The growth of the Work in Spain and the transfer of the General Council to Rome necessitated the formation of delegations dependent on the Spanish Regional Commission and Regional Advisory: Catalonia (January 1957), Andalusia (August 1957), and Pamplona (April 1960). The delegation of Catalonia had a retreat house near Barcelona, Castelladaura that had opened 1955. Andalusia opened one called Pozoalbero near Seville in 1958.

Relations between the central and regional governing bodies of Opus Dei were almost always close and cordial. The regional directors almost always acted promptly to put into practice the suggestions and indication they received from Rome. There were, however, two important exceptions.

The first, and perhaps the most painful for the Founder, involved Antonio Pérez Hernández, the councilor of Spain. Early on, Escrivá had come to appreciate his gifts for governing the Work and had found in him a valuable support in the development of Opus Dei's apostolic activities throughout the world. He had been secretary general of Opus Dei from November 1950 to September 1956 and regional councilor of Spain since then. It is not clear why things began to break down. Perhaps Perez Hernández felt Escrivá was pushing ahead too quickly or began to disagree with other aspects of how he was developing the Work. Whatever the reasons, the Founder began to notice that some directives from the General Council were not being put into practice in Spain. In an attempt to remedy the situation, he met several times with Pérez Hernández and wrote to him expressing his confidence in him. The situation, however, did not improve.

In January 1958, Escrivá spoke with the members of the regional commission in Spain about the suffering their failure to accept some of the directives sent from Rome was causing him. With the exception of Pérez Hernández, the members of the commission rallied round the Founder. The councilor, however, seemed to grow more distant from both the Founder and the General Council. Escrivá decided that for the good of the Work he needed to replace him. Rather than dismiss him, he waited until November 1959, when the term of office of the members of the Regional Commission, including the councilor, ended. At that point he named Florencio Sánchez Bella as the new councilor of Opus Dei in Spain. He appointed Antonio Pérez Hernández as the rector of the Pontifical Basilica of St. Michael in Madrid. Five years later, Pérez Hernández moved to Mexico, where he left Opus Dei and the priesthood.

The second case occurred in the mid-fifties, when the councilor, Salvador Moret, and some members of the Italian Regional Commission incurred debts that they did not show in the accounts sent to the General Council nor mention in meetings with members of the General Council. They also adopted a critical attitude toward the General Council. With the unanimous approval of the General Council, Escrivá dissolved the regional commission and appointed a new one with Juan Bautista Torelló as councilor and with Pedro Casciaro as *missus* or delegate. He disqualified almost all the members of the previous commission from holding positions of government in Opus Dei and assigned Fr. Moret to the region of Spain. Escrivá prohibited making public the warnings he had issued and asked that the people involved be treated with love and without suspicion, so that their wounds could heal. In Moret's case, this was successful. He carried out fruitful pastoral work as a priest of Opus Dei for the rest of his life. Two other members of the former commission, however, left Opus Dei.

To give breathing room to the new commission, the Founder moved its headquarters from Rome to Milan. To restore the region's finances, the general administrator devised a recovery plan and obtained a loan from the region of Spain. In the following decades, the region returned to economic health.

Escrivá and Del Portillo were actively involved in Opus Dei's relations with the Holy See, diocesan bishops, and other Church institutions. They paid special attention to the development of the Vatican's legislation and practice regarding secular institutes, but the most frequent contacts were with the bishops of dioceses where Opus Dei had a center or hoped to open one soon. The regional and local governments kept the Founder informed about their dealings with the bishops and worked closely with him in this area. Under Church law, Opus Dei needed the permission of the bishop to open a center in a diocese, and its priests needed to receive from him ministerial licenses to hear confessions. The bishop also needed to visit the centers to inspect the oratory and the way in which the Blessed Sacrament was reserved. For his part, the councilor, who was the Work's representative in each region, signed the legal act of erection for each center, which carried with it the right to have an oratory. Once a center of the Work was established, the regional directors frequently visited the bishop to keep him informed about Opus Dei's apostolate in his diocese.

Opus Dei also maintained regular contact with the nuncios in the countries where it was present. An exceptional case was that of Bishop Ildebrando Antoniutti, the nuncio to Spain. At his request, in May 1958 some women of Opus Dei took on the housekeeping at the apostolic nunciature. Since this was a direct service to the Church, Escrivá indicated that the Work would pay their salaries. In April 1962, a new nuncio arrived, Bishop Antonio Riberi, who publicly expressed his rejection of Opus Dei without giving reasons. Opus Dei, nonetheless, continued to provide housekeeping services at the nunciature for almost five and a half years, until September 1967, when a new nuncio was named.[30]

In countries where the law made it desirable, Opus Dei acquired legal recognition following the procedures each country had established. In countries where incorporation or some other form was required, Opus Dei took whatever steps were required to comply with the law. In the United States, for instance, Opus Dei currently exists as a New York religious corporation whose name is The Prelature of the Holy Cross and Opus Dei in the United States. These legal formalities had little effect on the development or day-to-day life of Opus Dei.

Notes

1. A report prepared in 1950 lists 2,954 members: 2,404 men and 550 women, three-quarters numeraries, and the rest supernumeraries. "Relación sobre el estado actual del Instituto Secular Opus Dei", en AGP, serie L.1.1, 11-3-5, dated Madrid, April 1, 1950/ Rome, April 16, 1950. Those numbers, however, are impossible to reconcile with numbers from earlier and later periods which seem more likely to be accurate.
2. *Crónica*, May 1969, p. 18. AGP Library, P01.
3. *Intimate Notes*, no. 169 (March 7, 1931).
4. *Crónica*, January 1971, p. 10. AGP Library, P01.
5. *Diary of Villa Tevere*, December 10, 1950. AGP M.2.2, 436-17.
6. Vázquez de Prada, *The Founder of Opus Dei*, vol. 3, p. 287.
7. *Diary of Villa Tevere*, December 10, 1950. AGP M.2.2, 436-17.
8. Adelaida Sagarra Gamazo, "Escrivá de Balaguer Albás, Carmen," in *Diccionario de San Josemaría Escrivá*, p. 410.
9. Pilar Urbano, *The Man of Villa Tevere* (New York: Scepter, 2011).
10. See Curso Formación de Servientas, 1952. AGP R.6.5, 2-18.
11. See AGP R.6.3, 1-3.
12. On Sunday schools, see AGP R.3.2.5, 1-4.
13. See AGP R.6.2.2, 1-10. Escrivá planned to erect a "Roman College of the Holy Family" in the area of the Administration of Villa Tevere. It would be an inter-regional center in which numerous women would be trained in accordance with their work. Although it only remained an idea, the women who worked in Villa Tevere had the opportunity to hear the spirit of the Work from the Founder himself.
14. See Recollections of Mónica Miguel Sancha, Valladolid, July 8, 2013, AGP U.1.2, 4-56.
15. Minutes of the First General Congress of Opus Dei (October 11, 1951). AGP D.1, 457-2-8
16. Josemaría Escrivá, Transcription of comments made in a family gathering, May 26, 1972, quoted in *Meditations*, vol. 2, p. 718. AGP Library, P06.
17. See Curriculum, January 9, 1951, AGP G.4.2.1, 131-3-2; and Curriculum, February 14, 1955, AGP G.4.2.1, 131-3-3.
18. See AGP G.4.2.1, 130-3-2.

19. Vázquez de Prada, *The Founder of Opus Dei*, vol. 3, p. 195. One day in 1951, he described the stay in the Eternal City of the students of the Roman College as a "second vocation. It speaks to us of flying very high, very high, with the two wings of education and holiness. We must feel doubly responsible for taking advantage of the formation offered us, because in the near future we will form our brothers and their flight depends on the safety and height of our flight." *Diary of Villa Tevere*, February 10, 1951, AGP M.2.2, 436-17.

20. Letter from Josemaría Escrivá to José Luis Múzquiz, Rome, September 30, 1952, AGP A.3.4, 264-2, 520930-1.

21. See Luis Cano, Colegio Romano de la Santa Cruz in *Diccionario de San Josemaría Escrivá de Balaguer*, pp. 235–241.

22. See Gertrud Lutterbach, "Colegio Romano de Santa María," in *Diccionario de san Josemaría Escrivá de Balaguer*, pp. 241–244; and María Isabel Montero Casado de Amezúa, "L'avvio del Collegio Romano di Santa Maria," *Studia et Documenta* 7 (2013), pp. 259–319.

23. *Instruction for Directors* (May 31, 1936), no. 26. AGP A.3, 89-4-1. This instruction is intended particularly for members of the local councils that govern individual centers. At that time (May 1936), Escrivá was preparing the first expansion of Opus Dei to Paris and Valencia. Since communication was relatively slow and expensive, the directors in those outposts would need guidance on how to go about their tasks. As we have seen, those first plans for expansion were thwarted by the outbreak of the Spanish Civil War. Escrivá finalized the instruction in the early 1960s.

24. *Instruction for Directors* (May 31, 1936), no. 27. AGP A.3, 89-4-1. See also *Constitutiones Societatis Sacerdotalis Sanctae Crucis et Operis Dei* (1950), nos. 293–436 and 450–479.

25. *Instruction for Directors* (May 31, 1936), no. 43. AGP A.3, 89-4-1.

26. See Minutes of the Second Session of the Second General Congress of Opus Dei (October 24, 1956). AGP D.1, 457-3-12.

27. See Minutes of the Second Session of the Second General Congress of Opus Dei (August 24, 1956). AGP D.1, 457-3-6.

28. See AGP D.1, 457-2-4 to 457-2-8.

29. Conclusions of the Second General Congress of Opus Dei (August 25, 1956, for men; October 25, 1956, for women). AGP D.1, 457-3-6 and 457-3-12, respectively.

30. See AGP E.4.1, 89-3-1.

CHAPTER 9

Worldwide Expansion

The 1950s witnessed an unprecedented spread of Opus Dei to new countries which would not be matched in any later decade. Between 1949 and 1962, the members of Opus Dei opened centers in twenty-two countries: In Germany (1952), France (1952),* Switzerland (1956), Austria (1957) and the Netherlands (1959), the United States and Mexico (1949), Argentina and Chile (1950), Colombia and Venezuela (1951), Guatemala and Peru (1953), Ecuador (1954), Uruguay (1956), Brazil and Canada (1957), El Salvador (1958), Costa Rica (1959) and Paraguay (1962). The opening of centers in 1958 in Kenya and Japan represented new continents and cultures very different from what members of Opus Dei had known until then. In Japan, Opus Dei also found itself for the first time in a country in which Catholics were a tiny minority. During the 1960s, Opus Dei focused primarily on growing in places where it was already established and less on starting in new places.

Section 1. Common Patterns

Before a group of members moved to a new country, someone would visit the country to prepare a report on its social and religious situation and to visit the bishop of the city where the Work hoped to establish its first center. In some cases, the bishop's enthusiasm and support sped up the process. In others, his disinterest or antipathy delayed it. After the General Council and the Central Advisory studied the

---

* This was a second attempt after an earlier unsuccessful effort. In all other countries, Opus Dei took root at the first attempt.

report, a proposal was formulated that included who could go to the new country, how they could finance the first steps, and what might be the first corporate activity.

The adventure of going with little money and sometimes little knowledge of the language to spread a spiritual message in a new and largely unknown place demanded boldness and a great deal of faith, but many members found it a stirring challenge. Their letters reflect a pioneering spirit. They felt moved by faith in God, the strength of the message they were trying to embody and spread, the inspiration and support they received from the Founder, and the prospect of being protagonists in a project to transform the world that, they were convinced, would eventually bear fruit.

The numeraries who accepted the challenge of moving were mostly recent graduates or college students, along with priests and domestic workers. To prepare for beginning in the new country, they usually attended a workshop in Madrid or Rome. The central directors who ran the workshops reminded them that the development of Opus Dei relied on God's grace. Whatever the conditions in their new country, what would make the Work go forward was their personal surrender of their life to God, rooted in prayer and personal mortification. They also urged them to reach out to the people they encountered without creating a closed circle made up of people from their native countries, as often happens to emigrants. The Founder urged them "to love [their new] country, to blend in, not to form a separate group."[1]

The majority of the people who carried out the first expansion of Opus Dei came from Spain, since it was the only region that had enough members to be able to send significant numbers of people to other countries without leaving the existing apostolates unattended. Although most were young, some of the older members of the Work took part in the expansion. Among the men, for example, there were José María González Barredo (United States), Ricardo Fernández Vallespín (Argentina), and Pedro Casciaro (Mexico); and, among the women, Narcisa González Guzmán (United States), Sabina Alandes (Argentina), and Guadalupe Ortiz de Landázuri (Mexico). Naturally, sending large numbers of people to other countries slowed the growth of Opus Dei in Spain, but this was the price of being part of the Church worldwide.

Although the majority of those going to new countries had to come from Spain, Escrivá was anxious to make clear that Opus Dei's message could be understood in any culture and society. God, he reminded his sons and daughters, did not want the Work to be Spanish. He warned against the danger of trying to transplant Spanish ways of being or losing sight of the universal character of the Work's message and mission, For that reason, he indicated that, as far as possible, the group starting Opus Dei in a country should not be made up entirely of Spaniards. From the mid-fifties on, men and women from other regions helped start the Work in other countries. The first Irish member, Cormac Burke, went to the United States in 1955. Kathleen Purcell, also from Ireland, moved to Japan in 1960. Several Mexican women went to the United States. Members from Germany played a decisive role in starting the Work in Austria and Holland. Some Portuguese members went to Brazil, and people from the United States moved to Australia, Canada, the Philippines, Japan, and Kenya.*

Although in the 1950s the number of women in Opus Dei was still relatively small, Escrivá understood that both sections had to be involved in the Work's expansion. At the 1951 General Congress, the Founder reminded his daughters that until then, because of the special circumstances at the beginning, his motto for them had been "Calm!" But now the moment had come to change it to "Hurry up! Go at God's pace!"[2] Beginning in the early 1950s, the women of

---

* "If, after the Lord has called me to account, somewhere some of my children would like to do an Opus Dei with the connotation of a nation—an Irish Opus Dei, a French Opus Dei, a Spanish Opus Dei, etc.—I would rise from the grave to anathematize that evil spirit, since it would be the origin of a diabolical division within this family in which we must all be very united, all of us interested in everyone, without ever putting up barriers of nationalities or discrimination of any kind." Quoted in Andrés Vázquez de Prada, *The Founder of Opus Dei*, vol. 3, *The Divine Ways on Earth* (New York: Scepter, 2005), p. 199.

Opus Dei began to carry out apostolic activities in various countries of Europe and the Americas. Usually the women opened their first center in a country two or three years after the men had done so. That way, the priests could give them ministerial attention and advice.

In the new country, women were needed to take care of the Administration of the men's centers, but they would also begin a corporate activity immediately, usually a residence for college students. The Founder stressed that they should not limit themselves to taking care of the Administration because they were called to work in the whole range of professions, no different in that respect from the men.

The number of men who went to a country varied depending on the circumstances, but it was usually fewer than five and in some cases only one or two priests. Ecuador was an exceptional case. Juan Larrea joined Opus Dei in Rome in 1949 and returned alone to Ecuador in 1952. As he was leaving, Escrivá recommended that he visit the archbishop of Quito to explain to him the core of Opus Dei's message; that he choose a pious priest to be his confessor; that he look for friends who could understand the message of sanctification in the midst of the world; and, with his mother's collaboration, that he suggest to some ladies that they pray for Opus Dei and contribute objects for the future oratory of the Work's center. Larrea remained in close touch with the Founder and with other members of the Work by correspondence, but it would be four years before anyone could come to join him.

In Canada, Chile, Colombia, Mexico, Ecuador, and Venezuela the initial group of women was made up of three or four people, but in some other countries (Costa Rica, El Salvador, Guatemala, and Paraguay) a larger group of numeraries and numerary servants were sent.

The members of the group that went to each country usually had very little money, just enough to cover their expenses during the first few weeks. Some of them might already have a scholarship or a job lined up. Those who did not immediately set out to find a job, in order to support themselves and the incipient center. At the beginning, the priests often worked in a parish or as chaplains. Later, when the members of the Work and local cooperators were able to support them, they usually dedicated all their time to the apostolic activities of Opus Dei.

The Work usually began in the capital of a country or in another city with a university, since many of the members were students, professors, or involved in one of the professions. In addition, they wanted to be near a university in order to carry out their apostolate with students from whom the first members from the country would usually come.

At the very beginning they might live in a modest hotel or a small apartment. As soon as possible, they would open a center of the Work in a larger apartment or rented house near a university. If it was not immediately set up as a university residence, establishing one was a priority. By the time they opened the first center, they had obtained from the local bishop permission to establish an official center with an oratory. In the process of requesting the bishop's permission, they explained Opus Dei and its message to him and gave him a summary of its 1950 constitutions.

Getting started was not easy. At the beginning, their economic situation was almost always precarious and often quite poor. To rent and furnish the early centers, they often had to ask people they had only recently met for furniture and money. They needed to adapt to the climate and food of the country, make its culture and idiosyncrasies their own, and learn to distinguish between customs and ways of behaving that shocked them simply because they were unfamiliar and others that were characteristic defects they should try to avoid. Those who went to countries whose language was different from their own had to make an extra effort to learn it quickly. They spoke the local language among themselves and in the get-togethers in the centers as soon as possible, even if they were far from being fluent.

Some of the people who started Opus Dei in a country stayed there for the rest of their lives. At the opposite end of the spectrum, some found it impossible to adapt to the new situation and returned promptly to their own country. Many stayed a number of years and eventually returned to their home country. Escrivá insisted that returning should not be seen as humiliation or failure.[3]

Members of the Work passed on its spirit primarily to friends they made at school or work, in the neighborhood, and in cultural, athletic, and other associations they joined. Although at first they often did not speak the language well, their way of life and their faith in God and in the spirit of the Work enthused others and helped make up for their poor communication skills.

The newly established centers promptly organized meditations, days of recollection, retreats, and circles, and arranged for high school and college students to teach catechism to children in poor areas. In developing countries where the gap between rich and poor was sharply marked, they had to organize separate activities for both groups.

As it had since the 1930s, *The Way* proved extremely helpful in spreading the spirit of the Work. Editions of the original Spanish version were published in a number of countries, starting with Mexico in 1949. Translations were published in Portuguese (1946), Italian (1949), English (1954), German (1956), and French (1957). Portuguese, Italian, and English versions of Escrivá's *Holy Rosary* also proved helpful, although the book had less impact than *The Way*.

To illustrate in concrete fashion what it means to strive for sanctity in the midst of the world, they often told people about Isidoro Zorzano. In 1949 they began printing cards with a picture of Isidoro, a prayer asking for his intercession, and a very brief biographical sketch. These were supplemented by ten- or twelve-page bulletins with brief articles about Isidoro's life, news of favors received through his intercession, and information about the progress of his cause of beatification. In 1949, ten thousand bulletins were published in English and as many in Italian. In 1954, a renowned Catholic writer in the United States, Daniel Sargent, published a biography of Zorzano titled *God's Engineer*.

Most of the contact between the various regions and the Founder, the General Council, and the Central Advisory was by letter, often on a weekly basis. Since international telephone calls were still very expensive, they used the phone only sparingly.

The Founder and the central governing bodies gave the members of the Work in the regions and centers great freedom. From Rome they sent broad general criteria and practical suggestions, but expected the regional and local directors to exercise their own judgment in implementing them, and to avoid asking the central directors to solve for them issues they could and should resolve themselves. This led to striking contrasts in approach among regions. For instance, in the United States, José Luis Múzquiz was anxious to begin in as many cities as possible as quickly as possible. This rapidly gave the Work a presence in a number of cities in both the Midwest and Eastern United States, at the cost of spreading it very thin. By contrast, in Brazil, under the leadership of Xavier de Ayala, the Work concentrated for years on increasing its presence in São Paulo before establishing centers elsewhere in the country. Escrivá also encouraged the directors to be daring and not to worry too much about making a mistake. He told Múzquiz, for instance, "It's better to have to turn back in two things then to fail to do 98 for fear of making a mistake."[4]

The Founder was well aware that the beginnings were usually hard, particularly from an economic point of view. He frequently encouraged his children, kept closely informed about their difficulties, and reminded them that they were not alone but accompanied in thought and prayer from Rome and from all the other places where members of Opus Dei were working.

The members' sense of closeness to the Father was fostered by the presence of the delegate in each region, by periodic trips of the regional directors to Rome, and by visits from numeraries and supernumeraries whose professional work brought them to the country for a few days or weeks.

As soon as possible, numeraries from the new regions went to Rome to study theology and to receive formation in the spirit of Opus Dei from the Founder himself. Often, before returning to their countries, they spent some time in Spain getting to know aspects of the Work's corporate and other apostolic activities which might prove useful in their home countries. Whether as priests or laypeople charged with tasks of government and formation, their in-depth knowledge of the spirit of the Work combined with being natives often made it possible for them to contribute decisively to the growth the Work and to its acculturation in their country.

Section 2. Western Europe

In Portugal, Opus Dei grew gradually in Coimbra, where the first center had opened in 1946, and in Porto. Some members lived in Braga and Viseu, and activities were held there, but there was no center in either city. One of the first Portuguese numeraries, Hugo de Azevedo, attended the Roman College of the Holy Cross and was ordained a priest in 1955. In 1958, the members of the Work opened a retreat house at Quinta de Enxomil, near Porto.

Lisbon was an unusual case. Cardinal Manuel Goncalves Cerejeira had heard bad things about Opus Dei and refused to allow a center in the capital until 1951. Five years later, he forbade Opus Dei from continuing its activities there. Álvaro del Portillo went to see him but was unable to persuade him. In November 1957, the Holy See confirmed that under canon law Opus Dei had a right to continue its activities in the three centers it had established in Lisbon, although it could not open new centers there. Eventually, the cardinal not only relented but asked Escrivá's forgiveness for having let himself "be carried away by an incomprehensible blindness."[5]

Somewhat similar problems arose in Ireland, where the archbishop of Dublin, John Charles McQuaid, a member of the Holy Ghost Fathers, felt that no more religious orders were needed in his diocese and considered Opus Dei a religious order. Both the apostolic nuncio and Pedro Casciaro visited him but were unable to change his mind. In August 1952, however, Del Portillo's visit led to permission for two centers in Dublin, one for men and one for women. A few months later, Nullamore Residence for university students opened its doors. Some years later Opus Dei added Northbrook and Ely centers in Dublin and Gort Ard residence in Galway.

In London, the men of Opus Dei opened in 1952 Netherhall House, a residence for forty students. A group of women moved from Spain in June of that year to run the Administration of the residence. Four years later they began Rosecroft House, a women's university residence. One of the first Irish members of Opus Dei, Anna Barrett, moved to London to work as regional secretary and director of the new residence.

In the early 1960s, the men of the Work set up a new headquarters for the Regional Commission of England, and opened a boys' club in South London and a new student residence, Greygarth, in Manchester. The women of Opus Dei opened three new centers: Ashwell House in London, Rydalwood in Manchester, and Derwen Deg in Bangor, Wales.

The second attempt to begin Opus Dei in France took place in 1952 when Francisco Lobato, Fernando de Silio, and José Vila moved to Paris. After some time spent in a dormitory in the Cité Universitaire, they rented an apartment. A few months later, Fernando Maycas, who had formed part of the first group to go to France in 1947–1949 and who had been subsequently been ordained a priest, joined them. Catherine Bardinet and Thérèse Truel began the apostolic activities of the women of Opus Dei in France in June 1958. Together with eight other numeraries who arrived a few weeks later, they opened a center called Rouvray.

In Rome, the men of Opus Dei opened Orsini in 1952; it was the first center in what would become the Italian region. Two years later, the women of the Work established the headquarters of the Regional Advisory. They also began to organize retreats for the mothers of some of the Italian numeraries at the oratory of the Administration of Villa Tevere. Escrivá was careful to avoid undermining the autonomy of the Italian region. For instance, although he handled relations with the Vatican Curia, the Founder allowed the directors of the Italian region to handle relations with the diocesan bishops and civil authorities.

Trips from Rome gave rise to centers in Naples (1952), Catania (1955), Bologna (1956), Verona (1961), and Bari (1964). The women of the Work opened a center in Milan in 1954. That same year, Marietta Pedretti joined Opus Dei as the first Italian numerary assistant and Maria Gatti became the first Italian associate member of the Women's branch.

Gradually Opus Dei established corporate activities in Italy. In 1955, the members of the Work acquired Castello di Urio, an old manor house on the shores of Lake Como, which they converted into a retreat house. In Rome, a women's residence called Villa delle Palme began operations in 1958, and the men's Residenza Universitaria Internazionale (RUI, University Hall of Residence) opened a year later. In Milan, a residence for university women, Viscontea, opened in 1954, and a men's residence, Torrescala, started in 1960. University residences for men started in Bologna in 1959 and in Palermo in 1956. A residence for university women opened in Palermo in 1966.

Fernando Inciarte, Fernando Echeverría, and Jordi Cervós, along with Fr. Alfonso Par, brought Opus Dei to Germany in 1952. They started a university residence in Bonn called Althaus. In 1958, they opened a center in Cologne that would serve as the headquarters of the regional commission.[6] In 1956, Carmen Mouriz, Ana María Quintana, and Hortensia Viñes came from Spain to start a residence for university women in Cologne. There they met Katharina Retz, Maria Elisabeth (Marlies) Kücking, and Helene Steinbach, who were already members of the Work.[7]

During summers, Escrivá, accompanied by Del Portillo, often traveled by car to spend a few days with his sons and daughters in the European cities where they were starting Opus Dei, or to carry out what he called the "prehistory" of the Work by studying on the ground the possibilities of starting up in new countries and by contacting local bishops. Between 1955 and 1958, the Founder made several trips to Austria, Belgium, France, Germany, Holland, and Switzerland. In Vienna, he began to say the aspiration *Sancta Maria, Stella Orientis, filios tuos audiuva!* (Holy Mary, Star of the East, help your children!), praying for the Catholics of the East, both in Asia and in the communist countries of Eastern Europe where they suffered persecution.

For five consecutive years, from 1958 to 1962, the Founder spent a large part of the summer in London. He was impressed by the economic and cultural power of the English capital and prayed intensely that the spirit of Opus Dei would take root in that non-Catholic country. One day, while walking around the City of London, he felt powerless to bring the message of the Work to people of so many different faiths and from so many different places. Suddenly, as he later recalled, "Inside me, in the depths of my heart, I felt the effectiveness of God's arm: 'You can do nothing, but I can do everything.'"[8] He urged the members of the Work in England to open an international college at Oxford University. Although at first things seem to be going well, the plan eventually collapsed because the opposition of Oxford's Catholic chaplain led the university authorities to deny recognition of the planned college. The Work had to be content with opening Grandpont House as a residence for graduate students in 1959.

Juan Bautista Torelló and Pedro Turull moved to Zurich in 1956. They were soon joined by Hans Freitag, the first Swiss numerary. Five years later, they opened the Fluntern university residence in Zurich.

Activities in Austria began in May 1957 when two priests, Joaquín Francés and Remigio Abad, moved to Vienna after spending a few months in Bonn learning German and getting a first taste of the culture there. Three years later Katharina Retz, María Josefa Elejalde, and Marga Schraml arrived in Vienna and started the Währing women's residence.[9]

The Work's presence in the Netherlands began in Amsterdam in 1959 with the arrival of Hermann Steinkamp, a German who had joined Opus Dei in Spain and was later ordained a priest. For the first two years, he was the only member of the Work living in the country, although he received regular visits from Germany. Shortly after more members arrived, they started the Leidenhoven university residence.[10]

Section 3. Latin America

In the 1950s, Opus Dei began in thirteen Latin American countries. Several factors favored this rapid development. All the countries had large Catholic majorities, and with the exception of Brazil, they were all Spanish-speaking. Many of them were accustomed to assimilating immigrants from Spain and other European countries, and significant aspects of their culture and customs were similar to those of Spain, making it relatively easy for Spanish members of the Work to adapt to their new circumstances.[11]

Countries like Argentina and Uruguay, which had large immigrant populations and major cities, had relatively flexible social structures with comparatively low barriers between social classes. In contrast, countries like Mexico, Ecuador, Paraguay, and Peru, with a high percentage of indigenous population, were characterized by a lack of social and economic mobility and marked differences between social strata determined primarily by ethnicity and income level. Although the women who started Opus Dei in those countries were mostly middle- or upper-middle-class, they found it relatively easy to deal with people from lower social classes because of their experience in carrying on activities for domestic workers in Spain.

Mexico was the first country of Latin America in which Opus Dei began activities. Fr. Pedro Casciaro, Ignacio de la Concha, a law professor, and José Grinda, an engineer, moved to Mexico City in January 1949. The archbishop of Mexico City blessed the oratory they built in a rented apartment. Although Mexico had a markedly laicist constitution, religious practice was high in most social sectors and Opus Dei developed rapidly. Less than a year after arriving, they had published the first Mexican edition of *The Way* and opened a small student residence.[12]

In 1951, a center was opened in Culiacán in the state of Sinaloa, 750 miles (twelve hundred kilometers) northwest of Mexico City. At the time, Culiacán was not an obvious choice. It was small and still had something of the Wild West about it. But a numerary, Gonzalo Ortiz de Zarate, had been assigned there by the construction company for which he worked. Two years later, activities began in Monterrey, one of the main centers of business and industrial growth in the country.

The women of the Work arrived in Mexico in 1950 under the leadership of Guadalupe Ortiz de Landázuri. They immediately began apostolic activities with women from both ends of the Mexican social spectrum, including married high-society women, university students, peasants, and other working women. Almost simultaneously they opened a residence for university women and a home arts school for women from rural, indigenous families. The bishop of Tacámbaro, who had a high opinion of Opus Dei, was instrumental in recruiting students for their home arts school.

Vocations of women came rapidly in Mexico. In January 1951, fourteen numeraries attended a course of formation. There were also vocations among the maids studying at the home arts school who were impressed by the fact that their teachers treated them as equals and were concerned not only about their professional education but about their personal development. Five of them attended a course of formation in January 1951.

This rapid growth made it possible for the women's branch to open centers in Culiacán in 1951 and Monterrey in 1953. In addition, some numerary women soon moved to Rome to work in the central offices of Opus Dei or in the Administration of Villa Tevere. Others went to Chicago to help develop apostolic activities there.

In 1951, a family donated an abandoned sugar plantation with seventy-five acres (thirty hectares) of land in the municipality of Jonacatepec, eighty miles (one hundred thirty kilometers) south of Mexico City. The rest of the land had been expropriated and the buildings burned during the Mexican Revolution of the early 1920s. The roofs of the buildings had collapsed, and what was left of the structures had been overgrown by tropical vegetation. After extensive renovation, some of the buildings became the Mexican region's first retreat house, Montefalco. In 1959 a farm school with thirty-three students opened in another part of the property. Initially, the school offered girls a two-year program in literacy, cooking, sewing, and wicker work. The students, whose parents were impoverished peasants, worked on their farms in the morning and took classes in the afternoons.[13]

Opus Dei followed a similar pattern in the other Latin American countries where it was beginning. The first centers, normally an apartment or small house in the country's capital, led to a university residence. The women of Opus Dei carried out two activities simultaneously in almost every country. Like the men, they opened university residences that also offered activities for high school students and married women. In addition, they created home arts schools for young women, mostly from rural backgrounds, who wanted to prepare to work in the field of hospitality. Examples were Lar (Santiago de Chile, 1954), Etame (Caracas, 1954), and Zunil (Ciudad de Guatemala, 1958).[14]

Once established in the capital, members of Opus Dei gradually established centers and student residences in other cities. In many countries, before the end of the first decade of the Work's activity, members had built a retreat house: for example, Guaycoral (Medellín, Colombia, 1956) and Altavista (Ciudad de Guatemala, 1959).

Section 4. The United States

José María González Barredo, a Spanish physical chemist, won a research fellowship in 1946 and came to work at Columbia University and later the University of Chicago. For three years he was the only member of the Work in the United States. He was joined in 1949 by Father José Luis Múzquiz and three laymen: Salvador Ferigle, Antonio Martorell, and José María Viladàs. The Founder urged them to be ambitious in spreading the message of the Work, not to be afraid of making mistakes, and to make American culture their own. They were impressed with the growth and organization of the Catholic Church in the country, the number of vocations to the priesthood and religious life, and the strength of Catholic Action. On the other hand, it seemed to them that American Catholicism had a certain ghetto mentality and sense of inferiority regarding the majority Protestant culture.[15]

In August 1949, they opened Woodlawn Residence near the campus of the University of Chicago. A year later, three women members of the Work arrived from Spain. At first they lived and worked in the Woodlawn Administration, but in 1952 they started a women's university residence called Kenwood, which was also close to the University of Chicago.

In 1952, a few members of the Work together with several other people created a small publishing house called Scepter Publishers. In 1953 it released an English version of *Holy Rosary*, and in 1954 *The Way*.

Múzquiz preached many weekend retreats for high school students at both Woodlawn and Kenwood. He was struck by the fact that so many of them found the ideal of holiness in the midst of the world daunting and unrealistic. He attributed this to their having received poor doctrinal formation.

In July 1950, Dick Rieman, a Navy veteran who was studying sociology, became the first American numerary. A year later, his cousin, Pat Lind, became the first American numerary of the women's branch. The first male supernumerary was Howell J. Malham, a commercial agent for a record company, who joined the Work in July 1953. Helen Healy, Marie Kenley, and Mildred Baird became supernumeraries of the women's branch in 1954. Múzquiz, who personally played a very active role in forming the new American members, was firmly convinced that it was essential for them to learn the spirit of the Work directly from the Founder and arranged for as many as possible to study in Rome. By 1957 there were twenty American numeraries studying in the Roman College of the Holy Cross or the Roman College of Holy Mary. This meant that a few years later Opus Dei could count on a significant number of priests and directors who were natives of the United States.

Opus Dei opened a residence, Trimount House, in Boston in 1953. A priest of the Work, Fr. Guillermo Porras, became the Catholic chaplain at Harvard University a few years later. Porras reached out to many people in all parts of the university community, and encouraged Catholic students to transmit their faith in the normal life of the university rather than shutting themselves up in a closed Catholic environment.¹⁶

Between 1955 and 1957, Opus Dei opened university residences for men in both Madison and Milwaukee, Wisconsin; Washington, DC; and St. Louis. The women of the Work opened residences in Milwaukee, Madison, Boston, and Washington, DC. Although Opus Dei still had no retreat center, a cooperator donated a small farmhouse in Vermont that was used for retreats and other activities.

Opus Dei's rapid growth and the geographic size of the country led Escrivá to divide the United States in 1957 into two quasi-regions, one with headquarters in Chicago and Fr. José Ramón Madurga as councilor, and the other in Washington, DC, headed by Fr. Cormac Burke. This was an organizational novelty. Up to this point, Opus Dei had not had more than one commission in a given country. Soon there were new centers in New York and in South Bend, Indiana, the home of the University of Notre Dame. In the fall of 1958 an interregional center of studies began in the outskirts of Washington, DC. The plan was for it to become a college specializing in journalism, and it took the name Maryland Institute of General Studies.

By 1961, between the two branches there were slightly more than four hundred members of Opus Dei in the United States: one hundred numeraries (including twenty-five priests, seven of whom had been born in the United States), a handful of oblates, three hundred supernumeraries, and about ten diocesan members of the Priestly Society of the Holy Cross. About half the members were located in the Chicago area, but a significant number lived far from any center. Giving formation to such a dispersed group presented a serious challenge.

Section 5. Kenya, Japan, and Australia

At the urging of local bishops who hoped that Opus Dei might be able to start a university with a Catholic focus, the Work began activities in Japan and Kenya in 1958. In both countries, the cultural and social structure was very different from anything that the members of the Work who went there had encountered. Although the percentage of Catholics in Kenya was much higher than in Japan, they were both what the Church considered "mission territories," and it was clear that much of Opus Dei's activity would have to be what Escrivá called "apostolate *ad fidem*," bringing people closer to the fullness of the faith through personal example, and the explanation of Catholic doctrine.

The Founder adopted the usual terminology of "mission procurator's office" as the name of the office Opus Dei created in Rome to aid its incipient apostolate in these two countries. He stressed, however, that the members of Opus Dei would carry on their professional work rather than traditional missionary activity: "Their activity there is no more missionary than what we do in all the other countries that are not called missions, and which perhaps are very much in need of a truly missionary work."[17]

Opus Dei's presence in Japan can be traced to the desire of the bishop of Osaka to establish a Catholic university in his diocese and his hope that Opus Dei could take on the task. Múzquiz traveled to Japan to look into it. He concluded that the Work was not in a position to start a university in Japan, but he was enthusiastic about beginning something there.

Escrivá asked Fr. Madurga, who was then the head of Opus Dei in Chicago, to lead the effort to begin in Japan. Before heading there, he spent a few days in Rome. The Founder urged him to try to find a house quickly, to obtain legal status in the country, and to prepare for the arrival of the women of the Work. He added that he was praying to our Lady as "Star of the Sea" for this new adventure. He was aware that it would not be easy, since only 0.3 percent of the population was Catholic, the language was notoriously difficult for Europeans to learn, and the culture and customs were very different.

Madurga arrived in Japan on November 8, 1958. A few months later, two other priests, Fernando Acaso and José Antonio Armisén arrived from the United States. Shortly thereafter, Múzquiz paid them a visit. He urged them to take care of themselves, to be patient and realize that learning the language and the customs would be slow, and to alternate Japanese with European food so that the "transplant" would not be too jarring. In July 1968, women of the Work arrived in Japan, led by María Teresa Valdés, an educator. They soon started a home arts school in Osaka.

Although the people of the Work could not begin to create a university, they did want to undertake an academic project which would also help to spread Christianity. They established the Seido Language Institute in the city of Ashiya, close to Osaka, to teach not only languages but Western culture and Catholic doctrine. Under the direction of an Irish member of the Work, Desmond Cosgrave, Seido developed its own method of language instruction specifically adapted to Japanese speakers.

During the following years, other young people of Opus Dei arrived in Japan. Some were second-generation Japanese from Brazil and Peru who had some knowledge of the language. In November 1960 the Japanese version of *The Way* appeared. The first two Japanese numeraries, Soichiro Nitta and Koichi Yamamoto, were converts to Catholicism.[18]

The beginnings of Opus Dei in Kenya were also connected with a request to establish a Catholic university. It came from the apostolic delegate of the Holy See for British East and West Africa. He felt there was a need for an institution of higher learning that would contribute to giving Catholicism a presence among African intellectuals. The time seemed right to him, because the United Kingdom had begun preparing Kenya for independence by establishing an interracial government.

Fr. Pedro Casciaro visited Kenya but concluded that, given the political situation, an institution of higher education would be in considerable danger of being expropriated by the government. Escrivá decided to start with something more modest, a pre-university preparatory school with a student residence which was called a "college" in Kenya. He said that it should be interracial, intertribal, and open to students of every religion. To avoid having the members of the Work confused with missionaries from religious orders, he insisted that the future school should not be considered a confessional Catholic undertaking. Finally, he said that all the students should pay at least a symbolic tuition, because in that way they would appreciate more the instruction they received.[19]

The first members of Opus Dei reached Kenya in 1958. Among them were several Americans. In March 1961, they opened Strathmore College, a sixth form college which prepared boys aged sixteen to eighteen to sit for the A-level exams required for admission to British universities. Its first headmaster was an American, David Sperling, a graduate of Yale, Harvard, and the University of London School of Oriental and African Studies. When Kenya became independent in 1963, the government confiscated many foreign-run denominational schools but respected Strathmore because it had been the first multiracial institution of its type in Africa, counting among its students Africans from many different tribes, Europeans, and Indians. In 1966, Strathmore added an accounting school. It proved enormously popular because the profession had been dominated by Europeans, many of whom left at the time of independence, and the country badly needed native-born accountants.

Eight women of Opus Dei arrived in Kenya in 1960. They were led by the philologist and educator Olga Marlin, who was born in the United States but had grown up and studied in Ireland. A year later they opened Kianda Secretarial College, the first multiracial girls' school in East Africa and the first school to offer professional secretarial training to Africans. Many people doubted that African women could succeed as executive secretaries, but Kianda's graduates soon proved them wrong.[20]

At the same time, the women working in the Strathmore College Administration opened Kibondeni Hotel School. It offered training in domestic arts, catering, and hotel services. Many of the first students came from remote villages and were impressed to see educated European women working side by side with them in providing cooking, cleaning, and laundry services in the Administration of Strathmore College. One of the central directors of Opus Dei who visited the country in 1962 observed that "no other similar case has been seen in East Africa."[21]

In Australia, the first member of Opus Dei was Ron Woodhead, a supernumerary who returned home in 1960. He had joined Opus Dei while pursuing a master's degree in engineering in Boston. At that time, Cardinal Norman Gilroy was interested in finding a chaplain for the newly established campus in Sydney of the University of New South Wales and eventually in establishing a Catholic college on the campus. After visiting Opus Dei's University Hall of Residence (RUI) in Rome, he asked the Work to come to his diocese.

Fr. Jim Albrecht and Fr. Chris Schmitt, American numerary priests, moved to Sydney in 1963. They were joined by several American lay members of the Work and soon opened Nairana Cultural Centre. Not long after, they began laying the groundwork for what eight years later would become Warrane College, a residential college on the campus of the University of New South Wales.

The first woman member of Opus Dei in Australia was also a supernumerary. Margaret Horsch, a schoolteacher, had joined Opus Dei in the United States in 1955. She returned to Australia in 1964. A year later, four numeraries arrived: Silvia Pons, Rosemary Salaz, María Inmaculada Berazaluce, and Janis Carroll.[22]

Notes

1. *Obras*, vol. 10, 1957, p. 11, AGP Library P03.
2. Quoted in Recollections of Encarnación Ortega Pardo, Valladolid, August 21, 1975, AGP A.5, 232-1-2.
3. See Letter 30, no. 33, AGP A.3, 94-2-1.
4. Quoted in John F. Coverdale, *Putting Down Roots: Father Joseph Muzquiz and the Growth of Opus Dei* (New Rochelle, N.Y.: Scepter, 2009), p. 45.
5. See Vázquez de Prada, *The Founder of Opus Dei*, vol. 3, pp. 244–248.
6. See Jordi Cervós, *Cruzando el muro: Recuerdos sobre los inicios del Opus Dei en Alemania* (Madrid: Rialp, 2016).
7. See Marlies Kücking, *Horizontes insospechados: Mis recuerdos de san Josemaría* (Madrid: Rialp, 2019), pp. 25–40; and Barbara Schellenberger, "Das Studentinnenheim Müngersdorf—eine Initiative des heiligen Josemaría: 1957–1966,"

Studia et Documenta 5 (2011), pp. 53–76. Retz and Kücking were numeraries, Steinbach a supernumerary.

8. Josemaría Escrivá de Balaguer, Meditation, November 2, 1958, quoted in Vázquez de Prada, *The Founder of Opus Dei*, vol. 3, p. 338.

9. See Maria Casal, *Una canción de juventud: Mi vida tras los pasos de san Josemaría* (Madrid: Rialp, 2019); and Ricardo Estarriol, "Die Vorgeschichte des Opus Dei in Österreich: Drei Reisen des heiligen Josefmaria (1949–1955)," *Studia et Documenta* 7 (2013), pp. 221–257.

10. Hermann Steinkamp, "Holanda," in *Diccionario de San Josemaría Escrivá de Balaguer*, pp. 595–597.

11. During and immediately after the Spanish Civil War, many Spaniards fled to Latin America. During World War II, people fleeing totalitarian regimes arrived in Latin America from many European countries. In the immediate postwar years, famine and the devastation the war left behind in Europe produced yet another wave of immigration. See María Estela Lépori de Pithod, "El contexto histórico de la posguerra y la expansión del Opus Dei en América Latina," in *La grandezza della vita quotidiana*, vol. 2, *St. Josemaría Escrivá: Contesto Storico, Personalità, Scritti* (Rome: Edizioni Università della Santa Croce, 2003), pp. 119–134

12. See Víctor Cano, "Los primeros pasos del Opus Dei en México (1948–1949)," *Studia et Documenta* 1 (2007), pp. 41–64.

13. See Lucina Moreno-Valle and Mónica Meza, "Montefalco, 1950: una iniciativa pionera para la promoción de la mujer en el ámbito rural mexicano," *Studia et Documenta* 2 (2008), pp. 205–229.

14. See Adelaida Segarra Gamazo, "Una iniciativa a favor de la integración social: La Escuela Hotelera Zunil (Guatemala)," *Studia et Documenta* 7 (2013), pp. 347–368.

15. See Federico M. Requena, "El Opus Dei en Estados Unidos (1949–1957): Cronología, geografía, demografía y dimensiones institucionales de unos inicios," *Studia et Documenta* 13 (2019), pp. 13–93; and Coverdale, *Putting Down Roots*.

16. See Federico M. Requena, "*Harvard and Catholic . . . Are Not Incompatible: Father William Porras' Chaplaincy at Harvard University, 1954–1960*," *U.S. Catholic Historian* 36 (2018), pp. 79–98.

17. Minutes of Meeting of the General Council, November 17, 1958, pp. 35–36.

18. See Antonio Mélich Maixé, "Koichi Yamamoto (1940–1983) and the Beginnings of Opus Dei in Japan," *Studia et Documenta* 1 (2007), pp. 127–159.

19. See Vázquez de Prada, *The Founder of Opus Dei*, vol. 3, p. 259.

20. See Olga Marlin, *To Africa with a Dream* (New York: Boissevain, 2011).

21. Comisión de servicio en Kenia, February 16, 1962, AGP Q.2.1, 2-51. See also Christine Gichure, "The Beginnings of Kibondeni College, Nairobi: A Historical and Sociological Overview," *Studia et Documenta* 5 (2011), pp. 77–129.

22. See Amin Abboud, "Australia," in *Diccionario de san Josemaría Escrivá de Balaguer*, pp. 145–148.

CHAPTER 10

Individual Action in Society

The numerical and geographic growth of Opus Dei in the period we are considering (1950–1962) and the growing professional maturity and prominence of some of its members meant members were carrying out an increasingly wide range of activities in many different fields. This suggests that it may be useful to review and expand on some of the ideas we have already touched on regarding the nature of Opus Dei and the characteristics of its members' activity.

As we have seen, joining Opus Dei does not change anyone's state in life, whether in the Church or in civil society. Members are called to exercise their rights and fulfill their obligations in the Church and in society just like their fellow citizens who do not belong to Opus Dei. In their place of work, their family, and the broader society, they strive to identify themselves with Christ and to spread the gospel message and the spirit of the Work by example and word, assuming their personal responsibilities. Escrivá reminded them:

> Each of my sons and daughters is a normal citizen and acts as such. This makes them courageously assume personal responsibility in their temporal activities. It leads them to be involved in the modern problems of the world and to seek loyally the good of their country. In this way, through an individual apostolate which is silent and almost invisible, they bring to all public and private social sectors the witness of a life similar to that of the first Christians.[1]

Escrivá highly valued autonomy and freedom in secular affairs. He thought that differences of opinion and disagreement among the members of the Work in temporal matters such as politics and literature, as well as in philosophical and theological matters, were signs of a good spirit in Opus Dei. At times, he used the example of an arithmetic fraction to talk about unity and diversity in Opus Dei. The common denominator of the members of the Work was small, he said, limited to the doctrine of the Church and the spirit of Opus Dei. The numerator was large, in fact limitless, since it respected the freedom of human thought and action.²

In political and public life, he asked the members of Opus Dei to take whatever positions they felt were appropriate and to give personal witness of Christian life there, in accord with their personal way of being and thinking. Similarly, the members enjoyed complete autonomy and freedom in their work. People of Opus Dei were increasingly to be found in all sorts of professions and jobs.

Although some would need to work in the government of Opus Dei or its corporate activities, in 1960 the Founder reminded the regional directors that all regions should "strive to have members of the Work who exercise their professions and work in positions of professional, social, and public responsibility. There they will sanctify themselves and carry out apostolate. With the money they earn, they will be able to help support apostolic activities."* Escrivá liked the members "to be spread out like a fan," not clumped together. In a given city or town, there might be only one member, but that was fine.

The immense majority of the members participated in professional and civil life purely as individuals and not as representatives of Opus Dei.†

---

* General Note 336, no. 2 (July 5, 1960), AGP E.1.3, 242-2. See also General Note 255, no. 2 (July 23, 1960), AGP s Q.1.3, 3-16. The idea of being present in many aspects of civil society appears often at this time. For example, in 1959, the Central Advisory encouraged women who wanted to be involved in the media: "A few will work in the leading positions of our publications and agencies [common works]. Many more will work professionally in many large-circulation influential newspapers, weekly magazines, and informative and cultural reviews in all countries." General Note 166, no. 2 (April 22, 1959), AGP Q.1.3, 2-14.

† Only the president general, the general secretary, and the councilors of the various regions represented the Work in civil or ecclesiastical society. The president general, the general secretary, and the councilors in each region maintained official relations on a periodic basis with the hierarchy and with other Church institutions. Concretely,

The spirit of Opus Dei required its members to speak discreetly and naturally about the Work and about their membership in it. Escrivá thought that secular Christians working in the midst of the world should be known among friends and colleagues mainly for their professional competence and their charity. They would not flaunt their Catholicism nor their membership in Opus Dei. But neither would they hide them, for they were not secret. The Founder pointed to the example of Jesus in his years at Nazareth, where he led a redemptive life hidden from the eyes of his contemporaries: "Let us be discreet; let us admire the fruitfulness of Jesus Christ's thirty years of hidden life."[3]

Naturalness and prudence were especially needed at this time to combat the tendency of some clergymen to treat the members of the Work as if they were consecrated members of a religious order. This was a serious issue, since it tended to undermine the secularity that was an essential characteristic of Opus Dei. The vocation of members of religious orders involves making their consecration to God public and expressing it through a distinctive way of dressing, speaking, and behaving. By contrast, as Escrivá stressed, "Our dedication to God is not public, in the manner of religious: we are dealing with different phenomena."[4] Because the members of Opus Dei were called to be secular faithful of the Church and normal citizens of their countries, it would have been inappropriate for them to have a distinctive way of dressing, speaking, or behaving. They wore no habit or insignia, but dressed and behaved like other members of their profession and social class.

The Founder emphasized that the discretion he asked the members of Opus Dei to practice "is never a question of secrecy or anything like it: I have always hated and rejected secrecy. [Discretion] is simply one more defense against being confused with members of religious orders and of keeping our centers, which are the

---

they met frequently with the bishops and other ecclesiastical authorities of the dioceses where Opus Dei had centers. The relations of other members of the Work with members of the hierarchy or other ecclesiastical institutions were friendly and personal, but not official.

family homes of professional men and women who are ordinary citizens, from being considered convents or religious houses."[5] In the nineteen-sixties, Escrivá decided to stop using the word *discretion* to express these ideas because it had taken on overtones of secrecy or pretense: "I don't even want to hear about discretion: it is better to say and do things *naturally*."[6] He also gradually modified his initial idea that it was better not to tell family members unnecessarily about one's membership in the Work and began to recommend manifesting it openly.

Escrivá was pleased with the personal prestige members gained in their various professional endeavors, but the Work did not take credit or blame for the professional, economic, or political successes or failures of its members, the result of their personal decisions and actions: "The Work can never be credited with the fame or merit of its members' activities. All the glory is for God and, in the human realm, for other associations."[7]

To avoid the danger of boasting, the temptation to believe oneself better than others, and the tendency to make comparisons with other ecclesiastical entities, Escrivá decided that Opus Dei as a whole should publish as few statistics as possible, generally limited to those it was required to send to the official Vatican yearbook, the *Annuario Pontificio*, which also published the names of the directors of Opus Dei. Escrivá often referred to this way of acting as a reflection of "collective humility." On the other hand, he encouraged Opus Dei's corporate apostolic activities to publish information about their domicile, nature, purpose, and activities.[8]

Section 1. Apostolate of "Friendship and Confidence"

Opus Dei's message is generally communicated one-on-one, in personal conversations of individuals with their friends, colleagues, neighbors, and relatives, without advertising, propaganda campaigns, or large gatherings or mass public events. Members of the Work take advantage of the opportunities that come up in the course of work and social relations to transmit Christian doctrine to their friends.

The Founder often referred to this way of bringing others closer to Christ in the private sphere of personal relations as an apostolate of "friendship and confidence." Members talk to their colleagues, friends, neighbors, and relatives about the joy of their Christian faith. If the other person shows interest, they invite them to deepen their lives as Christians and suggest practical ways of doing so, possibly including attending a day of recollection, a retreat, or a class on practical Christian life, or receiving personal spiritual direction from a priest of Opus Dei.*

In accordance with the express indications of the Founder, the directors of the Work respect the spontaneity and initiatives of the members in transmitting Opus Dei's message of holiness in the midst of the world by giving primacy to freedom over control. They encourage pluralism in the laity's action and make possible their presence in various areas of society.

This does not mean that the personal apostolate of Opus Dei's members is anarchic. It is "directed" in the sense that members receive in spiritual direction suggestions about possible priorities in their evangelizing activity with colleagues, friends, and family. In addition, to ensure the apostolate carried out in each center takes into account both the needs of the people coming for formation and the abilities and talents of individual members, each member is given a "personal apostolic assignment"—for instance, organizing a volunteer program or giving classes on Christian life. Starting in 1956, Opus Dei also "directed" the personal apostolate of its members by proposing each month a particular theme for them to read,

---

* The message was also spread within families. For this reason, among the members of the first generation there were close relatives and, in time, there were successive generations of relatives who belonged to the Work. None of this excludes the possibility of people receiving a vocation who have neither family members nor close friends in the Work. An early example is Maria Casal, who joined Opus Dei in Seville in 1950, at a time when there were no women members of Opus Dei in Seville. Casal had been a Protestant and was probably the first person to convert to Catholicism through Opus Dei. See Maria Casal, *Una cancion de juventud: Mi vida tras los pasos de san Josemaría* (Madrid: Rialp, 2019).

think, and pray about, and then spread in whatever way they saw fit in their particular circumstances with what the Founder liked to refer to as "the gift of tongues."[9]

All of this is compatible with the fact that Opus Dei does have, as we have seen, some corporate apostolic activities such as universities, schools, hospitals, and vocational schools which require institutional structures to give them continuity. Such undertakings, however, the Founder said "would be few and far between, since Opus Dei has no specific modes of external corporate action. Moreover, the spread of Christian life that takes place in these group activities is the sum of the personal apostolate of each of those who work there."[10] The fact that in a particular place Opus Dei has a certain type of corporate apostolic activity, for example a university, is no reason for members not to work in other similar institutions, even though they may compete with the corporate activity.

Section 2. Freedom and Responsibility in Public Life

During the 1950s, Franco's Spain gradually became less isolated from the rest of the world. Although the United States and its Western European allies continued to dislike the Franco regime, they came to see it as an ally in the Cold War. Spain was able to establish military and economic agreements with the United States (1953), signed a concordat with the Holy See (1953), was admitted to the UN (1955), entered the European Organization for Economic Cooperation (1958), and joined the World Bank and the International Monetary Fund (1958).

A 1947 law declared that Spain was a monarchy, but that General Franco was head of state for life. He governed with the help of a cabinet whose members came from the universities, business, the government-controlled trade unions, the army, and the upper reaches of the bureaucracy. From time to time, he shuffled his cabinet, responding to changing conditions within the country and in the wider world. Between 1939 and 1962, he formed seven cabinets, each time altering the balance among the various groups that supported him.

The Falange continued to be the only legally tolerated political party, and its national-syndicalist principles marked, to a greater or lesser degree, the boundaries of political life. Within those narrow limits, various political, intellectual, and religious groups and individuals associated with them strove for influence and power. The most important were the Falangists, the monarchist supporters of Juan de Borbón, who wanted a king who would reign but not govern, the Traditionalist monarchists who wanted a king who would both reign and govern, and the Catholic members of the National Catholic Association of Propagandists.

One of the most important intellectual and political debates of the period was framed as an attempt to identify the historical and cultural elements that defined the essence of Spain. On one side was a group of supporters of Juan de Borbón, linked to the cultural review *Arbor*. They sought the regeneration of Spain as a Catholic monarchy, following two conservative thinkers, Menéndez Pelayo and Ramiro de Maeztu. The most prominent figure in this group was Rafael Calvo Serer, a professor of the philosophy of history, member of the Superior Council of Scientific Investigations (CSIC), and editor of the review *Arbor*. Calvo Serer and some of his associates were members of Opus Dei.[11]

On the other side was a group of "left-wing" Falangists who defended much of the thought of the liberal intellectuals of the 1930s, including José Ortega y Gasset, Miguel de Unamuno, and the members of the Free Institution of Education. This group became famous in 1951 when the Christian Democratic minister of education, Joaquín Ruiz Jimenez, named one of its members, Pedro Laín Entralgo, rector of the University of Madrid, and another member, Antonio Tovar, rector of the University of Salamanca.

The clash between the groups reached a climax in September 1953, when Rafael Calvo Serer published in a French journal an article titled "*La política interior en la España de Franco*" (Domestic Policy in Franco's Spain). Calvo Serer criticized both the Falange, which had failed in its attempt to implement national-syndicalist principles during World War II, and the Christian Democrats, whom he accused of having stifled any attempt at political modernization in the second half of the 1940s. To overcome the impasse, Calvo Serer proposed a "third force" that would offer economic freedom and restore a popular and representative monarchy.

The article was harshly criticized in the Falangist press. Ruiz-Giménez removed Calvo Serer as editor of *Arbor* and from the other positions he held in the CSIC. Calvo Serer left Spain for a few months with the excuse of teaching in London. It seemed that the Falangists had won the battle, but their victory was short-lived. Franco was upset when Falangist and monarchist students clashed violently at the University of Madrid. As a result, Ruiz-Giménez lost his position in a government reorganization in February 1956, and Laín Entralgo resigned as rector.

A number of Falangists and others who found themselves out of power after the fall of Ruiz-Giménez said that Calvo had formed a political pressure group, centered around Opus Dei, that sought to impose its way of thinking on Spanish society. Escrivá asked the members of the Work not to give "too much importance to these scandalous articles which attribute to us political undertakings. Our Institute has nothing to do with those or any other political undertakings and never will."[12] "Attributing to Opus Dei the opinions of one of its members or his professional, political, or economic activities is," he said, "as illogical as attributing to the Association of Journalists the thought or activities of two or three of its members."[13]

In 1956, the head of Opus Dei in Spain, Fr. Antonio Pérez, began to think that it would be helpful if one or more members of the Work could become cabinet ministers. More specifically, he thought that a minister with economic responsibilities might be able to institute policies that would facilitate financing Opus Dei's apostolic activities and that a minister of the interior might be able to protect the Work from Falangist attacks.[14] Prior to his ordination, Fr. Pérez had been a prominent lawyer and a member of the Council of State, the Spanish government's most important legal advisory body. He knew many influential people, in particular Franco's number-two man, Luis Carrero Blanco. Fr. Pérez began to talk about this idea with Luis Valls,

Opus Dei's regional administrator in Spain. Valls, an assistant professor of economics, belonged to a prominent Catalan family and was beginning to position himself as a banker. He was building good connections in the small world of prominent people with political influence in Franco's Spain.

By this time it was becoming clear that the Falangist economic policies of large-scale government intervention in the economy and minimizing dependence on foreign trade had led Spain to a dead end, of stagnant production and rising inflation. The country needed to change course, which meant that Franco needed to shake up his cabinet.

In February 1957, Franco reshuffled the cabinet. Two of the 18 members of the new cabinet were members of Opus Dei, and both would play important roles in Spain's effort to revitalize its economy. Alberto Ullastres, a professor of economic history at the University of Madrid and president of a finance company, became the Minister of Commerce. Mariano Navarro Rubio, who had worked in the government-sponsored labor syndicates and as undersecretary for Public Works, became Minister of the Treasury.

Franco and the Cortes approved a National Plan for Economic Stabilization, developed by Navarro Rubio and Ullastres and the experts at the Ministries of Commerce and Finance. In a short time, the Spanish peseta strengthened on international currency markets, tax collection improved, inflation and public spending declined, and foreign investment increased. Ullastres and Navarro Rubio competed with each other for control of the Spanish economy, which each hoped his ministry would run.

Among the insiders who had advised Franco on drawing up the new list of ministers were Carrero Blanco and José Luis Arrese, minister secretary general of the Movement. In their search for suitable candidates, these high-ranking advisors consulted, among others, Fr. Antonio Pérez and Luis Valls, as well as Opus Dei member Laureano López Rodó, professor of administrative law, whom Carrero had appointed technical secretary general of the Ministry of the Presidency in December 1956.

It does not appear that Pérez or Valls consulted Escrivá, the members of the General Council, or the other members of the Regional Commission about whether they should respond to these inquiries, despite Escrivá's repeated insistence that Opus Dei should not get involved in politics.[15] We have not been able to determine what names they put forward, but Pérez's memoirs make clear that they not only responded to the government's request for input but also worked actively to promote the candidates they proposed.[16]

From the information we have been able to gather, it seems clear that neither the General Council nor the Regional Commission planned or approved Pérez and Valls' political activities.[*] The two of them may have thought that they were acting in their personal capacities, albeit in ways that would favor the apostolate of Opus Dei. Given the positions they held, however, their participation in overtly political conversations clearly violated Escrivá's admonitions against Opus Dei's involvement in politics.

It is not clear how or when Escrivá and the members of the General Council and the Spanish Regional Commission learned about these activities or how they reacted to them. Pérez ceased to be the councilor of Opus Dei in Spain in 1959 and Valls ceased being a member of the Regional Commission in 1961, but we have not been able to determine if their political activities played any part in Escrivá's decision to replace them.

The individual members of the Work who ended up as cabinet ministers did, of course, tell Escrivá about their appointments, just as they told him about family events and other big and small things that happened to them. They asked for his blessing and his prayers. López Rodó, for instance, wrote to the Founder shortly after his appointment as secretary of the Ministry of the Presidency by Carrero: "I continue to invoke St. Thomas More often, and there are always opportunities to make known the freedom we have in the Work in

---

[*] We focus here on Pérez and Valls because of the positions they occupied in Opus Dei's government. López Rodó did not hold a similar position and could therefore act freely in his personal capacity without implicating Opus Dei.

political and economic matters, etc."[17] They did not, however, consult him or keep him informed about policies they hoped to implement or problems they faced.

As we shall see, in 1962, when the media spread the idea that Opus Dei wanted to control the Spanish government, Escrivá responded by insisting, both within and outside the Work, that all members enjoy freedom in political and cultural matters, and that Opus Dei has a purely spiritual and evangelizing purpose. He explicitly reminded the members of the Regional Commission of Spain to avoid political interference. The priest who replaced Pérez as head of Opus Dei in Spain, Fr. Florencio Sánchez Bella, appears to have taken these injunctions very seriously.

Neither the intellectual debates between the Falangists and Calvo Serer's traditionalists nor Franco's appointment of ministers who belonged to the Work should have affected Opus Dei, for a number of reasons. Except for its corporate apostolic activities (schools, training centers, and student residences), the Work did not act in society as a group or collectively. The majority of its Spanish members did not participate in cultural and political debates. The few members who did play an active role in political life differed among themselves on important issues and repeatedly rejected the contention that members of the Work had a common political or economic project. Finally, members of the Work in other countries were not concerned about Spanish issues and in most cases knew nothing about them. From Franco's perspective, the important considerations were that his ministers were loyal to him and technically competent. He did not give privileged treatment to Opus Dei. For example, despite frequent requests, his government refused to grant significant subsidies to the Estudio General de Navarra, the nucleus of the future University of Navarre.

Nonetheless, many people began to connect these political activities to Opus Dei. In part this was because the Falange's own policies emphasized corporate presence in society and mutual aid among members, so its leaders assumed that Opus Dei must do the same. They said that Opus Dei had a collective political plan to shape the destinies of Spain and that its directors controlled the political activities of its members. This vision of Opus Dei was picked up by the national and international press in reports on Spanish politics. Quite a few European and American newspapers projected an image of the Work as a political-religious group that intended to occupy key positions in national life. They depicted it as an enemy of the Falange that used illicit and sectarian means. Opus Dei, they concluded, was the new force leading the regime's policy.[18]

These press reports adversely affected the spread of Opus Dei's Christian message. Bishops and other Church authorities in countries where the Work had been established were uneasy, particularly in the United States. Escrivá responded that he could not limit his children's freedom in social life, and that their successes or failures could not be attributed to the Work. When a cardinal congratulated him on Ullastres' appointment, he replied: "It doesn't matter to me. I don't care if he is a minister or a street sweeper. The only thing that interests me is that he becomes a saint in his work."[19]

Nonetheless, Escrivá understood that it was necessary to give an institutional response to public opinion and to the members of the Work. He asked the regional secretariats to send letters to the editors of newspapers and agencies that attributed political activity to Opus Dei, explaining the exclusively spiritual nature of the Work and the full freedom enjoyed by its members in their professional and political life. In addition, he told his spiritual children: "You should not give too much importance to these inevitable little things."[20]

In April 1957, Julián Herranz, prefect of studies of the General Council, published an article on "Opus Dei and Politics" in the magazine *Nuestro Tiempo*. Herranz stressed that the members of the Work enjoyed freedom of thought and action in civil society, and did not represent the institution. He added that it would be impossible to explain the rapid spread of Opus Dei in so many countries and among people of such diverse professions "if the Institute forced its members to follow a particular political opinion."[21]

A few weeks later, newspapers in several countries published an anonymous report, attributed to Opus Dei, which criticized some

Spanish interest groups. The regional directors of Opus Dei in Spain responded with an official note denying that the Work had anything to do with the report, repudiating the use of anonymous notes, and disavowing "any group or individual who uses the name of the institute for his or her political activities."[22]

In 1960, the theologian José Luis Illanes published an article in the Italian magazine *Studi Cattolici* commenting on the fact that some of Franco's ministers were members of Opus Dei. Illanes noted that the Vatican and the Spanish hierarchy looked favorably upon both Catholics who held positions in the Franco regime and those who opposed it. He pointed to factors which suggested that participation in the Franco regime was not immoral. Franco's dictatorship, which he described as paternalistic, was not based on terror and anti-Catholicism, as were communist dictatorships. Significantly, Spain claimed to have only fifty-one prisoners for every hundred thousand inhabitants, the lowest percentage in Europe after the Netherlands and Denmark. But he criticized the unjust concentration of power in Franco's hands and the limitation of political, informational, and press freedom, which he described as "an obstacle rather than a contribution to the exercise of power."[23]

Despite these and other clarifications, much of the international media continued to present Opus Dei as a leading political force in Franco's regime, and more generally as a conservative political group.[24]

Notes

1. *Instrucción de San Gabriel* (Instruction on the Work of St. Gabriel) (May 1935, September 1950), nos. 93–94, AGP A.3, 90-3-1.

2. "In the Work we all have our own ideas which are very different. Each one has his own way of thinking and being: a very varied numerator. As a denominator, in addition to the faith and morals of the Church, we have our *dedication to God*. In everything else, we are free!" Escrivá, quoted in *Obras*, 1963, p. 47, AGP Biblioteca P03.

3. *Statutes* (1941), "Espiritu," art. 59, AGP L.1.1, 1-3-3.

4. Josemaría Escrivá, Handwritten note, September 9, 1943, AGP L.1.1, 1-3-8.

5. Josemaría Escrivá, Handwritten note, September 9, 1943, AGP L.1.1, 1-3-8.
6. Letter to Jesús Martínez Costas, Rome, November 21, 1966, AGP A.3.4, 285-5, 661121-2 (emphasis in original).
7. *Statutes* (1941), "Espíritu," art. 10, AGP L.1.1, 1-3-3.
8. See *Catecismo* (Catechism) (1951, 2nd ed.), no. 76, AGP E.1.1, 181-2-1.
9. Nota general (General Note) 67, no. 15 (November 15, 1956), AGP E.1.3, 242-1. General Note 60, no. 15 (Novembere 15, 1956), AGP Q.1.3, 2-12.
10. General Note 182, no. 4 (December 6, 1959), AGP Q.1.3,2-14.
11. See Onésimo Díaz Hernández, *Rafael Calvo Serer and the* Arbor *Group* (Valencia: University of Valencia, 2008).
12. General Note 23, no. 1 (February 22, 1956), AGP E.1.3, 242-1; and 53, no. 1 (October 10, 1956), AGP Q.1.3, 2-12.
13. General Note 308, no. 2, c (March 16, 1952), AGP E.1.3, 242-1.
14. Pérez's memoirs cited in Alberto Moncada, *Historia oral del Opus Dei* (Esplugues de Llobregat: Plaza & Janés, 1992), p. 69.
15. We have consulted Mariano Navarro Rubio, *Mis memorias: Testimonio de una vida política truncada por el "Caso Matesa"* (Barcelona: Plaza & Janés, 1991), pp. 70–73; Laureano López Rodó (Barcelona: Memorias, Plaza & Janés, 1990), pp. 89–101; and Pablo Hispán Iglesias de Ussel, *La política en el régimen de Franco entre 1957 y 1969: Proyectos, conflictos y luchas por el poder* (Madrida: Centro de Estudios Políticos y Constitucionales, 2006), pp. 13–22; We interviewed Fernando de Meer and Jesús María Zaratiegui, January 30, 2021. (De Meer and Zaratiegui are historians of twentieth-century Spain, who interviewed Rafael Calvo and Antonio Fontán about these events.) We have also reviewed in AGP the minutes of the General Council and the letters of Josemaría Escrivá, Rafael Calvo Serer, Laureano López Rodó, Mariano Navarro Rubio, Antonio Pérez, Luis Valls Taberner, and Alberto Ullastres for the period 1956–57.
16. Pérez's memoirs, cited in Alberto Moncada, *Historia oral del Opus Dei*, p. 69.
17. Laureano López Rodó, Letter to Josemaría Escrivá de Balaguer, Madrid, March 16, 1957, AGP M1.1, 472-C1.
18. See, for example, *Daily Telegraph*, March 1, 1957; *The Observer*, March 3, 1957; *Daily Express*, March 12, 1957; *Time*, March 18, 1957; and *Le Monde*, June 6,1957.

19. Recollection of Julián Herranz Casado, quoted in Vázquez de Prada, *The Founder of Opus Dei*, vol. 3, p. 526.

20. General Note 90, no. 6 (March 7, 1957), AGP E.1.3, 242-1; and General Note 79, no. 6 (April 15, 1957), AGP Q.1.3, 2-12.

21. Julián Herranz, "El Opus Dei y la política," *Nuestro Tiempo* 34 (April 1957), p. 394.

22. Note from the Secretariat of the Regional Commission of Opus Dei in Spain, Madrid, July 12, 1957, published in Julián Herranz, "El Opus Dei," *Nuestro Tiempo*, 97–98 (1962), p. 12.

23. José Luis Illanes, "L'azione politica dei cattolici nella Spagna d'oggi," *Studi Cattolici: rivista di teologia pratica* 4, no. 17 (1960), p. 54.

24. General Note 236, no. 4 (June 18, 1959), AGP E.1.3, 242-2. General Note 167, no. 4 (June 18, 1959), AGP Q.1.3, 2-14.

CHAPTER 11

Institutional Apostolic Activities

As early as 1930 Escrivá was thinking about not only individual but also collective ways by which Opus Dei could spread its message. In his diary (*Apuntes íntimos*) he distinguished with respect to group activities between the Work itself and what he called "apostolic enterprises." Although the idea is not developed in his earliest writings, it seems that he already intended that Opus Dei itself would concentrate on spreading its apostolic message without getting involved in the ownership and operation of property. At some point, possibly even from the very beginning, he decided that Opus Dei would not even be involved in designing, creating, and operating educational, cultural, or social activities.

The DYA Academy and Residence, which opened its doors in a rented apartment in January 1934, was the first group activity created to spread the Christian message of Opus Dei. Today it would be classified as a "corporate apostolate" of the Work. At this stage, no foundations, corporations, or other legal entities were involved. Ricardo Fernández Vallespín signed the lease in his own name. As director of the DYA, he paid the bills and ran the activities. (There was still no legal entity that corresponded to Opus Dei. From the point of view of canon law, Opus Dei was still just Escrivá's personal apostolic activity.)

The first legal entity created to support the apostolate of Opus Dei was a private not-for-profit company called Fomento de Estudios Superiores (FES, Promotion of Higher Studies). It was founded in November 1935 to acquire and operate property to be used in the cultural and professional formation of students. Its incorporators were five professional men who belonged to Opus Dei. In June 1936, it purchased a property at 16 Ferraz Street in Madrid to house the future Ferraz Residence, intended to be the successor of the DYA

Academy and Residence. The Ferraz Residence project was cut short by the outbreak of the Spanish Civil War in July 1936.

In the immediate aftermath of the Civil War, a residence opened its doors on Jenner Street. The apartments which housed the Jenner Residence were rented in the name of Escrivá's mother and no operating entity appears to have been formed to run it. During the 1940s, in addition to a number of small centers in Madrid and in the provinces, the Moncloa Residence, Diego de León, and two retreat houses were opened. We have not been able to determine what arrangements were made for the lease or purchase of each property or for the operation of each of the centers, but various legal entities were formed to purchase and hold property. As we have seen, for example, in 1945 SAIDA (Sociedad Anónima Inmobiliaria de Andalucía) was created to hold and operate property for centers in the south of Spain.*

After the definitive approval of Opus Dei in 1950, the Founder distinguished both in Opus Dei's constitutions and in the *Catechism of the Work* between two types of group apostolic activities, which he called *corporate works* and *common works*. Corporate works would be organized by Opus Dei as a corporation and directed by members of the Work. Existing examples were retreat houses and student residences. Later corporate works would include educational and social centers. The common works would be projects developed by members of Opus Dei and others through professional entities that disseminated Christian values in publications and the media.[1]

Opus Dei's direct interest in these projects was as vehicles for promoting Christian values and spreading the message of sanctity in the world rather than in their other educational, informational, social, technical, or economic aspects. The individuals who created and directed the corporate and common apostolates took legal responsibility for them. Nonetheless, in order to guarantee that

---

* See chapter 6, section 2 ("Consolidation in Spain").

the projects focused on the spiritual and apostolic goals for which they were founded, the central councils of the Work oversaw their development, and the general president of the Work confirmed the appointment of the directors proposed by the entities that owned and operated them.

The line between providing spiritual, doctrinal, and formational guidance to enable the activities to achieve their apostolic goals and directing other aspects of the activities was difficult to draw in practice and even in theory. The concern of Opus Dei and its directors was the doctrinal and spiritual formation given through these apostolates. Their interest in other aspects of their operations was ultimately because of their impact on the formation given. Nonetheless, their apostolic effectiveness was closely linked to how well they achieved their other goals and to their economic viability. Especially in the early days, the directors of Opus Dei decided which members of the Work would run the corporate and common apostolates and supervised their activities. They focused on the doctrinal and formational aspects, but inevitably people outside the Work sometimes thought of them as responsible for the entire project. The situation was analogous to that of the owner of a company who might be interested only in its profitability and leave operating decisions to others, but whom people tend to think of as ultimately responsible for the entire undertaking.

Even in theory, the distinction was elusive. The 1951 version of the *Catechism* of Opus Dei simply says, without further distinctions, that corporate apostolates are carried out [*hechas*] by Opus Dei.[2] The 1959 *Catechism* goes into more detail, but the picture that emerges remains murky. On one hand, it says that "the *exclusive* activity of Opus Dei is the formation of its members"[3] and "the members carry out all the apostolic works."[4] On the other, it describes corporate apostolates as "directed [*dirigidas*] by Opus Dei as such, as a corporation."[5] Similarly, it states it is the members who "are responsible for them to the competent civil authorities,"[6] but also states that "the Directors are responsible for them to the competent authority."[7]

Section 1. Corporate Works

Historically, the first form of institutional activities were corporate apostolic works undertaken by Opus Dei "as such, as a corporation."[8] The Work organized them, declared them its own, and guaranteed that the teaching was in accordance with Catholic doctrine. As we have seen, because the directors of Opus Dei assumed ultimate responsibility for these corporate works, they appointed their leaders. Those individuals took on the legal and economic responsibility that the law imposed on the officers and directors of whatever type of legal entity was involved in a particular case. They discussed with the directors of Opus Dei the Christian orientation of the activity and periodically sent to the Regional Commission or Advisory Board financial information reflecting the progress of the projects.

From an economic point of view, each corporate work was a stand-alone entity. In some countries, educational or charitable projects requested public funding for their charitable and social projects in addition to requesting contributions from members of the Work and cooperators.

Escrivá stressed that corporate works were a means and not an end in themselves. Opus Dei's goal was to offer the formation individuals needed to seek holiness and bear witness to Jesus Christ in their professional, family, and social lives. Because corporate works were only one means among others of spreading Opus Dei's message, they could be modified, terminated, or expanded as dictated by experience and changing circumstances. Escrivá also stressed that each individual who worked in a corporate activity should see their work as a way to live and give witness to their faith: "I measure the effectiveness of these tasks," he said, "by the degree of holiness achieved by those who work in them."[9] On one occasion, Professor Ortiz de Landázuri said to the Founder, "Well, Father, you asked me to come to Pamplona to create a university, and we've done it." Escrivá replied, "I didn't ask you to come to create a university, but to become a saint, creating a university."[10] Over time, corporate activities sprang up in many different fields. They included student residences and retreat houses, secretarial schools, hospitals and dispensaries, training centers for farm and industrial workers, schools for domestic and hospitality workers, universities, high schools, and primary schools.

These later corporate activities combined in one way or another two elements that had been present in the first corporate activity of Opus Dei, the DYA Academy and Residence (1933–1939). On the one hand, it was a professionally managed academic undertaking that offered classes and ran a student residence. On the other hand, it provided Christian formation and transmitted the spirit of Opus Dei through doctrine classes, meditations, and personal spiritual guidance. It was a space for training in Christian life and spreading the message of Opus Dei, a place where Escrivá gave classes in doctrine and meditations and provided direction to interested students.

In 1939, the Jenner Residence took the place of the DYA Residence. During the nineteen-forties in Spain, Opus Dei established the retreat houses of Molinoviejo and Los Rosales, a student residence for women—Zurbarán (Madrid)—and eight student residences for men: Abando (Bilbao), Albayzín (Granada), Guadaira (Sevilla), La Alcazaba (Córdoba), La Estila (Santiago de Compostela), Miraflores (Zaragoza), Moncloa (Madrid), and Monterols (Barcelona).

At the beginning, the Founder did not consider it appropriate for the Work to establish high schools, colleges, or universities. Education in Spain at the time was either public or denominational. He understood that the spirit of Opus Dei would move its members to work in public institutions. Thus, the statutes of 1941 mentioned that only as an exception would the members of the Work dedicate themselves "to private education, which is always, only and exclusively, a means, never an end" (*Ordo*, 13, 10).

After obtaining provisional approval of Opus Dei as a secular institute in 1947, the Founder continued to maintain the principle that the purpose of Opus Dei was not to promote schools or universities, but he became open to the idea of establishing a few as another way of providing a service to society and spreading the message of holiness in the midst of the world. The schools would need to combine a Christian identity, professional quality, and sound management. Parents interested in giving their children an excellent education in accordance with Christian doctrine would play a key role in starting and operating primary and secondary schools.

The first two corporate works in the educational field were the Gaztelueta School (Bilbao, 1951) and the Estudio General de Navarra (Pamplona, 1952). In Bilbao, some parents decided in 1947 they wanted to start a high school for boys. Luis María Ybarra Oriol, vice president of the electric company Iberduero and member of the board of directors of the Bank of Biscay, established a committee. After studying several proposals, a company created by members of the Work bought a large house in a suburb of Bilbao and remodeled it to serve as a school. On October 15, 1951, Gaztelueta School began classes with sixty-three students.

The Work encouraged a number of members who were experienced teachers to join the faculty of the new school. Among them were José Luis González-Simancas, who had studied the British educational system, the geographer Pedro Plans, and the chemist Isidoro Rasines.

Escrivá suggested a number of ideas, including a system of personal mentoring for every student. He discouraged having an honor roll or class ranking based on grades and expressed his hope that the students' uniform would be "cheerful." Above all he encouraged the headmaster and teachers to see the school as an extension of the students' families and to create an educational community that involved parents and students, as well as teachers and non-teaching staff. He did not make any suggestions about the curriculum or instructional methodology of the new school. The directors and teachers of Gaztelueta developed their own educational style based on high-quality personalized teaching and an emphasis on truth and sincerity.

In a short time, Gaztelueta School became well-known in Bilbao for its quality teaching, individual mentoring system, and stress on physical education and extracurricular activities combined with Christian formation and an atmosphere of manly piety. In addition to its regular program, it offered a parallel night program which allowed students who had to work during the day to obtain a high school diploma.

Opus Dei's second corporate venture in the field of education was much more ambitious: creating a university from scratch. This would have been challenging anywhere, but it was made more daunting by the Spanish government's almost total monopoly on higher education.[11] The fledgling university was originally called the Estudio General de Navarra (General Course of Studies of Navarre), a name derived from the title given in the Middle Ages to institutions of higher education. It began in the city of Pamplona in northern Spain. With a population that barely exceeded seventy thousand, the former capital of the Kingdom of Navarre had no college or university, but it had a rich Catholic tradition and was proud of the privileges (*fueros*) it had enjoyed since the Middle Ages. Within the strict limits imposed by the centralizing Franco regime, the province of Navarre enjoyed a certain amount of financial and administrative autonomy.

In May 1952, a law professor, Ismael Sánchez Bella, was commissioned by Escrivá to launch the project. Sánchez Bella was as full of hope as he was short of means. The provincial government, the Diputación Foral de Navarra, granted an annual subsidy, which covered part of the operating expenses. It also allowed the Estudio General to use for its classes a thirteenth-century Gothic building located in the historical center of Pamplona. The incipient university began its activities in October 1952 with a School of Law. It had eight professors and forty-one students.* Two years later, it opened Schools of Medicine and Nursing.[12] In 1955 it began a College of Arts and Sciences with a history department.

In 1954, Opus Dei initiated a novel educational venture, a sports school in Barcelona called Brafa. Located in Nou Barris, a working-class neighborhood on the northern fringes of the city, Brafa offered playing fields and instruction in various sports. It taught physical

---

* In Spain students entered law school straight out of high school. There was no requirement of having first earned an undergraduate degree.

conditioning, organized teams, and stressed sportsmanship as a way of helping young men from disadvantaged backgrounds to develop character. It also offered Christian formation to those who were interested.

The next two educational corporate works were located in the small town of Culiacán, 750 miles (twelve hundred kilometers) northwest of Mexico City. In 1955, the Chapultepec School for girls started with a kindergarten that later developed a grade school and a high school. Chapultepec Institute for boys opened a year later. Both schools had an evening section for workers that offered training course for salespeople and bank clerks and supervisors. The same people who founded the schools also created a workers' cultural center that offered primary school certificate courses and private accounting and construction drafting courses.

Opus Dei's Second General Congress, held in 1956, focused on institutional activities. The congress members expressed their pleasure with the progress being made by student residences, the Estudio General de Navarra, the Gaztelueta School, and the two schools in Culiacán.[13]

For a number of years, Escrivá had been thinking about starting both a journalism school and a business school.* Shortly after the Second General Congress, Antonio Fontán, a specialist in journalism and a professor of philology at the University of Granada, was commissioned to create a journalism school as part of the Estudio General. He moved to Pamplona to become dean of the School of Philosophy and Letters in 1956. Two years later, he started an Institute of Journalism which would eventually become a School of Communications. The Institute of Journalism was a novelty in Spain. The state-sponsored schools of journalism which dominated the field were essentially trade schools and concentrated almost exclusively

---

* In November 1950, the General Council approved that the president general reserve to himself "all matters relating to the creation of a School of Journalism, a Social School and a School of Higher Economic and Commercial Studies in Spain." Minutes of the General Council, November 26, 1950, p. 9, AGP E.1.2.

on the practical aspects of journalism. Fontán's institute combined serious study of the humanities with practical training, making journalism an integral part of the incipient university rather than a trade school. Its goal was to educate journalists who wanted to shape public opinion through the media as a Christian service to the community.[14] Over the years, it helped raise journalism in Spain to the level of a profession.

Antonio Valero, an engineering professor and a director of Opus Dei, took the lead on the project of creating a business school. Although it would be part of the Estudio General, it would be located in Barcelona, the business capital of Spain and home to a sizeable number of Opus Dei members. Escrivá approved in March 1958 the creation of an Instituto de Estudios Superiores de Empresa (IESE, Institute of Higher Business Studies). The school's aim would be to prepare technically excellent business people who would try to incarnate gospel values in the world of business without limiting themselves to the search for economic success. Valero and the initial IESE faculty members decided to use the Harvard Business School case method. IESE's first activity was a Senior Management Program, which enrolled twenty entrepreneurs and executives in November 1958.

In 1959, the germ of the future College of Sciences and the Institute of Canon Law were inaugurated in Pamplona. The Canon Law Institute was associated with the Pontifical Lateran University in Rome.

Both the Provincial Council of Navarre and Founder wanted the degrees granted by the Estudio General to be officially recognized as having the same validity as the degrees granted by state-run universities. Spanish law, however, made no provision for private universities. Only the state and the Church could establish centers of higher education. Although Opus Dei would have greatly preferred to have the Estudio General treated as a secular private university, the only way for its degrees to be recognized was for it to become an official Catholic university. The Congregation for Seminaries and Universities erected the University of Navarre as a Catholic university on August

6, 1960, and appointed Escrivá its first chancellor and José María Albareda its first rector.

This did not automatically bring with it the right to grant degrees. Some leaders of the Falange and of the National Catholic Association of Propagandists continued to resist granting official recognition of the new university's degrees because they wanted to preserve the government's monopoly of higher education. The impasse forced Escrivá to travel to Madrid and complain to Franco. Finally, the Holy See and the Spanish state signed an agreement in April 1962 establishing the conditions for the validity of degrees awarded by Catholic universities. The conditions were very onerous. Above all, seventy-five percent of the full professors had to be people who had already won in a national competition a full professorship (*cátedra*) in a state university. Finally, in September 1962, the Ministry of National Education granted full civil effect to the degrees conferred by the University of Navarre.[15]

In Pamplona, the Estudio General de Navarra moved to a new one-hundred-acre (forty hectare) campus located south of the city. Over the next few years, it witnessed a flurry of construction, including an imposing Renaissance-style central building, a minimalist modern library, two residential colleges, the Medical School, and the first phase of the University Clinic, with twenty-seven beds. In 1961, the university established another campus in San Sebastián with a School of Industrial Engineering, which began its activities in a building ceded by the Provincial Government of Guipúzcoa.

Tuition and fees at the state-run universities, which dominated higher education, were almost symbolic. To be competitive, the Estudio General had to keep its own charges low. The financial situation was further complicated by the university's determination to provide substantial scholarship aid. The Provincial Councils of Navarre and Guipúzcoa granted some subsidies, but the national government offered only minimal support, mostly limited to construction loans. The absence of any tradition of substantial private giving to Spanish universities was a serious obstacle to the fundraising efforts of the Association of Friends the university formed to raise private funds.

In 1958 the Colegio Tajamar, a primary and secondary school for boys, was started in Vallecas, a shantytown in the middle of a wasteland on the southeastern edge of Madrid. The area lacked sewers and water and had few paved roads. A few years earlier, Tajamar had taken its first steps as a sports association for neighborhood boys. Many of the young people who came for sports instruction did not attend school, in part because the nearest schools were some distance away. The members of the Work and their friends who had established the sports association decided to start a school. The first year Tajamar had fifty-eight day students and eighteen night students, mostly apprentices who worked full-time during the day. The school rented and minimally remodeled an old, unheated cowshed. The addition of two prefabricated buildings increased capacity to 160 students. In 1962 a first group of new buildings was inaugurated. The minimalist but handsome low-slung buildings surrounded by grass contrasted sharply with the ankle-deep mud and shacks that made up the neighborhood. Five years later, enough other buildings were constructed to house all the school's primary, secondary and technical training courses. In addition to offering high-level education and hands on training, the teachers at Tajamar tried to transmit a Christian vision of life.[16]

In 1959, the women of the Work started the Guadalaviar School in Valencia, Spain. It began as a kindergarten and gradually added a primary school and high school.[17]

Section 2. Common Apostolic Works

As the twentieth century progressed, the Church became increasingly aware of the influence of publications and media of all sorts on thought and action. The hierarchy, religious orders, and some Catholic laymen responded by creating publishing houses, magazines, and newspapers, primarily of an overtly Catholic character, which sought readers almost exclusively among practicing Catholics. The Founder also appreciated the growing importance of the mass media, which he saw as "a channel—or even a source—of educational influence almost comparable to that of the family and the school."[18]

He was concerned that many of the most important media groups in the world were inspired by ideas far removed from Christian revelation and the truth about God and human nature. Specifically, he saw in the world three "waves" that turned individuals and institutions away from God and the Church. He described them as the red wave of Marxism, the green wave of pan-sexualism, and the black wave of materialistic secularism. In part, Escrivá attributed this situation to the failure of Christian lay men and women who had negligently allowed others to run the media: "Tell me, how many great newspapers that have millions of readers and make and unmake world public opinion are run by practicing Catholics? There are none."[19] The same thing, he continued, was true of international news and advertising agencies, and the film production and distribution companies.

The Founder was not content with sterile laments. The media was a positive reality. Catholics, and specifically members of Opus Dei, needed to be present in the places where public opinion was shaped, in order to "restore to temporal structures, in all nations, their natural function as an instrument for the progress of humanity, and their supernatural function as a means of reaching God."[20]

All Catholics, Escrivá felt, should aspire to contributing in one way or another to making the media and entertainment a positive influence in the lives of individuals and families. Most would limit themselves to choosing films, newspapers, and magazines whose message reflected a Christian view of life, or at least was not opposed to it, and perhaps by writing an occasional letter to the editor. Some would work professionally in one capacity or another in the media and entertainment, either individually or together with other likeminded people.

All of this applied *a fortiori* to members of Opus Dei. Escrivá encouraged them all to be aware of the importance of the media in shaping society and to contribute in whatever ways they could to making that influence a positive one. He also urged those with the appropriate talent and inclinations to consider careers in the media and entertainment fields. Finally, he suggested that some of the professional journalists who belonged to the Work could create corporate realities in the field of communication and entertainment.

Whether working individually or in corporate undertakings, he urged journalists who belonged to the Work and others to be not only competent but audacious, facing the great issues of their time with personal freedom and responsibility, transmitting a Christian view of life and events through modern, attractive, secular publications, films, and so forth.

As we have seen, well before the creation of a framework for common apostolic activities in the media, women of the Work had launched the short-lived experiment of Editorial Minerva. That first venture had been followed by Ediciones Rialp. A few years later, with Escrivá's encouragement, some women of Opus Dei began running a book distribution and sales company called DELSA, whose goal was to establish a network of bookstores.

Beginning in 1952, members of Opus Dei organized various common works of apostolate in the media as a way of bringing the Work's Christian message into the mainstream of society. The experiment proved short-lived because experience soon proved that activities in this area needed to be totally autonomous, without any institutional involvement of the Work. In 1966, Escrivá put an end to the category of common works of apostolate. The experiment, however, merits some attention. We will first explore the general framework and then mention briefly some of the publications and other ventures created within it.

The media ventures that were common apostolates of the Work, like other media companies, had a content side that implied an editorial policy, as well as an economic and commercial side The directors of the communications companies set the editorial policy, chose the journalists and writers, and were responsible for the publications' contents. They sought editors and writers who joined professional competence to a commitment to the Christian values of love of truth, pluralism, freedom, and charity.

Finances, labor, and contractual matters were the responsibility of the companies that owned and managed the publications, companies referred to in Opus Dei as "auxiliary companies," whose boards of directors were legally and economically responsible for the publications.

Media ventures, particularly those of a cultural or informative nature, such as magazines, often required a considerable initial investment and faced serious economic challenges. Some managed to become profitable or at least self-sustaining, while others were forced to close because they were not economically viable.

The directors of the Work were guarantors of the apostolic purpose of each initiative. For this reason, the president of Opus Dei ratified the appointment of the director of each one and appointed a spiritual advisor to the publication. Because they could not achieve their apostolic goals if they were not economically viable, the common works were asked to send their financial statements to the central or regional administration department of the Work, which offered advice on how they could become economically sustainable.

The governing bodies of Opus Dei, on the other hand, did not control the boards of directors or the editorial committees of the publications, nor did they give instructions on their information content. For this reason, unlike corporate apostolates, the common apostolates did not describe themselves as connected to Opus Dei. Nonetheless, the practical intertwining of the Work and its directors with these publications understandably tended to cast doubt on their independence. As we will see, this is one of the reasons why the experiment came to an end fifteen years later.

Turing to specific common apostolates, we have seen that the women of Opus Dei in Spain began in 1951 to establish a chain of bookstores. The first, called Neblí, was located on Ferraz Street in Madrid. In the following years, DELSA established more stores, run by women from the Work, and in 1958, established a subsidiary company, LINESA (Librerías del Norte de España). By the end of the nineteen-fifties, DELSA had a total of thirteen stores, including seven in Catalonia. LINESA had stores in Pamplona and San Sebastián. In 1960, DELSA's flagship store, Neblí, moved to Madrid's most prestigious shopping street, the Calle Serrano.

Each bookstore had a different name. They sold all kinds of books, from scientific to literary to religious, as well as textbooks. They also sold stationery and office supplies. The bookstores made available to their customers book reviews and bibliographies prepared by DELSA. DELSA also sold books through bookmobiles that traveled from town to town and through a network of about a hundred correspondents to whom they entrusted a supply of books to sell in their small towns.[21]

A financial company controlled at first by male members of the Work, ESFINA, handled the corporate-level accounting and legal and commercial side of DELSA. Women of Opus Dei hired and supervised the managers and other employees of each store and took care of store-level accounting. In 1960, women of Opus Dei took on leadership roles in ESFINA as well.[22]

In the 1950s, Escrivá encouraged members of the Work who had the necessary skills and interests to consider careers in the media. In addition he encouraged them to create cultural and graphic magazines which would offer a Christian perspective on events and ideas while avoiding controversy with other Catholics. Antonio Fontán, a university professor who had always been interested in journalism, created in 1952 a weekly magazine called *La Actualidad Española*. It was an illustrated family magazine, which covered current political and cultural events as well as human interest stories. Two years later, Fontán started *Nuestro Tiempo*, a monthly cultural and opinion magazine. Both magazines were owned by SARPE, the Work's publishing and media holding company.

At Opus Dei's Second General Congress in 1956, the electors noted with satisfaction the development of the eight common works that existed at the time. The Founder encouraged additional undertakings in the press, radio, television, and news agencies to spread the Christian message "among all social classes of civil society."[23] The congress set a goal of creating in each region a monthly cultural magazine and a daily newspaper in the country's capital.

In October 1957, a gathering was organized in Rome of academics and people working in communications. The participants reviewed the goals for common works set at the general congress and committed themselves to trying to reach them. The plan was relatively successful in Spain, but in other countries the results were modest to non-existent. At the end of the 1950s, there were thirty-eight common works in seven regions, mostly periodical publications. Five were cultural magazines: *Nuestro Tiempo* (Pamplona, 1954), *Rumo* (Lisbon, 1957), *La Table Ronde* (Paris, 1958), *Istmo* (Mexico City, 1959) and *Arco* (Bogotá, 1959). Five were university magazines: *Moncloa*, *Pórtico*, *Diagonal*, *Miraflores*, and *University Gazette*. Three were newspapers: *El Alcázar*, *Diario Regional*, *Diario de León* (all in Spain). Two were professional journals: *La Actualidad Económica* and *Revista de Medicina del Estudio General de Navarra*. There were also the weekly graphic magazine *La Actualidad Española*; the practical theology journal *Studi Cattolici* (Milan, 1957); the film journal *Filme* (Lisbon, 1959); and the popular neighborhood journal *Vallecas*. Also among the common works were the press agencies Europa Press (Madrid) and Anco (Bogotá); the publishing houses Rialp (Madrid, 1947), Scepter (Dublin-London-Chicago, 1953), Aster (Lisbon, 1955), Ares (Rome, 1956), and Adamas (Cologne, 1957); and various cultural forums, such as the Cine-Club Monterols.[24]

An unusual common apostolate was the religious goods house Talleres de Arte in Spain. It reflected Escrivá's desire to embellish the liturgy and the expressions of Christian worship. He saw the beauty of churches and vestments and the quality of tabernacles and sacred vessels as manifestation of adoration and love of God. He appreciated how the liturgical movement deepened Catholics' understanding of the nature of worship and its external manifestations. He did not propose novel forms but adopted those he felt helped the piety of the faithful.

In Madrid, in 1940, he began to purchase liturgical items from a company run by Fr. Félix Granda and his sister Candida Granda. They had workshops for goldsmithing, carpentry, enamels, and jewelry that produced extraordinarily high-quality items. As the years went by, however, the company began to suffer serious economic difficulties. Escrivá wanted it to continue contributing to the liturgy by offering beautiful sacred art and sacred vessels. In 1953, a society organized by members of the Work acquired the company, which was registered under the name Talleres de Arte, S. A. It was directed by the financier Tesifonte López. It added other facilities to the existing workshops. The factories were located on the grounds of two retreat houses: one that made and sold general clothing in Molinoviejo and another that made vestments and carpets in Los Rosales. In both cases, women from nearby villages worked and received training in tailoring and embroidery.

Talleres de Arte received numerous commissions from residences and schools run by members of Opus Dei around the world and also from other Catholic institutions. Over time, Talleres took on complex architectural and decorative projects for churches, oratories, and altars, in addition to making tabernacles, sacred vessels, medals, crucifixes and reproductions, in both classic and modern styles.[25] It also bought, in antique shops, images and other objects of worship which had been removed from churches, and recovered them for worship by restoring and selling them to religious entities.[26]

Section 3. Auxiliary Companies

Escrivá did not want the Work as an institution to own property or be involved in financial activities. In many cases, even the entities formed to sponsor and carry out corporate apostolic activities would not do so. Instead, the members would create companies, trusts, or foundations that would own and manage real estate and other property used in the apostolic activities. Financial and real estate professionals would set up and operate the companies, whose structure would vary from place to place depending on the laws of the country. The real estate and other goods they owned would not be ecclesiastical property regulated by Church law, but would belong to the company and be regulated by civil law. When the company was for-profit, the ultimate beneficiary owners would be the private citizens who had invested in it in the hope of receiving a reasonable return on their capital while supporting an apostolic activity.

Depending on local legislation and specific needs, the companies might be for-profit or not-for-profit corporations, foundations, joint stock companies, or trusts. They functioned autonomously, without forming a chain. There were, therefore, no consolidated accounts of Opus Dei or of all the apostolic undertakings.

The companies obtained the capital they needed through donations, loans, and sale of stock. Some of them also earned money through ownership and management of real estate and other economic activities unconnected with the apostolates of Opus Dei except through donations of the profits earned or their investment in new properties to be used in apostolic activities. Their officers, directors, and owners were members and cooperators of Opus Dei and other people who wanted to contribute to the social, cultural, charitable, and religious activities they supported.

Escrivá thought that the use of these various types of companies to finance and support apostolic activities was in keeping with the secular and lay spirit of the Work. Since they were not ecclesiastical entities, neither the Church nor Opus Dei had to be concerned about being liable for their economic and professional activities. Furthermore, they minimized the danger of losing property in a possible confiscation of ecclesiastical goods by the state, a danger Escrivá was especially aware of since he had experienced firsthand the expropriation of the Foundation of St. Elizabeth by the Spanish government in the spring of 1936.

Opus Dei was interested in these entities and called them "auxiliary companies" only because they mobilized people and resources necessary "to finance apostolic activities."[27] In Escrivá's words, "The Auxiliary Companies are a professionally managed economic framework that makes it possible to create, sustain, and develop the common apostolates, and at times, the corporate apostolates of our Institute."[28] He considered them the "ordinary means for the administration of goods and for the legal planning of our common and corporate tasks."[29] In order to ensure that the auxiliary companies would continue over time to contribute to the apostolic goals for which they were created, at least 51 percent of the company's capital was in the hands of people who were interested in the apostolic activities it supported, whether members of the Work or not.

In addition, the directors of the Work appointed a technical advisor with the mission of seeing to it that the auxiliary businesses fulfilled their apostolic goals. He was not always an officer, but he had a seat on the board of directors. To ensure that their capital was professionally managed in light of their apostolic purpose, the auxiliary companies periodically sent their accounts with an explanatory report to the regional administration department—or in the case of the women's branch, the regional procurator's office—so they could review the progress of their projects and make any appropriate suggestions.[30]

The Founder explained that this tutelage of the auxiliary companies by the directors of Opus Dei was due to the fact that some of the people involved in them still had little experience. It was a "circumstantial approach" whose only purpose was "to protect the use of the means that are used for the service of God."[31] This type of oversight of the members' business, financial, and economic activities was limited to the auxiliary companies. Escrivá clarified: "When I have written that the Directors control the economic activities of the members, I am referring exclusively to the proper administration of the apostolic instruments necessary to carry out apostolic activities."[32]

During the 1940s, a number of auxiliary companies were established in Spain. In the 1950s, some of them grew to significant proportions. The most important was ESFINA (Sociedad Española Anónima de Estudios Financieros), a holding company that owned the majority of shares in various commercial companies operated for essentially apostolic purposes. Alberto Ullastres was the president of the board of directors. The CEO was Fernando Camacho. Luis Valls Taberner and Andrés Rueda Salaberry were vice presidents. ESFINA held the majority of the shares of the publishing company SARPE (Sociedad Anónima de Revistas, Periódicos y Ediciones), which had been started five years earlier to hold shares in media companies. SARPE published the magazines *La Actualidad Española* and *Nuestro*

Tiempo as well as a weekly business magazine, *Actualidad Económica*. In the mid 1950s, it purchased majority interests in three newspapers: *Diario Regional de Valladolid*, *Diario de León*, and the Madrid evening newspaper *El Alcázar*. The ESFINA group also had interests in the book distributor DELSA, the film distributors Dipenfa and Filmayer, the advertising agencies Clarín and ALAS, and the news agency Europa Press.*

The auxiliary companies, like companies associated with other Catholic groups, served as a channel to transmit Christian values to society as a whole and to the many professional men and women who worked in them. Escrivá stressed that, in addition, they were called to be the specific means of personal sanctification for the members of the Work who worked there professionally.

Section 4. Office of the Apostolate of Public Opinion

The Second General Congress of Opus Dei (1956) set as a priority for the upcoming years the apostolate of public opinion; that is, spreading gospel values through the media, including the press and publications, radio, television, and films. In response, some people of the Work began working in existing media organizations or created new ones, started the School of Journalism of the Estudio General de Navarra, and began new common works related to information.

In 1957, Escrivá created the Office of the Apostolate of Public Opinion as an auxiliary office of the General Council charged with preparing information about the spirit and activities of Opus Dei, overseeing the Work's relations with the media, heightening awareness of the situation of Catholics in different parts of the world, and encouraging the use of the media to explain Christian doctrine on the rights and duties of the laity in the Church and civil society.

---

* In the conditions of the Franco regime, these undertakings contributed to a more open and pluralistic environment than that of the state-controlled media. See Carlos Barrera, "El Opus Dei y la prensa en el tardofranquismo," *Historia y Política* 28 (2012), pp. 139–165.

Initially, the office focused on three areas: providing information about Opus Dei to professional journalists; disseminating news about the Work's collective activities; and developing a documentation center on Christian doctrine and cultural topics. From 1959 on, it produced and distributed to Opus Dei's centers and to the directors of the common works a mimeographed monthly bulletin, SIDEC (Servicio Internacional de Colaboraciones). It offered news stories on current public, cultural, and religious life throughout the world, information on the Work's corporate activities, and articles on doctrinal and cultural issues, such as educational freedom, the activities of Catholics in public life, or intellectual discussions regarding Marxism.[33]

To facilitate writing articles about the Work and its apostolic activities, the central office of the Apostolate of Public Opinion sent to the regions an extensive file of short explanations of various topics such as secularity, love of freedom, the apostolic purpose of Opus Dei, and its corporate apostolates. Over time, it added to the file (referred to as the *Clasificador Informativo*) quotations, press clippings, and anecdotes.[34]

Starting in 1959, regional offices of the apostolate of public opinion were created. In most cases, they were quite small, often a single person who had other responsibilities as well. Depending on the circumstances and possibilities of each country, the regional offices carried out diverse functions: maintaining contacts with local journalists, writers, and press attachés at foreign embassies and sending them information about the Work and its apostolates; encouraging members to contribute in whatever way they could to the apostolate of public opinion, for instance by writing opinion pieces for local publications; encouraging students to study journalism at the University of Navarre; seeking subscribers for the publications that were common works of apostolate; keeping abreast of religious, public, and cultural events in the country and sending information to Rome for possible inclusion in SIDEC; or advising members about writing letters to the editor to clarify erroneous information about the Work and to express their appreciation for accurate and interesting articles.[35]

Occasionally Opus Dei issued official press releases to provide information about particularly significant events, like legal approvals from the Holy See, or to correct important errors in major publications—for instance articles attributing to the Work the professional or political activities of its members. These communiqués were signed by the General Secretariat of Opus Dei or by the Regional Secretariat in a particular country.

Notes

1. See also *Constitutiones Societatis Sacerdotalis Sanctae Crucis et Operis Dei* (1950), no. 365, AGP L1.1, 12-3-2; *Catechism* (1951, 2nd ed.), no. 339, AGP E.1.1, 181-2-1.
2. *Catechism* 1951, no. 420, AGP E.1.1, 182-2-1.
3. *Catechism* 1959, n. 530, AGP E 1.1, 182-1-4.
4. Josemaría Escrivá de Balaguer, handwritten note, September 9, 1943, AGP L 1.1, 1-3-8.
5. *Catechism* 1959, n. 529, AGP E 1.1, 182-1-4.
6. *Catechism* 1959, n. 530, AGP E 1.1, 182-1-4.
7. *Catechism* 1959, n. 530, AGP E 1.1, 182-1-4.
8. *Catechism*, 1951 (2nd ed.), no. 339, AGP E.1.1, 181-2-1.
9. Letter 24, no. 34, AGP A.3, 93-3-4.
10. Esteban López-Escobar and Pedro Lozano, *Eduardo Ortiz de Landázuri: El médico amigo* (Madrid: Rialp, 2003), pp. 200–201.
11. The only exception was the Universidad de Deusto founded by the Jesuits in the mid-nineteenth century. In the 1950s, it had only about five hundred students, who had to take exams at a state-run university because Deusto still had not obtained the required government permission to grant degrees.
12. Students also entered the School of Medicine straight out of high school.
13. In addition, the members of the Congress of the women's branch also reviewed other apostolic undertakings and proposals, including the nursing school of the Estudio General de Navarra, kindergartens, high schools, university residences, retreat houses, farm schools, home arts centers, and what they called "Sunday Schools" for domestic employees.

14. See Carlos Barrera, "Josemaría Escrivá de Balaguer y el Instituto de Periodismo de la Universidad de Navarra," *Studia et Documenta* 2 (2008), pp. 231–257. In 1957, the first steps were taken to create a freestanding university-level school of journalism in Washington, DC. A year later, it opened with the name Maryland Institute of General Studies, but it failed to attract students and closed a few years later.

15. These efforts benefited other institutions. In 1963, government recognition was granted for studies carried out in some schools of the Catholic University of Deusto (Bilbao)—which was also erected by the Holy See that year—and the Pontifical University of Salamanca. See Vicente Cárcel Ortí, *Historia de la Iglesia en la España contemporánea* (Madrid: Palabra, 2002), p. 493.

16. See Jesus Carnicero, *Entre chabolas. Inicios del colegio Tajamar en Vallecas* (Madrid:Rialp, 2011).

17. See AGP Q.2.1, 3-85.

18. Letter 12, no. 8, AGP A.3, 92-5-1.

19. Letter 12, no. 37, AGP A.3, 92-5-1.

20. Letter 12, no. 37, AGP A.3, 92-5-1. He added: "We must confess God, filling the world, as I often repeat to you, with printed paper, because that is a way of manifesting my children's dominant passion of giving doctrine." Letter 12, no. 49.

21. See AGP T.7, 1-7.

22. See AGP T.7, 1-2.

23. Conclusions of the Second General Congress of Opus Dei (August 25, 1956, for men; October 25, 1956, for women), AGP D.1, 457-3-6 and 457-3-12, respectively.

24. See AGP K.1, 186-1.

25. General Note 10/66 (January 21, 1966), AGP E.1.3, 244-5.

26. See General Note 74/65 (June 4, 1965), AGP E.1.3, 244-4.

27. *Instruction on the Work of St. Gabriel* (May 1935, September 1950), no. 126. AGP A.3, 90-3-1.

28. General Note 4, no. 2 (June 1952), AGP Q.1.3, 2-10.

29. General Note 239, no. 4 (June 28, 1959), AGP E.1.3, 242-2; and General Note 176, no. 4 (September 3, 1959), AGP Q.1.3, 2-14.

30. See General Note 56 (December 5, 1956), AGP Q.1.3, 2-10.

31. Handwritten note, January 9, 1943, AGP L.1.1, 1-3-8.

32. Handwritten note, January 9, 1943, AGP L.1.1, 1-3-8

33. AGP K.8, 872, 1125. In 1960, a "Supplement" was added to each issue. It contained both original articles and press clippings about corporate activities. SIDEC and the Supplement were merged in 1971 into a single biweekly bulletin called *Interpress*, which contained articles published in the international press about Christian life in various countries.

34. See General Note 506 (April 13, 1962), AGP E.1.3, 242-4.

35. See General Note 242 (July 1, 1959), AGP E.1.3, 242-1; General Note 310 (April 16, 1960), AGP E.1.3, 242-2; and General Note 352 (December 5, 1960), AGP E.1.3, 242-2.

EPILOGUE

This volume ends in 1962.

During its first third of a century, Opus Dei developed rapidly. From fewer than twenty members at the outbreak of the Spanish Civil War in 1936, it grew to some six thousand. The Work spread to many countries in Western Europe and the Americas and established its first centers in Africa (Kenya) and Asia (Japan).

A large number of priests were ordained and the ranks of married members also grew quickly. The growing diversity of its members, and the fact that increasing numbers of them were reaching professional maturity, meant that their personal apostolate of friendship and confidence was reaching wider circles of people.

Corporately, the Work had established student residences and conference centers in many countries and was taking its first steps in both higher and secondary education. It had received the definitive approval of the Holy See, although it was uncomfortable in the legal category of secular institute and was beginning for look for a new legal category.

Had it not been for the opening of the Second Vatican Council on October 11, 1962, that year would not have marked a turning point in Opus Dei's history. But the Work was, as its founder liked to say, a small part of the Church, so the changes in the life of the Church introduced by the Council were bound to have a profound effect on Opus Dei's development.

Two were especially important. First, the Council emphasized the universal call to sanctity and the role of the laity in sanctifying the world from within, thereby proclaiming central elements of Opus Dei's spirituality as part of the universal teaching of the Church. Second, the Council's call for the creation of personal prelatures opened the door to the change in legal categorization that Opus Dei was looking for.

In Volume 2 we will see how Opus Dei continued to grow and develop in the post-Vatican II Church.

INDEX

This index includes proper names in normal type and topics in small caps. Josemaría Escrivá de Balaguer Albás and Álvaro del Portillo y Diez de Sollano do not appear because they are mentioned so frequently in the book (495 and 77 times, respectively).

A

Abad, Remigio, 182
Acaso, Fernando, 188
Administration of the centers, 68nn, 87–91, 92n7, 104–06, 112, 129–30, 130n, 137–38, 142n34, 147, 150–52, 152n, 153, 158, 163, 170n13, 175, 180, 184, 186, 190
Aguilar, José Manuel, 64
Alandes, Sabina, 173
Alastrué, Eduardo, 43, 48, 50, 73, 80n21, 115
Albareda, José María, 45, 47, 49, 51n1, 59, 64, 66, 70, 72–73, 76, 80n17, 218
Albás, Carlos, xxv, xxvii
Albás Blanc, Dolores, xx, xxv, 83–84
Albás Blanc, Mauricio, xxv
Albás, Vicente, xxvii
Albrecht, Jim, 191
Alfonse XIII, 2, 14
Alonso Pacheco, Joaquín, 162
Álvarez Gazapo, Jesús, 166
Alvira, Tomás, 45, 131
Alvira, Visitación, 86
Amo, Álvaro del, 74, 76, 114
Andrés, Concepción, 91

Angelicchio, Francesco, 111, 119n20
Antoniutti, Ildebrando, 169
Aparici, Manuel, 75
Armisén, José Antonio, 188
Arrese, José Luis, 202
Ayala, Francisco Xavier, xxxn26, 128, 178
Azevedo, Hugo de, 119n21, 179

B

Baird, Mildred, 186
Balcells, Alfons, 65, 75, 81n25
Bandeira, Lourdes, 117
Bardinet, Catherine, 117, 162, 180
Barrett, Anna, 116
Berazaluce, María Inmaculada, 191
Berry, Chuck, 143
Bisleti, Giovanni, 157
Borbón y Battenberg, Juan de, 55, 200
Borobio, Luis, 149
Botella, Enriqueta, 84–85, 90, 92n3
Botella, Francisco, 45, 47, 50, 50n1, 59, 79n1, 128–29
Brosa, Jorge, 75
Bueno Monreal, José María, 64, 66, 95

Burke, Cormac, 115–16, 174, 187
Burke, Honoria, 116
Bustillo, Julia, 91

C

Cabellero Santos, Manuel, 166
Cabeza, Modesta, 18
Caggiano, Antonio, 109
Cagigal, Jesús Alberto, 166
Calasanz, José de, 138
Calleja, Álvaro, 116–17
Calvo Serer, Rafael, 50, 61, 72, 102, 115, 200–01, 204, 207n11, 207n15
Camacho, Fernando, 227
Canalejas, José, xx
Canals, Salvador, 74, 76, 78, 108, 118n17, 121
Carrero Blanco, Luis, 201–03
Carrillo, Ángel, 74–77
Carroll, Janis, 191
Casas Torres, José Manuel, 61
Casciaro, Pedro, 45, 47, 50, 50n1, 62, 75, 98–99, 103, 125, 128, 168, 173, 179, 183, 189
Castro, Fidel, 143
Central and regional government, xx, xvii, 12, 59, 65n, 66, 68, 96–97, 101, 125, 128, 131–32, 134–35, 150, 152, 155, 159–63, 165–66, 168–69, 179, 189, 195, 203n
Cerejeira, Manuel, 109, 179
Cervós, Jordi, 181, 191n6
Cicognani, Gaetano, 76, 81n29–30, 76, 103
Cirac, Sebastián, 14
Common Apostolic works, 209–12, 219, 221–22, 225–27, 229, 230n13

Concha, Ignacio de la, 128, 183
Corporate works, 173, 175, 179, 181, 195, 197, 199, 204, 209–16, 221–23, 225–26, 229, 232n33
Cuervo, Carmen, 18
Cummings, Paul, 116

D

De Filippi, Giorgio, 162
Delapuente, Fernando, 166
Díaz Gómara, Miguel de los Santos, xxvii
Duclaud, Gabriela, 162

E

Echevarría, Javier, ix, xiv, xvi, 31n
Echeverría, Fernando, 181
Eijo Garay, Leopoldo, 34, 51n6, 61, 66, 76, 80n21, 81n28, 95, 97, 99, 139
Elejalde, María Josefa, 182
Escarré, Aureli, 76, 81n28
Escolá, Rafael, 75
Escrivá, José, xx–xxv, xxvii
Escrivá, Teodoro, xxvii
Escrivá de Balaguer y Albás, Carmen, xxi, xxiii, 83, 85, 88–90, 107, 147, 157, 170n8
Escrivá de Balaguer y Albás, María Asunción, xxii
Escrivá de Balaguer y Albás, María de los Dolores, xxii
Escrivá de Balaguer y Albás, María del Rosario, xxii
Escrivá de Balaguer y Albás, Santiago, xxv, 43, 44, 157

F

Farri, Umberto, 136
Ferigle, Salvador, 185
Fernández, Bernardo, 162
Fernández del Amo, Concepción, 83, 85, 86
Fernández del Amo, Laura, 83
Fernández Vallespín, Ricardo, 29, 32, 33, 39n11, 50, 59, 64, 66, 72, 98, 173, 209
Ferreira, Nuno Girão, 162
Filippone, Gabriella, 112
Fisac, María Dolores, 44, 50, 51n3, 83, 84, 85, 91
Fisac, Miguel, 44, 45, 50, 51n1, 57n1, 73, 103
Fontán, Antonio, 72, 126, 207n15, 216, 217, 223
Francés, Joaquín, 182
Franco, Francisco, 2, 42, 49, 54, 55, 56, 71, 77, 199, 200, 201, 202, 204, 206, 218
Fraternity and family lives, 49
Freitag, Hans, 182
Frings, Josef, 109
Fuenmayor, Amadeo de, xvn, 40n16, 61, 62, 72, 80n10, 118n11, 126, 141n21, 142n29, 158

G

Galarraga, Juan Antonio, 115, 116, 129
Gama, Emérico da, 114
García Escobar, María Ignacia, 18, 23n44
García Hoz, Víctor, 131, 141n16
García Ruiz, Hermógenes, 18
García, Julia, 114
García, Alfredo, 149
Gasparri, Pietro, 2
Gatti, Maria, 181
Gomá, Cardinal Isidro, 57
Gómez Ruiz, Adolfo, 14
González Barredo, José María, 29, 33, 39n11, 43, 50, 173, 185
González Guzmán, Narcisa, 84, 85, 86, 90, 92nn3, 7, 129, 173
González-Simancas, José Luis, 214
Gouveia, Theodósio Clemente de, 109
Goyeneche, Siervo, 120
Granda, Cándida, 224
Granda, Félix, 224
Grinda, José, 183
Guardans, Ramón, 75, 103

H

Healy, Helen, 186
Hereza, María Jesús, 83
Hernández Garnica, José María, 19n8, 33, 39n12, 42, 43, 50, 61, 66, 78n1, 95, 98, 99, 106, 131
Herranz, Julián, 162, 208
Hitler, Adolf, 2
Holy See, xiin, 46, 55, 78, 81n32, 96, 108, 109, 110, 120, 121, 125, 127, 131, 132, 133, 134, 135, 136, 137, 138, 139, 142n31, 145, 158, 161, 168, 179, 189, 199, 218, 230, 231n15, 233
Hoyo, Dora del, 91, 91n

I

Ibáñez Martín, José, 70, 73
Ignatius of Loyola, Saint, 75, 94

Illanes, José Luis, xvn, xxixn3, 20n10, 21n11, 23n41, 40n16, 80n10, 118n11, 141n21, 142n29, 206, 208n23
Inciarte, Fernando, 181
Incorporation into Opus Dei, 36, 163, 169

J

Jato, David, 73
Jiménez Salas, María, 102
Jiménez Vargas, Dolores, 83, 85
Jiménez Vargas, Juan, 26n, 27, 33, 34, 39nn6, 11, 42, 43, 44, 45, 47, 50, 51n7, 57n1, 59, 63, 64, 65, 66, 72, 73, 83
John of the Cross, Saint, 26
José Miguel de la Virgen del Carmen, xxiii
Juncosa y Escrivá, xxi, xxii

K

Kenley, Marie, 186
Kücking, Marlies, xvii, 181, 191–192n7

L

Laín Entralgo, Pedro, 200
Lantini, Gioconda, 112
Lantini, Mario, 111
Larraona, Arcadio María, 120, 121
Larrea, Juan, 175
Lavitrano, Luigi, 139, 142n31
Lenin, Vladimir, 1
Lobato, Francisco, 180
Local councils, 104, 171n23
López Amo, Ángel, 113
López, Rosalía, 91
López Navarro, José, 116
López Ortiz, José, 64
López Rodó, Laureano, 75, 113, 202, 203, 203n, 207n15
Luis de la Palma, 30

M

Madurga, José Ramón, 115, 116, 129, 187, 188
Maeztu, Ramiro de, 71, 200
Maher, Eileen, 116
Malham, Howell J., 186
Marañón, Gregorio, 56
Mariani, Renato, 111
Marlin, Olga, 190, 193n20
Martínez, Francisco, 114
Martorell, Antonio, 185
Maura y Montaner, Antonio, xx
Maycas, Fernando, 116, 117, 180
McQuaid, John Charles, 179
Menéndez Pelayo, Marcelino, 71, 200
Moles, Odón, 126
Monterde, María José, 162
Monzó, Severino, 162
Morán, Francisco, 34, 47
More, St. Thomas, 203
Moret, Salvador, 168
Mouriz, Carmen, 181
Mulcahy, Dick, 116
Mulcahy, Olive, 116
Muñoz Aycuéns, José, 14
Mussolini, Benito, 2
Múzquiz, José Luis, 95, 98, 99, 107, 126, 129, 171n20, 178, 185, 186, 188

N

Navarro Rubio, Mariano, 131, 202, 207n15
Nicholas of Bari, Saint, 32
Nieto, Aurora, 106, 118n16
Nitta, Soichiro, 189

O

Ocáriz, Fernando, xv, xvn
Orbegozo, Rosario de, 129
Orlandis, José, 61, 78, 79n6, 80n19, 95, 108, 116, 118n17
Ortega, Alberto, 37
Ortega, Encarnación, 84, 85, 86, 90, 91n3, 92nn4, 8, 104, 147, 162, 191n2
Ortega, Gregorio, 114
Ortega y Gasset, José, 56, 200
Ortiz de Landázuri, Blessed Guadalupe, x, 106, 129, 173, 184
Ortiz de Landázuri, Eduardo, 104, 212, 230n10
Osuna, Francisco de, 102

P

Pacheco, Maria Sofia, 114
Pacheco, Mário do Carmo, 114
Pániker, Raimundo, 75, 102
Paternity, 31
Paul VI, Saint, 120
Pedretti, Marietta, 181
Peñuela, Antonia, 91
Pérez, Salvador, 166
Pérez Embid, Florentino, 102
Pérez, Antonio, 126, 164, 167, 168, 201, 202, 203, 203n, 204, 207nn14, 16

Peris, Salvador, 115
Pius X, Saint, xx, xxii
Pius XI, 2, 3, 7, 7n
Pius XII, 20, 54, 57, 96, 108, 109, 121, 123n, 133, 136, 138, 139, 140n3, 143, 144
Plans, Pedro, 214
Pons, Silvia, 191
Ponz, Francisco, 39n11, 72, 79n6
Porras, Guillermo, 186, 192n16
Pou de Foxá, José, xxviii, xxxn26
Poveda, Saint Pedro, 28
Presley, Elvis, 143
Priestly Society of the Holy Cross, 96, 97, 98, 99, 108, 109, 133, 134, 150, 154, 163, 187
Primo de Rivera, Miguel, 2
Purcell, Kathleen, 174

Q

Quintana, Ana María, 181

R

Rasines, Isidoro, 214
Retz, Katharina, 181, 182, 192n7
Reyna, Mercedes, 7, 15, 16
Riberi, Antonio, 169
Richards, Michael, 115
Rieman, Richard W., 162, 186
Rodríguez, Amparo, 48, 49, 50, 83, 85, 90
Rodríguez Casado, Vicente, 43, 48, 50, 59, 61, 72, 78n1
Rodríguez García, Norberto, 9, 30, 51n1
Romeo, José (Pepe), 9, 14, 17, 18, 21nn18, 19

Roosevelt, Franklin, 1
Rueda Salaberry, Andrés, 227
Ruffini, Ernesto, 109
Ruiz, Teodoro, 62
Ruiz Giménez, Joaquín, 200, 201

S

Sainz de los Terreros Villacampa, Manuel, 33, 42, 45
Salaz, Rosemary, 191
Salcedo, Pilar, 162
Samorè, Antonio, 140
Sánchez Bella, Florencio, 168, 204
Sánchez Bella, Ismael, 215
Sánchez de Movellán, Marisa, 162
Sanchez Elvira, Ramona, 82
Sánchez Ruiz, Valentín, 10, 13, 25, 39n5
Sanjurjo, Ramona, 106, 118n16
Sanjurjo, José, 18
Santos, Sister Lúcia, 113
Sargent, Daniel, 177
Schmitt, Chris, 191
Schraml, Marga, 182
Schuster, Cardinal, 137, 138, 142nn28–29
Sierra, Antonia, 18
Silio, Fernando de, 180
Soldevilla, Cardinal Juan, xxvii
Sperling, David, 190
Stalin, Joseph, 1
Steinbach, Helene, 181, 192n7
Steinkamp, Hermann, 182, 192n10
Stork, Richard, 115
Studium generale, 155, 155n, 158

T

Tapia, María del Carmen, 162
Tardini, Domenico, 140, 142n31
Tedeschini, Federico, 138, 139, 140, 142nn31–32
Teijeira, Ester, 114
Thérèse of Lisieux, Saint, 17, 23n40
Termes, Rafael, 62
Tirelli, Luigi, 111
Toranzo, Lourdes, 162
Torelló, Juan Bautista, 75, 168, 182
Tovar, Antonio, 200
Traglia, Luigi, 138
Truel, Thérèse, 180
Turull, Pedro, 182

U

Ullastres, Alberto, 202, 205, 207n15, 227
Unamuno, Miguel de, 200
Urbistondo, Julián, 116
Urteaga Loidi, Jesús, 102, 118n14, 149

V

Valdés, María Teresa, 189
Valero, Antonio, 217
Valle, Francisca Javiera del, 17
Valls, Luis, 201, 202, 203, 203n, 207n15, 227
Vea-Murguía, Lino, 14, 17, 30, 33
Vergés, Manuel, 75
Vila, José, 128, 180
Viladàs, José María, 185
Vince, Vladimiro, 108
Viñes, Hortensia, 181
Vives, Francisco, 148

W

Women in Opus Dei, 9, 89, 104, 174
Woodhead, Ronald, 191
Work of St. Gabriel, 27, 37, 59, 98, 126, 131, 162, 206n1, 231n27
Work of St. Michael, 27, 36, 98, 126, 162
Work of St. Raphael, 27, 34, 59, 69, 78n1, 98, 99, 100, 126, 162

Y

Yamamoto, Koichi, 189, 193n18
Ybarra Oriol, Luis María, 214

Z

Zedong, Mao, 2
Zorzano, Isidoro, 13, 22n33, 29, 33, 38, 39n5, 43, 44, 46, 50, 59, 65, 100, 113, 177

CPSIA information can be obtained
at www.ICGtesting.com
Printed in the USA
BVHW060053120123
655995BV00012B/478